WHAT TO DO WHEN THE IRS IS AFTER YOU

D1598182

Fast Facts When Dealing with the IRS

1. The revenue agent, tax compliance officer, and revenue officer cannot arrest you and put you in jail.
2. Never ignore a letter or phone call from the IRS. The IRS never forgets and never just goes away. Consult a CPA, Enrolled Agent or Tax Attorney if you are contacted by someone claiming to be from the IRS.
3. Always send a certified letter to IRS in response to any letter you receive, even if you think you have resolved the issue in a telephone call.
4. You have many rights, including due process rights, but if you do not exercise those rights, they go away in time.
5. If you move, file Form 8822 to officially change your address.
6. The IRS can seize and sell almost everything you own, but would rather talk to you and make an installment agreement or put a hold on your case if you have a financial hardship.
7. Be respectful to IRS employees, but don't be afraid. Never lie or tell half-truths. The IRS employee wants to close your case in the easiest way possible - usually this is an installment agreement.
8. Document every contact with IRS, with the date, employee name and number and what was discussed. This can benefit you later when IRS fails to do what it said it would.
9. You must be current in filing and paying all taxes before you can get an installment agreement.
10. Remember that the IRS is not in the business of being patient, reasonable or efficient.
11. The IRS has been known to make mistakes - don't back down if you think you are right.

WHAT TO DO WHEN THE IRS IS AFTER YOU

Secrets of the IRS as Revealed by Retired IRS Employees

Richard M. Schickel
Lauri H. Goff
William G. Dieken
With Valerie Porter

Disclaimer

None of the information in this book constitutes legal or tax advice. RMS Tax Consulting LLC and the authors of this book and their affiliates are not liable for any actions that you take based on any of the contents of this book. This information is a collection of the authors' experience, knowledge and training and observation in the tax field. This is not meant to be an all-inclusive book on the IRS. It will not be appropriate for all situations. IRS employees have varying types of experience as well as personalities, which can affect the outcome of your case as much as the facts of the case itself.

RMS Tax Consulting LLC is in the business of providing professional advice on a case by case basis. The goal of this book is to help you determine how the IRS thinks and to expose you to procedures of how the IRS works cases. Some cases may require the assistance of an Enrolled agent, Certified Public Accountant, or tax attorney.

What to Do When You are in Trouble with the IRS. Copyright 2016 by Richard M. Schickel and RMS Tax Consulting LLC. All rights reserved. Printed in the United States of America. No part of this book may be used or reproduced except in the case of brief quotations embodied in critical articles and reviews. For information contact RMS Consulting LLC at 520-448-3531 or Richard@RMS-Consulting.net

ISBN 13: 978-0692705612
ISBN 10: 0692705619

Dedications

This book is dedicated to the Civil Servants who help our country run. - WGD

This book is dedicated to all IRS employees past and present who tried to do the "right thing" and help taxpayers who had no idea how to respond to the IRS.

It is also dedicated to the National Treasury Employees Union (NTEU) who has helped many IRS employees over the last 77 years. – RMS/LG

Contents

Acknowledgements

Many people both still inside the IRS and those who have recently retired from the IRS have generously supported the need for this book and contributed their ideas and stories.

Lauri Goff did amazing work as co-author and Technical Editor, this book could not have happened without her efforts.

We are grateful to Valerie Porter for her patient and skillful editing of this book, her advice and other contributions.

We acknowledge and thank Deborah Bradseth of TugboatDesign.net for our cover and meticulous formatting work.

Thanks to author Florence Osmund for her advice and support.

Thanks to Rachel Theron of LaunchWebsiteDesign.com for her technical knowledge and advice.

Thanks to Dennis Farris of VisualCoolness.com for his graphic arts work.

Thanks to Larry Kent and Jean Gadea who have helped us all transition from IRS employees into the independent business people in our business RMS Tax Consulting LLC, where we help clients resolve their audit and collection issues with the IRS.

Thanks to Reina Fregoso who contributed stories to the Collection chapter.

Thanks to Kay Deters, Guadalupe Aguirre, Billie Ellefson, John Rohrback, Becki Grube, Cathy Howard, Juanita Morales, Derek

Burdsall and Frank and JoAnne Reichlin, Jessica Schickel, Monica O'Toole, Colleen Schickel and Marge Schickel for your editing, advice and support.

Thanks to all the readers of this book who probably have many IRS stories to tell. We support you in your efforts to resolve your IRS case and hope the information in this book will contribute to that.

Acronyms Used in this Book

ACS	Automated Collection System
CI	Criminal Investigation
DIF	Discriminant Index Function
EIN	Employer Identification Number
FTAW	First Time Penalty Abatement Waiver
ITIN	Individual Taxpayer Identification Number
HIRTI	High Income Fast Track Initiative
HNWI	High Net Worth Individuals
ICS	Integrated Collection System
IDRS	Integrated Data Retrieval Service
IRC	Internal Revenue Code
IRM	Internal Revenue Manual
MSSP	Market Segment Specialization Program
NTEU	National Treasury Employees Union
NRP	National Research Project
OIC	Offer in Compromise
PDT	Potentially Dangerous Taxpayer
RCA	Reasonable Cause Assistant
RA	Revenue Agent
RO	Revenue Officer
RRA	IRS Restructuring and Reform Act of 1998
SAR	Suspicious Activity Report

SFR	Substitute for Return Program
SSN	Social Security Number
TAS	Taxpayer Advocate Service
TCO	Tax Compliance Officer (Office Auditor)
TCMP	Taxpayer Compliance Measurement Program
TIGTA	Treasury Inspector General for Tax Administration

Glossary

Appeals Officer: This is a former revenue agent who now works as an appeals officer for audit related cases. As of late 2015, settlement officers (see below) are also called appeals officers but continue to work only collection issues.

Audit Statute of Assessment (ASED): This is how long the IRS has to conduct an audit and assess additional taxes. It is usually three years from the date the return was processed, but it can be extended to six years if you have omitted 25% or more of your income from your tax return. It can also be extended forever in the case of tax fraud.

Automated Collection System (ACS): This is the IRS telephone collection system.

Collection Appeals Program (CAP): Under the Collection Appeals Program, if a taxpayer disagrees with an IRS decision and wants to appeal it, he or she can ask to speak to an IRS manager to review his or her case. If the taxpayer disagrees with the manager's decisions, the case will then be reviewed by the Office of Appeals. The taxpayer will be notified if the Appeals officer agrees or disagrees with the taxpayer's claims or arguments.

Collection Due Process Appeal (CDP): After receiving letters, levies or a Notice of Federal Tax Lien, a taxpayer can file for a formal hearing with the appeals office.

Collection Information Statement (CIS): These include Form 433-A, 433-B, and Form 433F. This form lists all assets, income and expenses of the taxpayer. This is used to evaluate the taxpayer's financial situation when there is a tax balance due or an Offer in Compromise is being evaluated.

Collection Statute of Expirations (CSED): Ten years after the date that IRS legally assessed your tax balance it expires forever. Unless you have filed and offer in compromise, or filed suit against the IRS.

Computer Paragraph Notice (CP): This is the name of certain notices that are sent from IRS service centers telling you that IRS is making changes on your taxes.

Criminal Special Agent: This person works for the Criminal Investigation Division and has the power to detain, question and arrest taxpayers who have committed tax fraud. They carry weapons and if one appears at your door, you probably need to hire an attorney. Anything you say can be used against you.

Currently Not Collectible (CNC): This is the term used by Collection when they have reviewed a taxpayer's finances and determined that they cannot afford to make installment agreement payments towards the back taxes. The account is taken out of Collection and sits on the shelf accumulating penalties and interest. This collection freeze is usually for at least two years.

Direct Debit Installment Agreement (DDIA): An installment Agreement in which payments are automatically debited from the taxpayer's bank account.

Enrolled Agent (EA): Usually a former or retired IRS employee who now represents taxpayers before the IRS. They have years of technical knowledge and experience that can help the IRS system work for their clients.

Internal Revenue Code (IRC): This is the actual Income Tax law. This is what Congress creates to state what they want to tax and at what rate. It is very complex and is usually reviewed when creating the Internal Revenue Manual.

Internal Revenue Manual (IRM): This contains all the policies and procedures that guide the IRS employee in how to apply the law for audit and collection cases.

National Standard Allowable Expenses for Collection: These are the dollar amounts that the IRS allows taxpayers who have tax balances owed for their living expenses. Any income over these amounts is expected to be paid every month to the IRS.

Notice of Federal Tax Lien (NFTL): A federal tax lien is filed in the county where the taxpayer lives when there is a tax balance due. Credit bureaus attach the lien to the taxpayer's credit report. The lien attaches to all real and personal property. The lien is filed after the taxpayer fails to pay any tax due.

Notice of Levy: This is the Form that is used to levy (seize) wages, salary and other income and bank accounts and other assets of delinquent taxpayers.

Notice of Intent to Levy: This letter gives legal warning to a delinquent taxpayer that the IRS is preparing to seize their assets.

Reasonable Collection Potential (RCP): The amount that the IRS expects could be collected from a taxpayer in an Offer in Compromise. The RCP is the least amount that the IRS would accept to settle the case with an offer in compromise.

Revenue Agent (RA): The highly trained person who audits tax returns at the taxpayers' homes or places of business. Revenue agents have degrees in accounting and many also are Certified Public Accountants. They are trained to audit every type of business entity.

Revenue Officer (RO): This is the IRS name for tax collector. This employee is the last stage of collection. They can levy, seize and sell your assets.

Settlement Officer (SO): This is a former revenue officer, who now works collection related cases in the IRS Office of Appeals. As of late 2015, settlement officers are now called Appeals Officers, but continue to work only Collection cases.

Tax Compliance Officer (TCO): Also known as an Office Auditor. These employees handle 1040 audits only in the local IRS office, where they meet with taxpayers and their representatives.

Treasury Inspector General for Tax Administration (TIGTA): Special Agents with TIGTA carry weapons and are multi-functioned. In addition to investigating taxpayers for attempted bribery or other reasons, TIGTA agents investigate IRS employees for any reports of illegal acts per RRA '98 or other violations of the rules of conduct or ethical code. TIGTA agents have the power to detain and arrest and lying to a special agent in TIGTA or CI is in itself an offense.

Preface

—ɯ—

We worked for the Internal Revenue Service for many years and learned many secrets along the way that can benefit you when you are in trouble with the IRS. The intent of this book is to provide you with enough information to enable you to represent yourself in an audit or collection case before the Internal Revenue Service. We will provide you enough knowledge and information for you to know when you need a tax professional.

Hopefully, you can contact the IRS and find an employee who is professional, kind, courteous and helpful. If you find that employee, you are lucky and have won the IRS Lottery. Some taxpayers call the IRS and have reported feeling intimidated, bullied, bluffed. Some feel they were given misleading or incorrect information because the IRS employee was trying to rush to close their case and did not take time to listen to their story.

In this book we explain how your story should be told, what may have triggered the tax non-compliance, and all the other possible situations in your life that taken together show why you fell off the taxpaying wagon.

We stress how to complete the documents known as "Collection Information Statements" so that you get maximum credit for your monthly expenses, and you experience less harm when entering into an installment agreement.

Dealing with the IRS can be scary and frustrating and there has been abuse of taxpayers in the past.

There is a legal doctrine, often expressed as "The King can do no wrong." Historically, the King was the Sovereign Power and had authority over the people. In the United States the Sovereign Power is held by the United States Government. The Internal Revenue Service has long acted like it was the King; it did whatever it wanted without regard to the harm that it caused its taxpayers. It broadly ignored the Constitution and took away taxpayers' rights to not incriminate themselves, and to not submit to unreasonable search and seizure. The information you are about to receive will let you know your rights and how to claim them.

Every man shall stand equal before the law – even the tax law.

"We know the Internal Revenue Service, because we were the Internal Revenue Service" – The motto of RMS Tax Consulting LLC.

This book was written by former and retired employees of the Internal Revenue Service from audit, collection, appeals, taxpayer assistance, criminal investigation and the service center. We have the knowledge, experience and wisdom to help guide you through any contacts you have with the IRS. We want to help you pay the lowest tax, penalty and interest allowed by law. We offer you practical information so that you can respond to the IRS and resolve your case to the best advantage.

Introduction

Over our many years of experience, we have all had friends and relatives who have come to us because they received a letter or contact from the Internal Revenue Service and were scared and confused, not knowing what to do or how to respond. We calmed them down and listened to what had happened and then told them exactly what they needed to do. We offered them knowledge and hope. In compiling this book, we kept in mind that we would share our stories, experiences and knowledge with you, our reader, on the same level as if you were a friend or family. We may be retired from the IRS, but we still want to be of "service."

This book is organized to first help you figure out what the letter or personal contact from the IRS means. It will help you to determine how to respond and how important and urgent that it is to respond. Some letters come with various rights and if you do not exercise those rights they evaporate with time.

It is not only important to respond to the IRS, but to back up the response with other actions to support what it is that you want to see happen. For example, if you are being audited, you need to examine your return and collect all your documents, receipts and statements that prove what is on your return. It is important to respond quickly and with all the requested information. It is more important to not provide extra information that the IRS did not request. If you disclose information outside of the audit that indicates that you have more income or untaxed income, the IRS will conduct a more comprehensive audit. The same applies to collection matters. Disclose all of your income and expenses, but don't mention items that can harm your case.

The IRS is like a huge old house with many rooms. Tens of thousands of employees are busy working on cases, maybe even your case. They are doing what they were trained to do, in their specific jobs and program areas. The problem is that often "the right hand does not know what the left hand is doing." That means that you may be in the process of being audited for a recent tax year and also owe taxes for a different year. The auditor does not know you owe back taxes; they are trained to only investigate what is right there before them. They are trained not to look at the big picture, but to submerge themselves in the minute details of your financial statements and tax returns. Similarly, the tax collector is not concerned that you might be in the process of negotiating an installment agreement. This is short-sighted, because if an audit results in a new tax balance, the audit assessment will cause the negotiated installment agreement to default. At the same time, if you are not current with filing tax returns or making estimated tax deposits or do not have enough withholding, the IRS Service Center is charged with sending you letters to figure out why. It does not care about the audit, or the collection matter, just about what pertains to the Service Center case.

To most people, the manner in which the IRS is organized doesn't make sense. It appears confusing and massive and disorganized and illogical. Consider this book your roadmap to the IRS.

We will tell you how to be strong and survive your interaction with the IRS. We will offer recommendations on how to do effective tax planning that will help prevent future IRS problems and lower your tax exposure.

Chapter 1
The IRS Letter is in the Mailbox

Although dealing with the IRS is often confusing, this book should give you the information and ability to represent yourself and save time, money and frustration. You may be able to represent yourself in single issue audit cases and in most collection cases. This book will give you enough knowledge to know when you need to consult and perhaps hire a tax professional like a tax attorney, a Certified Public Accountant (CPA) or an enrolled agent who is licensed to practice before the IRS. We present information and references that will provide you with what you need to know to get the IRS off your back.

Your IRS trouble usually starts when you go to your mailbox and find a letter from the Department of the Treasury – Internal Revenue Service. Receiving the letter can scare the hell out of you. Just breathe and we will explain how to know what to do next.

The IRS can also send Field Examination Revenue Agents (RAs), Collection Revenue Officers (ROs) and Criminal Investigation Special Agents (SAs) to your door unannounced, but that is rare. Most people get a letter first. They don't get just one letter, but a series of letters which request information or remind you that you owe taxes or have failed to file tax returns.

Many people have reported feeling ill; they start shaking or sweating, their blood pressure goes up and they get a sick feeling inside.

They get so stressed out that some just stare at the letter for hours before they find the strength to open it. Some never open the letters, thinking that if they ignore the letters then the issue will just go away.

Once the IRS enters your life, your tax issues never just go away easily. If you receive a letter from the IRS, it may start as a small inquiry. If you fail to provide what is being requested, the issue can erupt quickly into your own full blown Federal Investigation. Your finances, business, and even personal life will be open to investigation. It is not pleasant when the IRS is after you. It is hard enough that they are in your paycheck every week. Being under the IRS microscope is painful, and for some unbearable.

Of course some of the letters from the IRS bring good news, for example that you have made a math error or other miscalculation and the IRS is increasing your refund and sending you more money. Maybe you learn that you could claim some tax credit that you did not list on your tax return. Some letters tell you that because your income is below filing requirements that you do not need to go to the time and expense of ever filing a tax form again, if your income and circumstances stay the same.

Every year the IRS issues 130 million letters to the taxpayers of the United States and at least 19 million (15%) come back undeliverable.

The IRS system begins with "the Pipeline", explained more fully in Chapter 2. The initial letter comes from an IRS Service Center Campus and if you write back and give them the information they request; the issue can sometimes be resolved at that point. If you do not receive the letter, ignore the letter or do not send the information that they request, it moves further along through the system.

The IRS letter stream is kind of like a train - if you fail to get on at the station because you are late, the train does not wait for you or back up to pick you up; it moves to the next station. The IRS operates the same way moving cases along until they ultimately reach a human being who will use whatever tools they have to resolve your case, usually in the Government's favor.

This ties in perfectly with a statement made by Nina Olsen, the IRS National Taxpayer Advocate. She reported "The IRS collection process is the same as it was 30 years ago. It relies on bulk processing of correspondence and systemically generated actions - letters, etc." She reported that "The IRS system is unproductive and inappropriate to the taxpayer who simply cannot pay."

She continued, "The IRS collection strategy appears to assume in far too many situations that delinquent taxpayers have made a conscious decision to not comply with tax obligations. They use the 'full force of the law' to correct problems in a manner that is premature in many cases. The IRS should adjust this mindset and achieve a better balance between the use of enforcement tools and other collection tools, including reasonable payment agreements and offers in compromise. Collection treatments should be tailored to the needs of each taxpayer, with the goal of not only addressing the delinquencies at hand, but also promoting future compliance."

The IRS does not make telephone calls demanding that you send payments via MoneyGram, Western Union, Walmart-2-Walmart or any other money wiring method. The IRS does not demand that you secure iTunes cards or other prepaid debit cards to pay your taxes. The IRS does not threaten to send the police or sheriff out that day to seize your home, remove your children or throw you in jail. The people who make these calls are scam artists who have already collected at least $36 million from gullible taxpayers. The IRS Field Examination and Office Audit Departments are required to first send an audit appointment letter to the taxpayer. Due to identity theft concerns the IRS will not call a taxpayer to set up an initial appointment.

So that leads us to ask, if you got a letter from the IRS, how do you know it is real? The fastest way is to call the number on the letter. One of the numbers that IRS uses is 1-800-829-1040. This is the standard greeting you will hear. A recorded voice will say "Welcome to the Internal Revenue Service. You can also visit us at www.irs.gov. To continue in English, press one or to continue in Spanish, press two."

This is the real IRS number and, then once you make a selection, it will take you to an endless number of other menus. The important part is that the IRS, due to short staffing, usually will not pick up your call for at least 30 minutes to an hour and a half. They have music playing that puts you to sleep and you often get what is called a "courtesy disconnect." In 2015 the IRS automatically hung up on over 7 million callers.

In 2015, the IRS incoming phone operators only answered 38% of incoming calls. In 2016, they only expect to pick up 20% of the incoming calls. In the 2015 filing season there was a three-week period in which the IRS only picked up 10% of the calls and that was after the taxpayers had been on hold for an average of 60 minutes or more. Later in the season this improved to 24% of the calls being picked up after only an average of 29 minutes. Some members of the taxpaying public have suggested that the word "Service" be removed from the Internal Revenue Service agency name, to reflect the low levels of service being provided.

In contrast, the bogus callers will usually pick up the phone right away, may speak with heavy accents, not understand your slang words, and are intimidating and want to force you to do something.

According to J. Russell George, Treasury Inspector General for Tax Administration, (TIGTA), callers who commit this fraud often:

- Use an automated "robocall" machine.
- Use common names and fake IRS badge numbers.
- Know the last four digits of the victim's Social Security Number.
- May make caller ID information appear as if the IRS is calling.
- Send bogus IRS e-mails to support their scam.
- Call a second or third time claiming to be the police or department of motor vehicles. (Again, caller ID may support their claim.)
- The fraudster usually will tell the potential victim that they owe taxes and they will use threatening language if you do not pay immediately. That is a sign that is not the IRS calling, and is your cue to hang up.

The Inspector General reports that the scammers often demand that the "tax balance due" be paid immediately using a prepaid debit card or wire transfer. It has been reported that the scammers threaten those who refuse to pay with being charged with a criminal violation, immediate arrest and being put in jail, deportation and loss of business or driver's license.

The IRS never asks for debit or credit card numbers over the phone. It does not accept wire transfers, unless authorized by the IRS management. This tactic has already scammed 4,550 people out of 23 million dollars. One person sent in $500,000 to the scammer. Over 736,000 people have been contacted. Perhaps tens of thousands more were also scammed, but were too embarrassed to report it.

If you get a call asking for payment from someone claiming to be with the IRS, here's what to do: If you owe federal taxes, or think you might owe taxes, hang up and call the IRS at 1-800-829-1040.

Just the fact that you have a letter in your hands that appears to be legitimate is not enough. The IRS letter is not going to ask you for your Social Security number, your children's names and Social Security numbers or other information that it already has available to them. The IRS never asks for your credit card information.

The IRS does not have nor need your credit card numbers; it does not use credit cards like other businesses. The IRS does not take them over the phone, you have to go to www.irs.gov and then click on "Pay your tax bill" and then you can have your payment direct debited (withdrawn) from your bank account or credit card - securely and directly. There are service charges for either method, but it is important to know that all credit and debit payments go through this special IRS system and not through talking to an IRS employee. Once you have verified that the letter is genuine and what the IRS is asking for is reasonable, then you need to determine **what** they want? **Why** do they want it? **Where** are they located and what you can send them to adequately respond to the letter.

Figuring out where your letter came from and what it means is essential. Some letters have audit, collection and appeals rights that expire if you do not respond in a timely manner. Some letters are more important than other letters. Some letters are sent certified mail, but contain no appeals rights. Some letters just make threats. One taxpayer who was 46 years old was terrified when he received a letter that said that the IRS was going to seize his Social Security benefit check. This was an empty threat since he did not even qualify for a Social Security check for another 16 years, long after the tax would have legally expired.

The most important thing that you need to do is to know how to look at the IRS letters and find out the letter number. All letters from the IRS are coded. All CP (computer paragraph notices) and LTR or LT (letters) are supposed to be found in the upper right corner of the letter. That is not always true.

Some letters numbers are in different locations. Some are across the bottom of the letter or on the lower left side. Figuring this out is important. That way you can figure out what the letter is all about. You might think that you could use the official IRS website to find this information. You can, but not easily. It is not useful for outside inquiries because it does not use a "Google" type search engine. It will give you 30 places to look instead of the most important place. We strongly suggest throughout this book that you use Google or Bing to search for the term that we suggest. For instance, if you receive a CP 2000 letter you would search Google or Bing for: Understanding Your CP 2000 IRS. We have underlined what you can search. That will take you directly to the IRS webpage that can best help you. When you search, you will be directed to a screen that tells you what the letter is about and if it gives you the right to appeal as well as what the letter is proposing to do.

Because the IRS is pushing hard for more taxpayers to use their website instead of calling them or coming into the office, they have totally updated the material on the website and it is very helpful, if you can find it. We acknowledge how useful this information has been in creating this book.

The letter may start a mail audit, or send you to a local IRS office where a Tax Compliance Officer (TCO - formerly known as an office auditor) will ask to see all of your tax records. Or it might direct your case to the Examination (Audit) Field branch. There it will be worked by a Field Revenue Agent (RA) - a highly trained tax professional who specializes in audits of higher income individuals and businesses. The revenue agent is trained to examine the deductions and credits listed on the tax returns. They can question everything on your tax return. Most revenue agents will come to your home or place of business to perform the audit; however, we will cover more about that in our Audit Chapter 7.

When you have a tax balance due, collection letters will be sent to you. We will show you how those cases eventually end up being worked by a Field Revenue Officer.

Letters are the first notification that you will receive from the IRS in most cases. Some of the letters you receive are called notices, but the importance is the same and the terms are simply part of the name. The IRS also uses forms, publications, and other items to take actions against you or send you information.

Once you have determined where your case is currently located in the system, then you will know what section to go to in this book.

The following chapters will explain exactly how to respond, what to say and, most importantly, what not to say. You will then be directed to the chapter that deals with the IRS section that is working your case.

It is so critical to respond within the timelines that the IRS gives you to prevent the case from travelling further down the IRS pipeline system.

The Most Important IRS Letters and Notices - Because They Offer Appeals Rights

LETTERS

Letter 11 – Final Notice of Intent to Levy and Notice of Your Right to a Hearing (Automated Collection System/Collection)
This letter provides you notice of your unpaid taxes and that the IRS intends to levy to collect the amount due. The letter and publications explain how to request an appeal if you do not agree. You need to file Form 12153, Request for a Collection Due Process hearing, and send it to the address shown on your levy notice within 30 days from the date of the letter in order to appeal the proposed action with the Office of Appeals. This letter is very important because a lien or levy will soon follow, if you do not respond.

Letter 525 – General 30 Day Letter (Audit)
You will get this letter accompanied by a computational report of proposed adjustments to your tax return. It outlines your options if you do not agree with the proposed adjustments. If you agree with the adjustments, you sign and return the agreement form. If you do not agree with the adjustment, you can submit a request for an appeal to the office/individual that sent you the letter. This letter contains information and lists IRS publications on how to file an appeal/protest. You need to file your protest within 30 days from the date of this letter in order to appeal the proposed adjustments to the Office of Appeals.

Letter 531 – Notice of Deficiency
You will get this letter if you owe additional tax or other amounts for the tax year(s) listed in the letter. Often called a "Statutory Notice of Deficiency", the letter explains how to dispute the adjustments if you did not sign an agreement after an audit was completed. If you want to dispute the adjustments without payment, you have 90 days from the notice date to file a petition with the tax court. This time period cannot be extended.

Letter 692 – Request for Consideration of Additional Findings
This letter is a computational report of proposed adjustments to your

tax return. It outlines your options if you do not agree with the proposed adjustments. If you agree with the adjustment, sign and return the agreement form. If you do not agree, you can submit a request for appeal to the office/individual that sent you the letter. The letter contains information and lists IRS publications on how to file an appeal/protest. You need to file your protest within 15 days from the date of this letter in order to appeal the proposed adjustments with the Office of Appeals.

Letter 915 – Letter to Transmit Examination Report

This letter explains adjustments in the amount of tax. The letter explains that if you agree with the adjustment, you sign and return the agreement form. If you do not agree, you can submit a request for appeal/protest to the office/individual that sent you the letter. The letter or referenced publications explain how to file a protest. You need to file your protest within 30 days from the date of the letter in order to appeal the proposed adjustments with the Office of Appeals.

Letter 950 - 30 Day Letter - Straight Deficiency or Over-Assessment

This letter is used for unagreed, disputed straight deficiency or mixed deficiency and over-assessment cases. This letter may be used for various types of tax. If you agree with the adjustment, you sign the agreement form. If you do not agree, you can submit a request for appeal/protest to the office/individual that sent you the letter. The letter or referenced publications explain how to file a protest. You need to file your protest within 30 days from the date of the letter in order to appeal the proposed adjustments with the Office of Appeals.

Letter 1058 – Final Notice - Reply within 30 days

This letter is to notify you of your unpaid taxes and that the IRS intends to levy (seize) to collect the amount owed. The letter and referenced publications explain how to request an appeal if you do not agree. You need to file Form 12153, Request for Collection Due Process hearing and send it to the address shown on your letter within 30 days from the date of the letter in order to appeal the action with the Office of Appeals. This is a very important letter, never ignore it!

Letter 1085 – 30-Day Letter Proposed 6020 (b) Assessment

This letter is to notify you that the IRS has prepared and enclosed tax returns for you based on information provided to them. These returns will become legal tax returns with tax balances if you do not file a protest/appeal. Copies of the returns are included with this letter and you can file your own returns at any time, before these IRS-created returns are legally assessed. The letter and referenced publications explain how to request and appeal if you do not agree. You need to file Form 12153, Request for Collection Due Process hearing and send it to the address shown on your letter within 30 days from the date of the letter in order to appeal the action with the Office of Appeals. This letter could affect you in two ways. If the IRS underestimated your tax liability, you can legally pay the assessment and then even though the tax is lower than what you might truly owe, you are legally protected. If the IRS overestimated how much you owe, you should immediately prepare tax returns. If you do not have all of the tax data, but most of it, you can also estimate the tax, and file that using your documentation.

Letter 1153 – Trust Funds Recovery Penalty Letter

This letter explains that the IRS's efforts to collect the federal employment or excise taxes due from the business named on the letter have not resulted in full payment of the liability. Therefore, the IRS proposes to assess a penalty against you. If you agree with this penalty for each tax period shown, you are asked to sign Part 1 of the enclosed Form 2751 and return it to the person/office that sent you the letter. The letter contains information and lists IRS publications on how to file an appeal/protest. You need to file your protest within 60 days from the date of the letter in order to appeal this decision with the Office of Appeals.

Letter 3016- IRC Section 6015 Preliminary Determination Letter (30 Day)

This is the preliminary letter giving you 30 days to appeal the determination for innocent spouse relief under IRC Section 6015. If you do not agree, you can submit a request for appeal/protest to the office/individual that sent you the letter. The letter or referenced publications explain how to file a protest. You need to file your protest within 30 days from the date of the letter in order to appeal the proposed adjustments with the Office of Appeals.

Letter 3172 – Notice of Federal Tax Lien Filing and Your Rights to a Hearing under IRC 6320

This letter is to notify you that the IRS filed a notice of tax lien for unpaid taxes. If you do not agree you can request appeals consideration within 30 days from the date of this letter. The letter and publications explain how to request a hearing from Appeals. You need to file a Form 12153, Request for a Collection Due Process hearing, and send it to the address shown on your lien notice within 30 days from the date of the letter in order to appeal the action with the Office of Appeals. If a lien is filed, you could lose your job, your security clearance, your good credit. This lien is against everything that you own.

Letter 3391 – 30 Day Non-Filer Letter

This letter advises you that the IRS believes you are liable for filing tax returns for the periods identified in the letter. It includes a report giving you a computation of the proposed adjustments to your tax return and explains the adjustments. The letter explains that if you agree with the adjustments, you sign and return the agreement form. If you do not agree, you can submit a request for appeal/protest to the office/individual that sent you the letter. The letter or referenced publications explain how to file a protest. You need to file your protest within 30 days from the date of the letter in order to appeal the proposed adjustments with the Office of Appeals.

Letter 3727 – 30-Day Letter Notifying Taxpayer No Change to Original Report Partially Disallowing EIC Based on Failure to Meet Residency Test for 1 Child

This letter explains why the IRS will not allow your Earned Income Credit (EIC).

The letter states that if you agree with the adjustment, you sign and return the agreement form. If you do not agree, you can submit a request for appeal/protest to the office/individual that sent you the letter. The letter or referenced publications explain how to file a protest. You need to file your protest within 30 days from the date of the letter in order to appeal the proposed adjustments with the Office of Appeals.

NOTICES

CP 90 – Final Notice of Intent to Levy

This letter notifies you of your unpaid taxes and that the IRS intends to levy to collect the amount owed. This notice and referenced publications explain how to request an appeal if you do not agree. You need to file a Form 12153, Request for Collection Due Process Hearing, and send it to the address shown on your letter within 30 days from the date of this letter in order to appeals the action with the Office of Appeals.

CP 92 – Notice of Levy upon your State Tax Refund

This letter notifies you that the IRS has levied (seized) your state tax refund to pay your unpaid Federal taxes. If you did not have a state refund, you have nothing to worry about. If you agree, you do not need to reply. If you do not agree, you can submit a request for appeal/protest to the office/individual that sent you the letter. The letter or referenced publications explain how to file a protest. You need to file your protest within 30 days from the date of the letter in order to appeal the proposed adjustments with the Office of Appeals.

CP 242 – Notice of Levy upon your State Tax Refund

This letter notifies you that the IRS has levied (seized) your state tax refund to pay your unpaid federal taxes. If you did not have a state refund, you have nothing to worry about. If you agree, you do not need to reply. If you do not agree, you can submit a request for appeal/protest to the office/individual that sent you the letter. The letter or referenced publications explain how to file a protest. You need to file your protest within 30 days from the date of the letter in order to appeal the proposed adjustments with the Office of Appeals.

CP 523 – IMF Installment Agreement Default Notice

This letter notifies you that the IRS intends to terminate your installment agreement in 30 days. If you do not agree, you can submit a request for appeal/protest to the office/individual that sent you the letter. The letter or referenced publications explain how to file a protest. You need to file your protest within 30 days from the date of the letter in order to appeal the proposed adjustments with the Office of Appeals.

CP 2000 - Proposed Adjustment

You receive this letter when the IRS receives information from W-2 forms or Form 1099 which report that you earned income that does not match your tax return. This information can also affect deductions or credits that you claimed on your tax return. If you do not agree, you can submit a request for appeal/protest to the office/individual that sent you the letter. The letter or referenced publications explain how to file a protest. You need to file your protest within 30 days from the date of the letter in order to appeal the proposed adjustments with the Office of Appeals. This letter must be investigated and responded to within 30 days or you will next enter the IRS collection process, either through the Automated Collection (telephone) office or with a field collection revenue officer.

Count the Days Correctly

Many people do not count the number of days that they have to file an appeal correctly. Some might think that with a letter dated July 30, they can file an appeal by August 30 and it will be timely. It will not be timely; that is 31 days later. Your appeal will be rejected. You can use a website that counts the days for you. Timeanddate.com has such a feature under the heading "calculate duration between two dates." You must send in the appeal via certified mail, since some offices do not count Fed Ex or UPS mailing dates as legal. Some offices accept faxed appeals and some do not. The eFax address for an IRS employee is hard to obtain. Some employees do not use their eFax numbers.

Typically, the IRS will only need a response if you don't agree with the information, or they need additional information, or you have a balance due. If the IRS changed your tax return, compare the information that the IRS provided in the notice or letter with the information in your original return. If the IRS receives a return that they suspect is identity theft, they will ask you to verify your identity using the web address provided in the letter.

Respond within the Required Time Frame

If the IRS asks for a response within a specific time frame, you must respond on time to minimize additional interest and penalty charges or to preserve your appeal rights if you don't agree. If you do not resolve the matter on the first notice, a chain of letters will begin with the service center and end in collection. That chain of letters will become a chain around your neck.

Contact the IRS by Phone if you have a Question or You Disagree with What is Being Proposed in the Letter

The IRS provides their contact phone number on the top right-hand corner of most of their correspondence. Be sure you have your tax return and any related documentation available when you call. You can also write to the IRS at the address in the correspondence to explain why you disagree. If you write, allow at least 30 days for a response. If you call, be sure and get the name and employee ID number of each person you talk to during every call. All IRS employees are required to give this ID number to each taxpayer or representative.

Always keep a copy of all correspondence with your tax records.

Failing to Respond to the IRS is a Pain in Your Neck

If you do not respond to the IRS letters, then you may eventually think in time that the issue has been resolved and they will not bother you anymore. This is usually incorrect. When the IRS opens a case, it stays open until you or the IRS does something to close it. It might take 6 months or 2 years for the next letter or next action to occur, but it will occur. You can be sure that your inattention to the letter will bring a less than desirable outcome to you. If your case is closed as an installment agreement or as "currently not collectible" (CNC) then you will receive a letter confirming that status.

We have, in our years with the IRS, heard many stories of taxpayers who were damaged because they either never received their IRS letter or never responded to it.

The most common situations are that refunds are lost due to lack of information needed to confirm that a dependent really is your legal dependent or that some expense you listed on your tax return can be proved by you.

In audit situations, the IRS letters will request many items. The IRS might request proof of income earned, expenses paid, filing status, a copy of your marriage certificate or divorce decree and child support statement. If you provide that information quickly, it will save you money.

In collection situations, the letters can result in the IRS issuing notices of levy on your wages, salary and other income and your bank accounts along with almost every other asset that you own. In the private business world, these are also known as wage garnishments. By whatever name, the IRS will take your hard earned money, suddenly and without further notice. Employers may fire you on the spot, if they receive a levy. They do not want to have anything to do with the IRS. At the very least, the levy will cause you great embarrassment and is likely to be talked about by your coworkers. If you open the IRS letters, you have rights within the collection process and have less chance of losing all of your money overnight.

We will explore which types of IRS letters and types of IRS inquiries that you may be able to handle with minimal effort and which ones are more complex. The more complex ones, especially, should be handled by a tax professional. Money spent in hiring a professional will likely save you money in the end.

Nine Things to Know about IRS Notices and Letters

Each year, the IRS sends millions of notices and letters to taxpayers for a variety of reasons. Here are nine things to know in case one shows up in your mailbox.

1. Don't panic. You often only need to respond to take care of a notice.
2. There are many reasons why the IRS may send a letter or notice. It is typically about a specific issue on your federal tax return or tax account. A notice may tell you about changes to your account or ask you for more information. It could also

tell you that you must make a payment.

3. Each notice has specific instructions about what you need to do.
4. You may get a notice that states the IRS has made a change or correction to your tax return. If you do, review the information and compare it with your original return.
5. If you agree with the notice, you usually don't need to reply unless it gives you other instructions or you need to make a payment.
6. If you do not agree with the notice, it's important for you to respond. You should write a letter to explain why you disagree. Include any information and documents you want the IRS to consider. Mail your reply with the bottom tear-off portion of the notice. Send it to the address shown in the upper left-hand corner of the notice. Allow at least 30 days for a response. Always keep a copy of everything you mail.
7. You shouldn't have to call or visit an IRS office for most notices. If you do have questions, call the phone number in the upper right-hand corner of the notice. Have a copy of your tax return and the notice with you when you call. This will help the IRS answer your questions.
8. Keep copies of any notices you receive with your other tax records.
9. The IRS sends letters and notices by mail. The IRS does not contact people by email or social media to ask for personal or financial information.

It might seem like the IRS does not want to see you in person or respond to you, even though you are trying to contact the IRS. If you think that, then you are correct and now know the IRS strategic business plan for the future.

Report Phishing and Online Scam

The IRS cautions taxpayers on its website that if they think their letter looks suspicious they should call the IRS at 1-800-829-1040 or go to the IRS Report Phishing Page at https://www.irs.gov/uac/Report-Phishing.

The IRS doesn't initiate contact with taxpayers by email, text messages or social media channels to request personal or financial information. This includes requests for PIN numbers, passwords, Social Security numbers or similar access information for credit cards, banks, or other financial accounts.

What is Phishing?

Phishing is a scam typically carried out through unsolicited email and/or websites that pose as legitimate sites and lure unsuspecting victims to provide personal and financial information. The IRS cautions taxpayers on its website that if they think their letter looks suspicious they should call IRS at 1-800-829-1040 or go to the IRS Report Phishing Page at: https://www.irs.gov/uac/Report-Phishing.com

Report all unsolicited email claiming to be from the IRS or an IRS-related function to phishing@irs.gov. Recent scams have used the Electronic Federal Tax Payment System (EFTPS) to attract potential victims. Also, if you've experienced any monetary losses due to an IRS-related incident, please report it to the Treasury Inspector General for Tax Administration (TIGTA).

IRS Phone Scam

If you receive a phone call from someone claiming to be from the IRS but you suspect that they are not an IRS employee, then you should get their name and employee identification number, telephone number and tell them that you need to verify who they are first and you will call them back. Then you should call 1-800-366-4484 to determine if that caller is a legitimate IRS employee. If they are, call them back. If not, report them to phishing@irs.gov.

This Woman Never Opened IRS Letters and It Nearly Destroyed her Life

The following story is told by Richard Schickel in his book *IRS Whistleblower:*

This is the story of a woman who was a prominent and wealthy corporate attorney. She was a widow who had no family and was very private. When her husband died, she stopped working and started doing day trading of stocks. This involves a lot of buying and selling stocks and making short-term profits. She suffered from depression and was unable to cope with daily life. She could not even bring herself to open the mail or pay bills. She had a 200-acre ranch worth $1 million, a $200,000 house that was paid for, and a very large retirement account. She should have been set for life. Then the IRS got involved in her life.

The IRS received reports that she had large amounts of stock sales and no tax returns were filed, so it sent her many letters and tried to contact her. When she failed to contact the IRS, they sent a new letter to her, which, again she did not open.

She was so completely overwrought with anxiety and depression that she was not taking care of her business affairs. The most shocking part was that a few years before, the IRS had sent her a letter advising her that they were issuing a backup withholding order that required her stockbroker to do backup withholding, or 28% of the value of her account needed to be liquidated to pay to the IRS on her behalf, but she had never opened that letter. She should have been exempt, but she had not responded.

Her IRA account was $4 million at the beginning of the week, consisting of $2 million cash and $2 million on margin (borrowed from the brokerage house for investment purposes.) The IRS back up withholding order was issued which required the broker to pay 28% of the value of the account to the IRS. The broker was afraid of the IRS but was legally required to do what was ordered.

The broker had to liquidate the stocks and send the IRS $1,120,000 within a two-day period. The broker issued a margin call which meant if she did not have more money to put into her account they would start selling stocks to protect their loan. She lost another $2.1 million due to those sales and commissions. (She was heavily invested in small startup companies' stocks). The stock she sold made other investors sell their stock as well. The stock sales almost triggered a stock collapse of two small companies. Everyone thought that bad news about the companies must be circulating so a selling spree of their stocks was triggered as well. Then the remaining stocks lost an additional $780,000 in value over three days. The brokerage house sent her letters at the time, but again, since she did not open her mail, she did not respond. This woman lost $3,758,000 in a week.

All this happened without the IRS ever contacting her in person and offering due process rights or giving her any appeal rights and without the case ever having been seen by an IRS employee.

Then nothing happened because she did not yet have a tax assessment against her, but she was left with only $242,000 in her brokerage account. She had several hundred thousand dollars in other bank accounts. Due to her emotional instability, she was incapable of working. Later, the IRS seized $400,000 from her other bank accounts.

The IRS stopped receiving tax returns from her so they made up tax returns for her under the Substitute for Return Program (SFR). In two years, the IRS assessed her $4.5 million in taxes. They based this on all the stock sales that she made, but because the IRS did not know what was paid for the stocks, it was a very unjust calculation. The tax balances were legally assessed, and due and owing to the United States Government.

The SFR program produces huge tax assessments for people who have failed to file returns, but when this happens they do not get credit for any exemptions, or filing status. It is very harmful to anyone who is assessed under the program. The IRS does this right before a Notice of Federal Tax Lien is filed, which destroys one's credit for ten years.

Although the Internal Revenue Code does have exceptions for financial hardship situations, if the person cannot advocate for himself or herself and cannot prepare forms and financial statements required by the IRS, there is no one who can help them. The IRS just plods along like a hungry bulldozer gobbling up assets without regard to ethical correctness.

Eventually, the woman connected with a sympathetic CPA who prepared corrected tax returns. Instead of owing taxes she actually was due refunds for the years that the IRS had assessed. However, if you do not file a tax return within three years of its due date, you lose your refunds without recourse - forever. When all was said and done, she had over $800,000 in lost refunds.

She is not alone. There are many cases of people who are afraid or unable to respond to the IRS notices and letters. They fail to provide what is requested or demanded by the IRS because they either cannot or will not. Some had physical or mental illnesses. It does not matter because the IRS will continue taking what they can find for at least the next ten years. This is just one case where fear of the IRS, or incompetence, led to a person's ruin.

There are many stories of taxpayers who fail to respond to IRS notices and many stories of people who respond, but with incorrect information.

We frequently hear stories about taxpayers being too afraid to even open their IRS letter and then when they do and talk to friends, family or a tax professional, find that the time has passed for filing an appeal. They might write a letter, but the case is no longer being worked by the IRS group that had its address on the first letter, so the matter, no matter how small it seems at first, quickly turns into a Federal Case.

The question is - can you adequately respond to the letter that the IRS sent you? The advice we give in this book regarding mail (correspondence) audits is that maybe you can respond, if the IRS is questioning just one item. If the IRS wants to question your charitable deductions, send copies of cancelled checks and receipts. Or if they are questioning your car expenses, send copies of your mileage log and car maintenance records. Never send your original documents. You should be pretty safe doing that yourself.

We have seen taxpayers who sent in more than the IRS asked for and this led to an increased audit that questions many other items on the tax return, just because you may have sent them bank statements that shared too much information with them.

You can usually represent yourself on most collection letters with balances under $50,000; however, if you feel uncomfortable you should hire a tax professional.

Chapter 2
Understanding the IRS Process and IRS Employees

When the IRS is after you, you probably will be contacted by the IRS Master Computer in the form of a letter first. This computer is called IDRS, the Integrated Data Retrieval System, and it was the state of the art for computers...in 1961. IDRS computers are located in the IRS Service Centers. This computer system is 55 years old and very secure because it is so obsolete. It runs on the old IBM 370 computers from the 1960s and uses the computer languages of BASIC, FORTRAN and COBOL. The computer is programmed to spit out 170 million letters a year, questioning your filing status, items on your return, questions about your dependents, and many other issues. It also sends a series of notices if you do not file or pay your taxes. Any IRS employee who has access to IDRS has unlimited access to the tax records of every business, trust, partnership and small business and every United States citizen - *everyone*. This includes sensitive personal and business information.

The IRS is losing tens of billions of dollars because of its antiquated master computer system. The IRS and its old computer system cannot keep pace with modern demands. The IRS reported that it had paid out $5.2 billion in false/fraudulent refunds in 2011 and paid out $3.6

billion in 2012 and $6.5 billion in 2013. The IRS has announced that it expects refund fraud to rise 223% to $21 billion in 2016.

The old computer system did not pick up that 5,500 fraudulent returns were filed by a single tax preparer for refunds totaling $27 million and a payout of $490,000 to a single address in Bulgaria that filed 700 returns. This is all because of an old computer system, reduced and inexperienced staffing, and poor internal controls.

All audit and collection cases start in the Service Center Automated Processing Section, which is known as the "Pipeline." This is where all letters originate. At this stage, IRS employees do not ever speak to taxpayers. If their cases are not resolved at this level, then they move to Service Center Accounts Management.

This section is divided into Audit and Collection cases and is where telephone calls are answered (when they feel like picking up the phone) and where incoming correspondence from taxpayers is read and responded to. This unit is reached throughout the United States by dialing 1-800-829-1040. All the letters that you receive will be issued from the Pipeline and responded to by Accounts Management.

Most audit cases in this section are resolved by the taxpayer either sending in proof of something that they listed on their tax return and closing the audit or they result in new tax balances which flow into the collection letters.

Collection Letters

On collection cases, Accounts Management collects financial information and tries to collect full payment of the tax debt. It gives installment agreements or defers collection until the taxpayer is able to pay. Service Center Accounts Management just answers calls and letters from taxpayers; it does not issue levy/seize bank accounts or wages, salary and other income. This unit does not file Notice of Federal Tax

Liens. They are only able to resolve business tax cases under $25,000 and income tax balances under $50,000.

If Accounts Management is unable to resolve the case, it moves next to the telephone collection system which is called the Automated Collection System (ACS). Cases here are worked with dollar amounts from $25,001 to $100,000.

There are many ACS call sites and they send you the letters with the required information needed before they are allowed to issue levies. If they cannot contact you, they will take enforcement collection actions, such as seizing your bank accounts and wages and filing Notice of Federal Tax Liens against you and your credit.

Anything owed over $100,000 will be eventually transferred to the Field Collection Section. These will be worked by a field revenue officer (RO). If you owe this much you should seriously consider writing a letter and/or calling the number on most recent notice that you received and request that your case be transferred to a revenue officer. The caseworker will ask you where you bank and where you work. Provide this information but do not offer any other information. Then the case will either be transferred directly to a revenue officer or go into a Collection Queue - a massive database where cases are held pending assignment into the field revenue officer's inventory.

The Collection Queue is a great place for your case to be, because the ten-year statute of limitations for collection continues to run and nothing is happening to your case. Your case can stay there for years and never be assigned to a revenue officer. But there is a ticket for admission - first you must file current taxes and you must fully pay all tax balances for current year and future years' taxes. That suggests to the IRS that you are not actively trying to avoid paying your taxes.

Revenue officers are tax collectors who can and will seize anything you own presently along with anything that comes to you in the future. This includes your car, truck, personal residence, vacation home, rental property, commercial property, cash, artwork, jewelry, stocks, bonds and other income as well as any rights that you have to any other assets like lottery winnings and inheritances. RO's can also file Notices of Federal Tax Lien against you in counties where you reside or own property.

Audit Letters

Audit cases are worked in the Service Center Accounts Management Section. That area works mail audits (correspondence audits), math error notices, proposed adjustment cases and handles the simplest types of audits. If they are unable to resolve an audit, it will go to a local IRS office to be worked as an office audit case by a tax compliance officer (TCO). If it is expected to yield higher dollars in an audit, it will be assigned to a field revenue agent (RA) who will conduct the audit at your home or business, or at the office of your authorized representative.

Due to a declining labor force, it is getting harder and harder to get into contact with any branch of the IRS. As of November, 2015, IRS Commissioner Koskinen reported that the IRS is down to 74,580 employees – a decrease of 61% from their all-time high. Fifty-two percent of all IRS employees are over the age of 50 and 25% can retire today, with an additional 15% eligible to retire by the year 2019. Half of IRS management has retired in the last five years. Only 1,900 employees are under the age of 30 and only 384 under the age of 25. This is traditionally where the "new blood" comes from and the IRS has only a drop in a bucket.

Koskinen claims that "This situation makes it extremely difficult, if not impossible, for the IRS to properly develop its next generation of leaders. We estimate that by 2016 41% of our front-line managers and 61% of our executives will be eligible to retire."

There are:

- 10,657 revenue agents who do the field audits; this is expected to drop to 10,165 in 2017. A drop of 64% since 1997.

- 3,719 revenue officers (tax collectors); this is expected to drop to 1,700 in 2017. A drop of 77% since 1997.
- 2,139 criminal investigators (down 36% from their peak of 3,358 in 1995.) Because of attrition and retirements, this is expected to drop to only 1,600 IRS criminal special agents.
- 1,307 tax compliance officers (TCO) (formerly known as office auditors) - down 18%.

These are the front-line field enforcement employees. The number of IRS employees assigned to answer taxpayer telephone calls fell from 9,400 in 2010 to 6,900 in 2014 - a 26% decline. The IRS announced that it lost another 1,800 enforcement personnel through attrition in 2015.

Now you may think that is good news: the IRS is finally going to get off your back and you won't need to file or pay anymore because there aren't enough field agents to worry about. But the IRS still has its powerful computer that will pursue you with a flurry of audit and collection letters.

The people who are causing economic problems for our government are not being investigated, which leaves the law-abiding taxpayer to shoulder the burden.

The IRS has not done any major replacement hiring in over 7 years. The staff that it does have is new, inexperienced, inflexible and insufficiently trained to meet the demands of the Internal Revenue Code and the many tax law changes that occur every year. The more experienced employees are generally looking forward to retirement and the overall morale is terrible.

Every day more IRS employees retire. These employees are the backbone of the agency and when they retire they take with them years of tax wisdom, knowledge, and technical skills in administering the tax laws.

The IRS suffers because it does not offer accessibility to data for its customers; it is not directly accountable to anyone for the way it treats individual taxpayers (their customers); and they no longer offer customer service- just customer confusion, frustration, inconvenience and pain.

Taxpayers do not have the ability to access their tax accounts online and directly interact and communicate with the IRS on-line. The IRS is still working cases the same way that they did in 1980.

The IRS is in serious trouble due to fewer employees, less audits, less collection, and fewer dollars collected. The tax system is under so much stress, it is now affecting long-term compliance. People hear their friends talk about the fact that they have stopped filing and paying taxes and then they try it also. Some rural and low population areas of the United States are referred to as "tax free zones", because other than sending out letters to those delinquent taxpayers, the IRS doesn't have enough staff to drive 2-10 hours to make field calls not to mention conducting audits and collection work.

The IRS Employee

In many cases should you not respond to a letter received from the IRS, it will eventually lead to a contact with an actual IRS employee, either on the phone, in the office or in person.

Just like there are many trees in a forest, there are many different people in the IRS:

- Some IRS employees are well trained and dedicated to providing quality customer service. Since the IRS has severely cut its training budget in recent years, these are usually the employees who have been at the IRS for more than ten years. They know the system and how to move cases through the system. Many of them are caring, decent individuals who are trying hard to serve not just the government, but also the taxpayers they are assigned to work. They will be balanced, polite, respectful and firm but fair in their interviews.
- Some IRS employees want to get their cases closed, because that is the top priority for IRS management - closing cases - not making new audit assessments or collecting tax dollars. The

latter may occur, but it is closing cases that these employees care about. Some employees will do whatever it takes to close cases. Usually they stay within the bounds of the Internal Revenue Code; sometimes not. Some IRS employees have been known to harass, badger, and stalk their taxpayers, which makes all employees look bad.

- Most employees in the Service Center Campuses may have good intent, but they are trained only to do very narrow jobs. They are not paid as much because the campuses are usually in remote areas where labor is cheaper. The employees just do what they are instructed; no more, no less. Production is the most important goal to them. They need to input, process, and close as many cases as they can on their shifts. They are not trained to look at the "big picture". Most of them do not have contact with taxpayers, except through the mail. Even if they are trying to do the right thing and make a difference, they cannot, because they lack the training, knowledge and experience to do so.
- Some IRS employees are just plain mean, cold and uncaring. They wake up grumpy and go to work grumpy and just don't seem to care what happens to anyone else in the world other than themselves. They can be rude, formal, and officious and cause you a great deal of frustration, worry, fear, and anger.
- Some IRS employees exhibit characteristics of anti-social, psychotic or sociopathic behavior. Some employees allow their personal beliefs and prejudices to influence how they "lay down the law" with respect to certain taxpayers. This can include racism, being anti-African American, anti-Hispanic or anti-Semitic. This has no place in tax administration.
- Some employees practice economic discrimination. This can go both ways, treating the poor and working class taxpayers in an impatient or degrading manner, or as though they were not worth the time of day. This has also been known to work

against people who are well off or wealthy. Some employees think that just because people have money, they should just quietly pay audit assessments and penalties. One IRS employee defended this by saying: "because they can afford it."

Most IRS employees are good, decent people. Some are competent and some are not, some are like aggressive robots. A bad IRS employee can be the meanest, nastiest person that you will ever meet. They will seek to destroy your life to collect money for the government. They will poke around your life asking your friends, family and coworkers the most intimate details about you, your life, your business and your financial circumstances. They will look for money and assets they want to seize.

Many employees working in the IRS do not take anything personally. They don't care if people are hurt because of their actions. They are so tired, pressured and stressed out trying to follow the IRS procedures which sometimes do not reflect the intent of the actual tax laws that they have no time to think. They have to hurry on to the next case. The IRS Service Center Pipeline system effectively prohibits many employees from thinking or using their good judgment. They do a few tasks and then just move the case forward. They have no ability to help and no incentive or ability to do the right thing. Many managers in the Service Centers will actually use the phrase "you are not being paid to think".

How the IRS employees feel about themselves will likely be reflected in how they treat you. Of course, the different attitudes reflect humanity in general, because IRS employees are simply human. They can be overworked, demeaned, depressed, disrespected, and demoralized and that is all before you talk to them.

Some employees may try to do the "right thing" in your case, but many are simply too burned out to even try.

The attitude of the IRS and the attitude of the IRS employee will influence how your case is worked. IRS employees are under a great deal of pressure to close cases exactly the way their managers want them closed.

One revenue agent was assigned a business to audit. The RA limited her audit to just one part of the tax return. She made a proposed tax adjustment and the taxpayer agreed to and paid the entire amount. When she went back to the office, she hoped her manager would give her positive recognition in her employee file. Instead, the manager demanded that she go back and expand the audit to dispute a $1,200 depreciation expense that he contended should have been treated differently on the return. The revenue agent was shocked. She had not only done her job, but she had collected the tax, too! After she pulled back from the situation, she remembered that the manager would soon be going on Christmas vacation for two weeks. She held on to the case and then submitted it to the acting manager who immediately reviewed, approved and closed the case, without comment. The secret here is that most managers are on vacation the last two weeks of the year, since they accrue so much vacation leave. This is when most revenue agents and revenue officers are able to close the majority of their difficult cases.

Many employees who were hired within the last ten years lack the knowledge, training and experience of those employees who are about to retire. They were trained more like robots than human beings. Many of those employees are frustrated, because the IRS has not hired or promoted employees to higher graded jobs. As the economy improves, many are starting to leave.

The IRS used to like to hire people who were fresh out of college because they did not know anything about the job and were very trainable. There is some abuse in the training and most of it is psychological. The IRS makes you feel like they are doing you a favor by letting you work there. At the same time, they infer that no one else would hire you. This is common across the whole IRS.

Many of the more recent hires (7-9 years ago) had previous careers in the military and in private business and do not like nor allow themselves to be treated like the IRS commonly treats its employees. They've mostly left the IRS for other jobs.

Often IRS employees will gain power and authority through their jobs. The employees will think that they are better than other people and they hurt people in large and small ways because they received some power. Power can drive a person crazy by corrupting the basic human idea that we should love other people, not destroy them. This does not represent most IRS employees, but the ones who have the most authority and power are often in control of hundreds, or even thousands, of employees or taxpayers.

There is a widespread "collective spirit of inadequacy" with IRS employees. They are constantly berated by IRS management, told that they are not good enough, smart enough, productive enough, or have any value. It is inferred almost daily that they are disposable.

Fear gives the IRS even more power than Congress gave it. When you take away the fear, the IRS is just like the Wizard of Oz, a little man in a secret room trying to control everything and everyone with fear and intimidation.

You are not completely alone in presenting your case before the IRS. The Revenue Restructuring and Reform Act of 1998 (RRA 98) offered taxpayers a Taxpayer Bill of Rights. They are:

1. The right to be informed about how to comply with the tax laws
2. The right to quality service
3. The right to pay no more than the correct amount of tax
4. The right to challenge the IRS's position and be heard
5. The right to appeal an IRS decision in an independent forum
6. The right to finality (how much time the IRS has to increase your taxes or collect balance dues)
7. The right to privacy
8. The right to confidentiality
9. The right to representation
10. The right to a fair and just tax system

In the current IRS climate, good luck getting these rights. You will have to be aggressive to pursue your interests and rights.

The Collection Due Process and the Collection Appeals Program are examples of that. Appeals officers are seasoned and trained professionals in the IRS; they have the authority to make settlement agreements when a taxpayer has grounds for going into tax court and if the IRS believes that it will lose its case, the appeals officer will often make decisions that benefit both the taxpayer and the government.

This book will assist you in how to structure what you prepare and present to the IRS employee to make it easier for the IRS to understand what you want it to know, to make clear what you want to happen, and to take back some of your power and prevail in the situation. We will show you how to deal with the IRS from start to finish in order to increase your chances that the IRS employee assigned to your case will make a decision which is favorable to you.

—∞—

Chapter 3
What Does the IRS Do and Why Do We Need It?

The IRS collects $3.3 trillion a year. That amount represents 93% of total receipts for the federal government. This is primarily derived from income taxes and excise (add-on taxes on products) taxes for both individuals and corporations, as well as Social Security and Medicare/Medicaid taxes.

The IRS is the primary collector for the whole U.S. Government; it collects much more than just income and employment taxes. It collects penalties on people who fail to carry health insurance or who default on their student loans, child support and alimony. Other taxes collected include gasoline and diesel taxes, taxes on liquor and weapons, and tariffs and other excise taxes.

The IRS budget was $12.1 billion in 2010 and has been cut year after year. The 2016 budget proposal is $10.9 billion (down 17%). In the same time, inflation has been 9.4%, which effectively cuts the IRS budget by almost 26%. It is hard to run the nation's tax collector on dwindling dollars.

President Obama, in talking about the IRS budget, stated, "The real scandal around the IRS budget is that they have been so poorly funded that they cannot go after these folks who are deliberately avoiding tax payments."

"If taxpayers ever lose confidence that their friends, neighbors and business competitors are not paying their fair share of taxes, then they become less willing to pay taxes themselves", said James R. White, Director of Tax Issues, General Accounting Office. The effect of the budget cuts has a direct impact on the number of returns audited. The audit rate is down, tax collections are down, and criminal investigations are down.

Tax attorney Robert E. McKenzie stated that "IRS enforcement in examinations, collections and criminal enforcement produces $6 for every dollar spent. In other words, the misguided Congressional budget cuts have only served to increase the federal deficit. Tax cheats and scofflaws now have 20% less chance that the IRS will discover their non-compliance. Those who choose not to pay their taxes know the IRS will be much less likely to levy their wages and bank accounts." So the most dishonest Americans are being richly rewarded for non-compliance with tax laws.

Taxpayers have been trained to file and pay income taxes and the IRS claims a 98% rate of voluntary compliance. That is what they advertise. They quietly admit this is only on 84% of people with income in the United States. IRS audit and collection efforts resolve 2% more cases and the other 14% do not file or pay. Some reports indicate that 14-20% of people in the underground cash economy do not file or pay taxes at all.

The Treasury Inspector General for Tax Administration (TIGTA) reports that:

- 99% of W-2 earners report their income.
- Only 44% of self-employed people report their income.
- Only 11% of people who operate on a cash-only basis report their income.
- Only 53% of taxpayers are even required to file income tax returns and owe taxes.
- Forty-seven percent of people in the USA do not even owe income taxes, because they make too little income or have exemptions and deductions that lower their income.

Congresswoman Barbara Mikulski from Maryland claims that "Whatever you feel about the IRS…you can't have tax compliance without the IRS."

The National Taxpayer Advocate Nina Olson said:

> "The IRS is a system that treats all taxpayers and non-taxpayers as if they cannot be trusted, as if they all did something wrong. The computer system and the letters march forward progressively getting more aggressive and harassing. The system is designed with the belief that the people receiving the letters have already done something wrong- cheated on their taxes, provided false information on their tax returns or deliberately failed to pay their taxes. In most cases this is not true. All taxpayers are treated by the IRS as if they are guilty. Just trying to defend yourself is hard since you don't know the rules of the game. Just trying to get to the stage of "Guilty, until you prove yourself innocent" is difficult and can sometimes come after a lot of tears and anger on the taxpayers' part."

The IRS is supposed to be the agency which verifies information taxpayers put on their tax returns though its audit process. This is supposed to be fair and balanced and neutral. When the IRS manager and IRS employee get involved in their own interpretation of the Internal Revenue Code (the tax law), it turns into a nightmare of subjectivity, discrimination and recriminations.

The standard IRS approach to tax administration is that the taxpayer did something wrong and now the IRS has to find a way to punish him, possibly by putting him through a grueling audit or collection process.

Just trying to respond to the IRS can be exhausting and abusive to taxpayers who go into the office, or attempt to correspond with the IRS whether in writing or over the phone.

IRS employees are overworked, exhausted and short of patience after dealing with taxpayers who have been waiting on the telephone for 20 minutes to 2 hours, just to talk to someone. It is an exasperating experience to wait all that time and some hostility does often flow out of some taxpayers who feel disrespected and mistreated. They want to ask questions to determine whether to either agree with the letter that they received or to protest and find out what they can do to disagree with the letter.

Oftentimes these phone calls are handled by the lowest graded IRS employees, who have minimal training, knowledge and experience. They can be rude, short, officious, mean, uncaring and nasty. The whole process is one of frustration and is very unpleasant for both the IRS employee and the taxpayer.

It would take a whole book to spell out all the ways that the IRS abuses, harasses and mistreats its customers. You just need to be aware that it can and does happen on a daily basis and that you should try not to take it personally. It is only by acknowledging the power that the IRS has that you can hope to work within the system.

The best way to approach the IRS is in the same cold, uncaring and unemotional position that they treat you. Reviewing this book before you contact the IRS will give you enough IRS procedural knowledge in the examination and collection process to try to get the IRS to do what you want to see happen to resolve your account.

How the IRS Views You

Abuse and the IRS go both ways. One of the reasons that the IRS takes such a negative view that all taxpayers are liars and tax cheats is because there is a certain segment of society that is all that and more.

Fear is what often motivates taxpayers in their dealings with the IRS. Many people want to do the right thing and pay their fair share of taxes in support of their country and provide for the welfare of less fortunate people. Some taxpayers look at the tax system and life in a different way. There are many emotions that come to people as they think about taxes or having anything to do with the IRS. The IRS is the most hated government agency because it causes United States citizens to live in fear - fear of getting caught, fear of loss and fear of punishment. These emotions are accompanied by honesty, anger, greed, worry, anxiety and depression. Even talking about the IRS can suck your energy away!

Taxpayers may evaluate the situation as follows: Will I get caught? Will I get punished? How badly will I get punished? Then they make a risk assessment based on the answers. This is a very small percentage of delinquent taxpayers. Then there are those people who may pay the least amount of tax that they are legally entitled to pay (tax avoidance) which is legal, versus those who do not want to pay taxes at all - or pay less than the legal amount that would be due (tax evasion) which is illegal.

The Internal Revenue Service has many employees who are trying to "teach a lesson" to the taxpayers that they think are all cheaters and liars, thieves and scoundrels. They take the position that the actions of the taxpayer were deliberate, planned and were to their personal benefit. Some taxpayers who owe the IRS have expensive cars, awesome homes and vacation homes, the jewelry collection, the gun collection, the stocks and bonds, and fat bank accounts. These were the people who were living large, mostly on the government's money – your money.

But many other hard-working, honest Americans have saved their money and have these items. That is why some IRS employees need an attitude change. Most people did not set out to get audited or have a tax balance due. Eighty percent were just people who were pursuing their dreams and trying to make the best of their lives and then bust!

The IRS calls people who do not file or pay "Delinquent Taxpayers." This promotes a negative connotation. The word delinquent usually means a person or situation that is bad, failing, or a person who is an offender or guilty.

Most of the reasons why people owe taxes come down to the

following. Taxpayers have experienced death, depression, divorce, drugs, drinking, deception, dumb choices, or dumb behavior. Add to these reasons illness, a gambling addiction, adultery, bad luck, stupidity, and incompetence. Some people say they are too busy, or too afraid to open the IRS letters. They are so overwhelmed with their daily lives and the whole tax filing system that they try to hide. Sprinkle greed and deliberate tax evasion in, and it makes for an interesting cast of characters. There was always plenty of blame to go around as well. Blame the economy, the market, their competitors, their partners, their spouse, their employees, the President, Congress and the IRS. Rarely did they blame themselves for having any part in their financial collapse.

No one in their right mind would ever choose to be in any situation with the IRS. Those taxpayers who might be classified as psychopaths and sociopaths who seek confrontation with the IRS will soon find out they cannot win. You don't want to bring a butter knife to a gun fight.

Taxpayers receive letters and are unaware that the IRS does not care to respectfully consider the circumstance which may have given rise to the tax assessment. The IRS can be reasonable and fair and make sound decisions as to how to resolve tax issues, but that is often the exception not the rule. Most taxpayers think that the IRS is like a business where you can make proposals and offers that would be in the best interests of the IRS and get things done.

You need to remember that the average IRS employee couldn't care less about you or your circumstances; they only care about making their manager happy and closing cases as quickly and as legally as possible.

The actions of IRS employees are often unreasonable or even illogical, but they are procedural. They do things as they have been taught to do, as they have always done them. It does not matter if they make sense or not, it is just important to follow the rules which will lead to the case being closed.

Many people who have dealt with the IRS have said that "the left hand does not know what the right hand is doing." This means that there is no connection between various parts of the IRS. Examination does audits and Collection does collections, often on the same person, but they do not have any means to communicate or coordinate actions taken on your case.

There are many things wrong with the IRS. That is not the point of this book. We want to show you how to get the IRS off of your back. We want to show you how to navigate through the bureaucratic wreckage that defines how the IRS is run on a daily basis.

Chapter 4
How to Respond to the IRS

Upon verifying that you actually have received a letter from IRS, as outlined in Chapter 1, then you need to know how to respond.

When you receive a notice from the IRS, you have options, a few of which are as follows:

- Call the IRS
- Speak to an IRS employee in a local Taxpayer Assistance Center (TAC, also known as walk-in office), or at your business or home.
- Send a letter providing the IRS with additional information.
- Ignore the letter and hope that the IRS will go away.

Many people are afraid and do not respond to letters or phone calls from the IRS and they suffer greatly in the end.

The IRS has procedures, processes and protocols for everything that it does. You, being an outsider, must first figure out what that means. This chapter will help you with that. You must follow the IRS system in the way that you respond, or your case simply will not be resolved. The way that the IRS does things may not make sense to you, and may appear to be unreasonable. Don't worry about that. Not your problem. The IRS does those things, not because the procedures make sense, but because that is the way that the IRS has always done things. IRS employees face disciplinary actions if they don't follow those antiquated procedures.

Before you contact the IRS, you need to organize all your tax and financial income records and figure out the best way to present your case. You need to explain it to the IRS representative in a way that will cause the representative to understand your situation and, hopefully, help resolve it in your favor.

After presenting your case to the IRS, the IRS representative will decide how to resolve your case. It could be in your favor or not. Make sure that they understand your case and any special circumstances, because that can help you. Excuses seldom work, like telling the IRS that you "just don't have the money to pay your income taxes." At some point you had those dollars in your hand; it was your income. You just chose to spend those dollars, instead of paying the IRS.

If the IRS does not understand your case and does not offer you a reasonable solution that you can live with, you have the right to speak to the representative's immediate manager. For audit cases you have this right at any time. For collection cases you may also speak to the manager informally or file Form 9423 Collection Appeal Request. The manager must call you within 24 hours and discuss the case. This may or may not get you what you want. You need to know that the manager of that representative used to do that same job, before they became manager. If you cannot find a solution that you can live with, then your case will be forwarded to an appeals officer for review.

Stick to the Internal Revenue Code (IRC) or the Internal Revenue Manual (IRM) and use the laws and procedures to support your case. In addition to this book, you can conduct research on irs.gov, Google and Bing and find additional forms and information. There are many tools available to assist you. The IRS policy statements, letter rulings, tax court cases and many other sources can provide you with so much information.

The problem is that if you are not used to doing tax work, then it quickly becomes overwhelming and frustrating. The information is available, but you don't know how or what to ask for or have a clue as to where to find it.

Responding to IRS Letters

Although the IRS has tried to make some of its letters more understandable to its customers, the letters are still confusing, go on for 6-10 pages and you still cannot figure out what the IRS wants or is instructing you to do. As previously stated the letters are all coded with information that the IRS can understand, but is not easy for you to understand. As we said earlier, just trying to figure out which letter number you are holding in your hand can often be difficult.

All letters will address one of three areas:

- Directing you to do something – go to the office for an audit, or to request receipts or other proof of what was on your return, or
- Asking you for more information, or
- Requiring you to do something, such as requiring you to act or be somewhere by a certain deadline.

This can be confusing, because the IRS often does not just specifically ask you about something that they are disputing in the letter. The IRS will say that they have changed your return and now you owe increased tax, penalties and interest, all without waiting for you to respond. Many people do not even try to reply or to fight what the IRS is disputing; they simply send a check thinking that this will prevent further audit or collection action. This is not always true. Many people do mail a check in, after receiving a letter from the IRS claiming that they owe additional taxes. They believe that this will stop any further IRS interest in their tax file or it will prevent future audits or collection work. Nothing could be further from the truth. That is because the IRS is so huge and so compartmentalized, that the old saying "the right hand does not know what the left hand is doing", always applies. Paying off an audit letter does not prevent future audits. Paying a collection amount for one year does not prevent future collection actions.

The most important thing to remember is that you have the right to understand any changes that the IRS proposes making on your tax return.

It is important to respond to IRS letters and provide them with what they ask for. Do not provide anything more than what they specifically request. Additional information might get the IRS employee interested in exploring your tax case more thoroughly.

You will need to review the letter several times to determine what it is asking for. Use Google or Bing to query Understanding My (insert your letter number here) Letter (using the applicable letter number). This will take you to irs.gov and hopefully tell you everything that you need to know about why the letter was issued or what is required next. It is recommended that you gather the information that they are requesting and photocopy it and then write a simple letter explaining what your answer to their letter is and what proof you have of your position. Again, we stress that you never send original documents as the chances are high that you will never see them again.

Your response to the IRS should be sent back via certified mail. This does not get your case worked any faster, but it does prove that you sent something to the IRS address. If your letter is lost or destroyed by the IRS, this can make the difference between getting a levy on your wages or bank account lifted or not. Otherwise the IRS will take the position that you did not respond at all.

With the IRS you need to remember the standard is "You are guilty until you prove yourself innocent of whatever the IRS is claiming you did wrong."

You have to know what you want to achieve before you can figure out how to get it. In the case of a letter where the IRS is proposing to raise your taxes, you want to verify what is on your tax return so the tax remains the same. This could be verifying that you are married or that your dependents are actually people you can legally claim on your tax return.

If you owe a tax balance, you need to figure out what your rights are and how to get yourself in the best financial position you can be in according to what the IRS allows for you. To start, this may depend on how much you owe and for how many years.

Just because you received a bill from the IRS, it does not mean that it is correct. Check your records and see if you made an error on your tax return - see if the numbers were transposed or if you made a math error. These are increasingly rare, because so many people use automated tax programs. In 2014, 145,230,429 tax returns were filed and only 1.4% (2,035,463) had math errors and 2.6% (3,777,000) had under-reported income.

It may seem that there is no rhyme or reason for how the IRS operates. It may seem that way to you, a person outside of the IRS, but the IRS runs on procedures and manuals so everything that they do is part of an overall system. Everything eventually leads to your case being closed. Just because the computer sends you a letter, does not mean that you owe the tax. Private tax practitioners suggest that the error rate is 5-20%.

Math error notices are deceptive, because they adjust your tax, show you a balance due and tell you to pay it – now. The math error notice does not make it clear that you have either have 30 days to respond with an explanation or 60 days to ask for an abatement of the proposed tax and penalties.

Notices and Letters are available in other languages if you so request. They are available in English, Spanish, Russian, Vietnamese, Chinese and Korean. Many instructions and forms also are available in these languages.

There are many solutions that can come from your contact with the IRS. However, each IRS employee has limited authority which depends upon the employee's job description.

Responding to Telephone Calls

How do you know you are speaking with the IRS? As stated previously, if you suspect that the person calling you is not from the IRS or the letter that you have received does not appear to be genuine, then call the IRS directly at 1-800-829-1040. You will have to wait, but at least you can verify that the IRS is trying to contact you. The important thing to know with the IRS letter or phone call is that they already know most of your data. They will try to confirm who you are by asking you questions, but you will not be threatened that the sheriff is coming out to arrest you.

You may try to call the IRS in response to a letter, and that can be frustrating, because the IRS does not pick up 60-80% of incoming calls. You might receive a phone call from the IRS. Although this may be unexpected and inconvenient, don't ignore it completely. If it does not appear to be a legitimate call from the IRS, then you should tell the caller that you are going to hang up and verify that the IRS is calling and that you are going to need their employee identification number to do that.

When you contact the IRS, the IRS employee needs to know your story and the reason that you are talking to them. Be brief! Be clear and concise. You need to wait until they ask you, don't just blurt it out. The first thing to know is that they do not want your whole story and all your reasons at first. They first have to identify themselves and give you their employee identification number. Then they will ask for your name, Social Security number, date of birth, and maybe your adjusted gross income on your most recently filed Form 1040 Income Tax return. This is all before you can say anything at all about why you are calling.

When they ask how they can help you, do not start the conversation by telling them how much you dislike the IRS or how many hours you were on hold before they answered your phone call or how many months/years you waited for someone to be assigned to work your case. IRS employees do not need to know how long you waited and how frustrated you are. They are just picking up the next call, all day long, and are frustrated as well. They just want to do the work, resolve your case and move on to work the next case and then go home and hide at the end of the day. Customer service work has a way of depleting the energy of the IRS employee. It can be especially frustrating because they are talking to taxpayers who are afraid to call the IRS, who are worried about what the IRS employee will tell them and who are angry because they have been on hold for so long.

Don't try to figure out the IRS employee; sometimes your idle chatter just upsets them. All that you need to know is that they are under a significant amount of daily unremitting pressure to perform, to pick up the calls, to close the cases. Some employees are almost robotic in their interview. This is how they were taught. We see this especially with employees hired in the last ten years who were given a much different training standard than older employees.

Instead of helping you, some IRS employees will judge you, blame you, and condemn you for your actions, inactions or other choices. Don't get into a power match with them. Stay relaxed, balanced and professional. Focus on your case being resolved in the best possible way. It might seem like they want to provoke you, and usually they have some power position over you – they can give you many deals that will either be in your favor or not. Many IRS employees just don't care; as your tax issue is not their problem. It's your problem.

Even employees who may want to help you cannot make the adjustment themselves online of what they told you that they would do to help you. All input to the Master Computer System (IDRS) is done directly from various Service Center Campuses located around the United States, unless you are working with the Taxpayer Advocate Office. This is not an online system. It is updated once a week.

It is important to not be angry or inject attitude in your response to the IRS, because that will only increase the amount of attention that they pay to you and your case. As you will see later, if the IRS labels you as a troublemaking tax protestor, or as a potentially dangerous taxpayer, you will have more trouble than you can imagine.

If you don't know the answer to a question that the IRS employee is asking, then don't make stuff up; never lie. Just tell them that you will have to find out the answer to their question. It is better to be silent than to lie to an IRS official.

After you answer the initial round of questions that are asked of you, the IRS employee will automatically start asking you additional questions, such as your home, cell and work phone numbers. They will also ask the name of the place where you work and the address, and where you bank and the account number. This can seem very intrusive, but in cases where the IRS claims you owe money, they have the right to ask this. Unfortunately, when you failed to pay your taxes, it was like inviting the IRS into your life for the next ten years.

If you are calling to find out more information about a letter that you received, you must be very clear in your request. If you have a letter showing that a W-2 form was received from your employer which shows that you received $200,000 in income, but in fact you only received $20,000 in income, you can verify that with the IRS, but the IRS employee can do nothing to help you. You have to go back to the issuer of the W-2 form and get it corrected. The same applies to Form 1099, the form that reports to the IRS other income that you received; this could be from interest, dividends, gambling winnings, and self-employment income. If there is an error, it must be corrected by the issuer, not the IRS. The same applies to audit changes that come from other government agencies. These can come from the Social Security Administration, defaulted Small Business Administration loans, your state's Unemployment Commission, a state court that is collecting past due alimony or child support, defaulted student loans and hundreds of other government agencies.

If you default on your student loan, then your Social Security retirement benefit or disability may become subject to levy from the IRS to the extent of 15% of your money. This is called the Federal Levy Payment Program (FPLP). This can be avoided if Social Security makes up most of your benefit. The U.S. Department of Education has a program which you can apply for that will allow you to pay a reduced payment based on your income or even make no payment at all in the event that paying would cause you a financial hardship. Use Google or Bing to search for "Student Loans, Forgiveness at ed.gov."

Out of the blue, other phone calls will be with regard to late filing or non-filing of tax returns, identity fraud and lost refunds.

Speaking to the IRS in Person

One IRS representative who was dealing with a delinquent taxpayer was being rude and the taxpayer reminded her that "she worked for him and all the other taxpayers." She told him "I don't work for you, I work for the IRS," and then refused to stamp his tax return as accepted by the IRS. The IRS is supposed to be the people working for the "We the People" described in the U.S. Constitution. All people who pay taxes pay their salaries. There are five ways that you may speak to an IRS employee in person:

- The first is if you go to an IRS office for information or advice. These employees work in the area called the Taxpayer Assistance Center (TAC) and they are the first line of IRS customer/taxpayer service. If you search Google or Bing for this term, "Contact Your Local IRS Office" you should be able to find the nearest IRS office. Not all towns or even cities have a TAC. Some TAC offices work on an appointment-only basis.
- The second is if you are told to appear at an IRS office for an office audit. You will speak to a Tax Compliance Officer/ Tax Auditor (TCO), an employee who is required to have only limited accounting skills but is highly trained in IRS tax matters who will audit some part of your Individual Income tax return/Form 1040. Some tax compliance officers do have more experience or education than the job requires, so do not dismiss them or assume they don't know the law.
- The third type of contact will be a Field Revenue Agent, (RA), who will come to your home or business and will audit your personal or your business returns. Revenue agents have extensive accounting and tax law experience. Some also

have Masters' degrees in Taxation or are Certified Public Accountants. Chapter 7 will discuss your rights during an audit, including the right to have your audit handled by an enrolled agent or CPA.

- The fourth type will be a Field Revenue Officer, (RO), who will come to your home or business to view what you own and try to collect tax balances from you.
- The fifth type is an IRS Criminal Special Agent (SA). Dealing with a special agent can be the most dangerous contact you have. They have the power to arrest and jail you. Be polite, but ask to speak to your attorney first, and then stop talking. The special agent works your case and anything you say can and will be used against you in a criminal case. The criminal special agent refers their conclusion for prosecution to the U.S. Attorney which is part of the Department of Justice (DOJ).

When you make contact with the IRS, you may be angry, confused, and frustrated all at the same time. These are all typical emotions for a person in their dealings with the IRS. You need to know that these are also feelings and reactions that the IRS employee may also have many times throughout the day.

IRS employees are responsible for administering the tax laws passed by Congress. In fact, their Mission Statement is:

> "To provide America's taxpayers top quality service by helping them understand and meet their tax responsibilities and enforce the law with integrity and fairness to all."

This mission statement describes the role of the IRS and the public's expectation about how the IRS should perform that role.

In the United States, the Congress passes tax laws and requires taxpayers to comply. The taxpayer's role is to understand and meet his or her tax obligations. The IRS role is to help the large majority of compliant taxpayers with the tax law, while ensuring that the minority who are unwilling to comply pay their fair share.

IRS employees are evaluated on how they treat their taxpayers, how they apply the tax laws and how they follow IRS procedures. There are many laws and procedures and many people watching what each employee is doing, then grading them on it. For starters, they have their direct line manager reviewing their work then another two levels of management that will review an employee's cases. When the case is closed it is reviewed by Quality Review, National Office or maybe IRS National Taxpayer Advocate. IRS employees are forever living in fear that they will do something wrong and get disciplined.

Finally, the greatest worry that an IRS employee has is the U.S. Treasury Inspector General for Tax Administration (TIGTA). TIGTA causes IRS employees to get caught, arrested and jailed. TIGTA is divided into two parts.

Internal Audit - the people who actually look at the IRS employee's case work, audit each IRS employee yearly, review the systems and procedures and seek to determine if they followed the law. The other half of TIGTA is Internal Security. This consists of special agents who monitor employee contacts, employee conduct and have the power to charge and arrest IRS employees who they claim have violated the law while doing their jobs. Types of violations include the employee accepting a bribe or filing false refund claims or other identity fraud.

Special agents also investigate taxpayers who threaten or attempt to bribe IRS employees and have the power to arrest those people. TIGTA special agents also have the right to arrest and detain taxpayers and lying to any IRS employee is a crime.

There is a lot of pressure on employees of the IRS to do the right thing for the government and taxpayers every day on every case. The problem comes down to the employees and their respective managers' subjective interpretation of what constitutes the right thing to do on each case. It can be very stressful for the IRS employee knowing that they have someone looking over their shoulder all of the time.

Now that you have determined what letter you have received and who is contacting you, you can go directly to the chapter that deals with that section. The Index at the back of this book can help you to find your letter number and where it is located in the IRS.

Chapter 5
Service Center Processing

—~—

There are ten IRS Service Centers located around the United States and one Master Computer (IDRS) which collects all the data and organizes it. The Master Computer is 55 years old, but it is still efficient and hack proof, since it is not online.

The Submission Processing Section begins the "Pipeline System" used by the IRS. The IRS receives paper tax returns and has to convert that data by hand to data the computer can process. This takes time and manpower. The electronic filing (E-filing) of tax returns is the IRS alternative to paper tax returns; those returns mostly bypass this pipeline. Now the majority of information and payments are arriving electronically.

The tax returns are examined for errors or inconsistencies, for example, if the return was not complete, was not signed, or is illegible. To fix this, the IRS will send the return back with letters telling the taxpayer what needs to be done to make the return "processable." Your return may not be considered as timely filed if it is returned to you for correction or especially for a missing signature.

The return data is then transmitted to the IDRS, (Integrated Data Retrieval System) which is located at the IRS Martinsburg Computing Center. There, the tax returns are subjected to math error and other validity checks before processers attempt to upload them to the Master Computer.

No matching is done at this point between what the taxpayer puts on the return and what was reported to the IRS. This is because when the returns are received, much of that information has not even been submitted or processed by the IRS. It will be compared to the returns later, usually 12-16 months after the due date of the return. Then letters will be issued that tell the taxpayer there was an error and they forgot to report a certain amount of money and owe a new balance due.

All income tax returns are "coded" when they are input to the computer. This code is called the Discriminate Index Function (DIF) score; it compares what you put on your return with what other people put on their returns. This DIF score then decides your potential to be audited. The IRS is looking for items that are very different from what other taxpayers in similar circumstances have reported on their returns. This statistical scan identifies which cases should be considered for audit.

If you owe a balance, a series of letters will be sent to you over a six-month period. If you are being audited, it will begin with a letter from a Service Center. The simplest audit is called a "correspondence audit." You send in proof of whatever item that is being questioned and the IRS lets you know if they agree or disagree. Or the IRS can send the case to a local office for an office auditor (tax compliance officer) to review or send it to a field revenue agent who does audits at your home or business.

From this point on the cases will move to the Accounts Management Section. This unit responds to taxpayer inquiries for advice on a variety of tax law and how the IRS process works, and to clarify for the taxpayer the data contained in letters they have received. This unit is divided into two sections which we will call Service Center Audit and Service Center Collection. You will only have a telephone number on your letter, you will not know where your IRS agent is located, and you will never be allowed to speak to the same person twice. The system is designed that way, but it makes people mad that if they have to call more than once, they have to retell their whole story.

The IRS is divided into numerous Business Units; however, most taxpayers deal with two- one is called Wage and Investment (W&I), and the other is called Small Business-Self Employed (SB/SE). This makes no difference to you, but it does to the IRS. If you are a wage earner only, your case will be worked by a Wage and Investment employee, a person who was narrowly trained to work cases on wage earners. If your case is being worked by an SB/SE employee, they have more specific training about people with small businesses or a mixture of business and wage earners. Both types of employees work:

- Math error notices.
- Balance due notices.
- Tax adjustment notices (where your tax is being increased).
- Offset notices, where your refund is taken to pay some debt that you have, such as child support or delinquent student loans.
- Information notices related to some item on your tax return.
- Credit transfer notices when your refund is being transferred to pay your back taxes.
- Annual Reminder Notices, known as CP 71 notices, are letters that are required by law to be issued yearly reminding you that you still owe taxes. You do not ever have to respond to these notices. They do not affect what is happening with your case. They are just reminders that you still owe the taxes.

Cases go into different "pipelines" at this point. But they do not stay long. They process to the next stage, the next letter, or the next action about every 6-8 weeks.

If Service Center Audit or Service Center Collection are unable to resolve your case after an almost endless stream of letters, they send your case to the IRS Telephone Collection Unit which is called Automated Collection System (ACS) or put it in a hold file (the Queue) waiting to be issued to ACS or to be issued to a field revenue officer.

Some exam cases are closed after they have been worked by Service Center Audit; they are marked as "surveyed by National Office." This means that you should have been audited, but because not that much additional tax would have resulted or IRS does not have the staff to do an audit, they will put your case aside and not audit it. If you keep making the same mistake year after year, that scores more points on the IRS computer and makes it more likely for you to be audited.

Another way both collection and exam cases are closed in the Service Center pipeline is called "shelved by National Office." Again this means that the case might be worthy of work, but the IRS does not have the resources to work the case. So they put it figuratively on a shelf waiting for a time that may never come for it to be worked.

If you receive a balance due letter and it is for under $1,000, you might just receive that one letter and not hear from the IRS again. That means that they will collect any balance due from future refunds that you might get, but otherwise they will not bother you. Another way that the IRS closes cases is called "Tolerance", where the balance is under a certain amount and the IRS leaves the balance on the computer, but makes no other effort to collect it. Each part of the IRS has various dollar criteria for when they will do this. Sorry we cannot share that with you; it is all classified information.

The important thing to know about Service Center audit and collection is that they do take notes that you responded to their letters. They share this with the ACS site and also with the taxpayer service employees. But if the case is sent to office audit or field audit or field collection, none of these units have access to the notes from your phone call. This is another example of how in the IRS, "the left hand does not know what the right hand is doing."

The problem with any communication with the service center is that the IRS employees do not explain anything to you about the process. They are so busy asking you questions like where you work and bank they will not tell you how long you have to pay the amounts due. Service center employees treat everything like it is a secret. The secrets include - how long you have to pay, what options are available, and what credits they will allow you on the financial statement you submit. A review of the IRS work procedures guidebook which is called the Internal Revenue Manual (IRM) is also censored to remove reference to what payment plans are available to you based on your circumstances. IRS is pretty consistent in wanting to keep itself in a cloud of mystery.

If you call the Service Center, be careful what you say, otherwise you might paint yourself into a corner. You will give up some of your rights, because you give vague answers to them. Saying that you don't know or don't remember or need to get back to them is acceptable. You can also say that you want to consult with a tax professional and will call them back.

Before you give any financial information, you should read Chapter 12 which explains how to get maximum credit for your expenses when completing the IRS financial statements.

Service Center audit and collection offices are in 25 locations around the United States; they are open from 7am to 7pm in whatever time zone that you are in. Hawaii and Alaska are in the Pacific time zone.

This book will explain exactly what you need to know to protect yourself and give yourself the best terms of whatever settlement you reach with the IRS. We want you to know all the alternatives and benefits available to you. The IRS is not your "friend." They don't see things from your position, just from the government's position. When you speak to people in the Service Center, you will usually feel like you are not being treated well. They are often rude and insensitive to the circumstances of your life.

Audit Letters

The first audit letters you receive asking for information are Letter 566, Letter 566-D, Letter 566-E, CP 75, CP 75A, CP 75D, and CP 06, Letter 566(CG), all signaling an upcoming correspondence audit. When you receive any of these letters, look at your tax return and go through all the numbers. Compare what the IRS is showing in your letter to what you put on your return. Pull out all your receipts and records that support what you put on your tax return.

There are hundreds of letters and CP notices that are sent out. This is because the IRS wants to issue letters that protect its right to assess the tax. The IRS Service Center never issues personalized letters to taxpayers – they are all computer generated. When the IRS gives written advice, it can later be used by the taxpayer to support their case. That is why they use the boilerplate form letters to respond to taxpayers.

This is why it is important for you to locate the letter or CP number first and then Google or Bing search - Understanding Your (Insert Your Letter Number Here), or whatever is your letter or notice. Some of the letters are not found on the irs.gov site. That is why we have included them here.

These are listed numerically; it makes no difference to you, the taxpayer, if it is a computer paragraph notice (CP) or a letter (LT) or a form. So look for the number on your letter, and then find that on the following list.

CP 05 **Initial Audit Review Notification Letter**

CP 06 Same as **CP 05**

CP 11 **IRS Made Changes to Your Return.** This is also issued as **CP 11A** and **CP 11M**. You have 60 days to file an appeal.

CP 21 **Change to Your Tax Return.** This is the same as a **LT 4364 C**

CP 22 Same as **CP 21**

CP 71 **Annual Letter to Remind You That You Still Have a Balance Due.** This letter is required to everyone who owes a tax balance every year. You do not have reply to it. If you have an installment agreement, offer in compromise pending or your case has been declared as "currently not collectible" then this letter does not affect any of that. This letter generates tens of thousands of unnecessary phone calls to the IRS.

CP 75 **Return Audit Notice.**
Notice that return is under audit questioning Earned Income Credit, dependents and filing status. Letter will include Form 886-H telling you which items are being questioned. Also issued as **CP 75A** and **CP 75D.**

CP 87-A **Verify a Claimed Dependent.** This indicates that you may have suffered identity fraud. The IRS is questioning why you claimed someone who was already claimed by someone else.

LT 239C **Identity Fraud Notification letter.**

LT 525 **General 30 Day Letter.**
This informs you that the IRS is proposing to make changes to your tax return. This can be the result of a math error or something else that does not appear correct on your return. It will also come with a Form 886-A Explanation of Items (of the audit) and Form 4549 Income Tax Examination Changes which shows the calculations for the proposed changes. This letter is written telling you that you owe a balance as a result of those changes. In fact, it is not a balance due letter, it is proposing changes. Because of this you have 30 days from the date of this letter to appeal it in writing. There is no form, this is an inside IRS appeal. You tell why you do not agree and send any information to make clear your case. Send your response certified mail to the address that you received the letter from. If you appeal the case it should be assigned to an auditor next.

LT 531 **Notice of Deficiency.** This is a letter legally telling you that now the IRS has decided that you owe taxes. This will come with a Form 886-A and Form 4549. You can agree and sign a waiver consenting to this. At this point, you must file a petition with the tax court within 90 days from the date you received the notice. This is very important! You cannot get an extension longer than the 90 days unless you can prove that you are out of the United States and then you get up to 150 days.

LT 566 **We Are Examining Your Federal Tax Return.** There are many variations of this letter. There are many boxes on the letter and the IRS will check off those that they are questioning. Also issued as **LT 566 C, LT 566 D** and **LT 566 E.**

On this form the IRS will question:

- Filing status and exemptions.
- Adjustments to income.
- Alimony paid.
- Moving expense deduction.
- Schedule C – itemized deductions.
- Medical and dental expenses.
- Interest you paid.
- Gifts to charity.
- Casualty and theft losses.
- Unreimbursed employees expense.
- Schedule C - expenses and gross receipts
- Other miscellaneous deductions.
- Tax credits.
- Foreign tax credit.
- Earned income tax credit
- Child care credit.
- Education credit.
- Adaption credit.
- Credit for the elderly and disabled

They will also include anything else they are questioning. At this point you need to reconstruct all of the data you put on your tax return originally and make sure it was accurate. Then photocopy it all (never send your originals) and return to the address on the letter within 30 days from the date of the letter. Form 886-A is usually included with this letter also.

LT 692 **Request for Consideration of Additional Findings.** This letter is sent along with a report of detailed adjustments that the IRS has made to your tax return. It will come with a form detailing the changes. You will receive the Form 886-A and Form 4549 with this letter also. You have **15 days** from the date of this letter to appeal the proposed adjustments with the Office of Appeals.

Form 886-A

Explanation of Items.
This tells you exactly what records and for what time periods you need to gather and send to the IRS. This is always attached to a **LT 692**, or other letters as described above.

LT 915 **Letter to Transmit Examination Report**
If you agree you can send a check. You have **30 days** from the date that you received the letter to submit your appeal/protest to the office that sent you the letter. This letter also includes a Form 886-A and a Form 4549.

LT 950 **30 Day Straight Deficiency or Over Assessment.** This letter is sent after IRS field audits and is used for unagreed, straight deficiency and straight assessment cases. Those are where you either owe more money or the IRS is saying that you will be getting money back. If you agree, you sign the form and return to the address on the letter. If you don't agree, you have **30 days** to file an appeal/protest.

LT 1912 **You Have Not Responded to Our Earlier Request for Information.** This is a second chance letter, where the person conducting the audit believes that you might have some information that will prevent a new increased tax assessment, if only you would send it.

CP 2000 **Automatic Adjustment Notice**
This is not an audit letter, this is a notice that the IRS has matched information that was provided to them by third parties like your W-2's, Form 1099's that report stock transactions, bank interest, sales of your home, self-employment income, etc. and they have found that you did not list something on your return. This is part of the IRS Matching Program. These letters usually come out in August, September and October in the year after you file a tax return. Many times this notice is incorrect. Carefully review what the IRS is sending to you. If you agree, pay the balance as soon as you can. Please note that paying a balance that is not correct will not prevent an IRS audit for this same tax return up to six years after you filed it. If you do not agree, then you have **60 days** to file an Appeal/Protest in writing to IRS, otherwise the balance proposed becomes your new balance due.

LT 2201A **You are being Audited - Call Us Within 10 days to Schedule an Appointment.** This letter indicates that you may be audited for Schedule C – self-employment expenses and income, or for Schedule E Real Estate Gains and Losses. Same as **LT 2202.**

LT 2202B **Correspondence Examination.** Send proof of everything that you claimed on the tax return. Similar to **LT 2205A.**

LT 2205 A **Your Return Has Been Selected for Audit.** There are many reasons you will receive this letter. They include, but are not limited to the following.

- Schedule A - Home mortgage interest and points from Form 1098

- Schedule A - Employee Business Expenses
- Schedule A - Miscellaneous Expenses and other expenses
- Schedule C - Gross Receipts and Sales
- Schedule C - Depreciation and Section 179 Expense
- Schedule C - Hobby Losses
- Schedule C – Rents Received
- Schedule C – Depreciation and Section 179 expense
- Schedule C - Other expenses
- Schedule C - Contract labor expense
- Schedule C – Insurance, Car and Truck Expenses, Interest Expense, Office Expense

LT 2205B **Audit Notice.** Regarding Schedule F Sales and Expenses.

CP 2501 **Tax Return Information Does Not Match the Information the IRS Has On File.**

LT 2566 **You Have Not Filed Your Taxes.** This is not an audit letter. This is worse, it tells you that the IRS has reason to believe that you have taxable income that you are not reporting and it is preparing "Substitute for Returns" (SFR) for you. This is always bad for you, because the IRS files you as single or married filing separately and does not allow any dependents, credits, deductions, or exemptions. If you receive this letter, run, don't walk to the nearest tax preparer and then send your version of the tax return not through normal IRS processing but to the address on the letter.

LT 2645C **We Have Received the Items That You Sent Us.** This is a delay letter, the IRS is acknowledging that they received the information you submitted, but they need up to 90 days to review it and then they will respond to you. Sometimes they never respond.

LT 3016 **IRC Section 6015 Preliminary Determination Letter (30 Day).** This letter gives you **30 days** to appeal the determination for innocent spouse relief under IRC Section 6015. If you do not agree, you must file a written appeal of the proposed adjustments to the office/individual who sent you the letter within 30 days from the date of the letter.

CP 3219 A **Increase in Tax and Notice of Right to Challenge.** This is a very important letter. If you do not agree with the changes, you have to respond to it with a written protest. You have **90 days** to respond with your protest. This would be a good time to consult with a CPA or tax professional.

LT 3391 **30 Day Non Filer Letter.** The IRS sends this letter when they believe that you will owe money on a tax return that you have not filed. They will calculate it and tell you how much you will owe. If you agree and pay it, the IRS cannot come back at you later. If it is in error, you need to file your tax return now. You have 30 days from the date of this letter to file an appeal with the Office of Appeals.

LT 3401 **Audit No Change Letter.** This is the best letter you could ever receive. It means that the IRS is not changing your tax amount.

LT 3541A **Documents Requested to Support Alimony Deduction.** This usually means that the IRS does not know to whom you paid alimony; it also indicates that the person who received the alimony did not report it either.

LT 3572 **Return Selected for Examination.** This is another letter that tells you that you are going to be audited. Issues that this type of audit looks at include any line on your Schedule A, C, E, or F. This is usually an audit that will be conducted by an office auditor or field revenue agent. This is likely to be more serious and more far reaching. You should gather your records and consult with a tax professional at this point.

LT 3727 **30-Day Letter Notifying Taxpayer No Change to Original Report Disallowing EIC Based on Failure to Meet Residency Test for Children Claimed.**
You have **30 days** from the date of the letter to file an appeal with the Office of Appeals.

LT 3728 **30-Day Letter Notifying Taxpayer No Change to Original Report Partially Disallowing EIC Based on Failure to Meet Residency Test for 1 Child.**
You have **30 days** from the date of this letter to file an appeal with the Office of Appeals.

LT 4364C **Thank You for Your Amended Return – Here is How Much You Owe.** This is the same as a **CP 21** and **CP 22** letter.

LT4464 C **Your Case Has Been Selected for Audit.**

Form 4549-E
Income Tax Discrepancy Adjustment. Your tax has been adjusted because of a match with your state tax agency information. This usually has to do with some benefit you receive from your state like taxable benefits or unemployment. It can also include an unreported state tax refund.

Form 4564 **Information Document Request.** The IRS will be very specific in what records it wants to review. This is usually sent along with a Form 886-A.

Form 4700 **Examination Work papers.** This is used by the person conducting the audit as a history sheet and it reviews all of the facts of your case and why they are auditing you. This can sometimes be obtained when you request a transcript of your tax account and the "auditors or revenue agents work papers." Or you can also file a Freedom of Information Act Request.

Form 5278 **Proposed Notice of Deficiency.** This is similar to Form

4549 and it offers you specific rights. You can agree with it and pay the balance proposed. You can appeal it to the employee's manager, you can file a written appeal to the IRS Office of Appeals, or you can wait for the tax to be assessed and then file a petition in tax court. You will have **90 days** from the Notice of Deficiency date to file in tax court, if you do not, you never will have the chance again. If you have lost in the IRS appeals office, you can then go to tax court and the IRS attorney assigned to the case will try to settle the case outside of court. If that does not work, then you have the right to have your issue heard by the court.

Resolving Your Audit Case in Service Center Audit

It is best for you to always resolve your case as quickly and easily as possible. Sometimes what the IRS is questioning is easy to correct. It may be that you wrote down the wrong Social Security number for your child or a dependent parent. You need to check the numbers on your return and then copy the Social Security card and mail it to the IRS. Or if you are claiming the Earned Income Tax Credit and the IRS shows that someone else is also claiming the child or children that you are claiming, this can be reviewed. Many times the father or mother of the children will in divorce or separation cases take the deduction even though their joint custody agreement does not allow them to do that. This is quite common and the bad news is that whoever files their return first will be allowed by the IRS to claim the children, whether it is legal or not under state law.

The IRS employee working your case will sometimes acknowledge that yes, by rights you should have been allowed to take the child or children as your dependents, but there is nothing they can do to help you. The IRS will tell you that you need to go back to divorce court and clear it up with your ex.

Many taxpayers receive one or more of the above letters and dutifully reply by sending back their original receipts which the IRS then loses. **Never send any original documents to the IRS.** We cannot say that often enough.

Many taxpayers mail the information and then call the IRS to see if they received the information or if what they sent was sufficient to resolve the problem. Sixty-two percent of these taxpayers called 4 times or more. The IRS stated that for 13% of people it took eight or more telephone calls to get some response to that question. For most taxpayers it takes 2-4 phone calls and they wait 1-2 hours on each call. Then the person picking up the phone is not the same one you spoke with the last time. You need to know that you will never speak with any of those people again. That is how the pipeline is designed. Also the person picking up the phone is not the one who has access to your information that you mailed in. We suggest you stick to providing everything in writing and mailing it certified mail and then following up in writing also.

Often audit letters are issued for only one item on your tax return, like a request for charitable deductions or for a copy of your real estate tax bill. This is because the IRS has some audits that only want to test a certain number of returns and see if they were done correctly. This is taking a statistical sampling. If you have the proof they want, that will allow the matter to be closed. We believe that you may be able to represent yourself in a correspondence audit if only one issue is involved. More than that and we suggest that you consult with a tax professional.

It is important to understand who the person is who is working on your audit. In the service centers those employees are called *correspondence examination technicians*. These are grade 5 employees who may be part time or just hired for the tax season. This is an employee who is making $13.58 an hour evaluating the work of CPAs. These are usually lower paid employees who have been trained to do the work, but are not auditors or accountants in any way and may or may not understand the information that you provide them. If you think that may be the case, you should request in writing that your case be transferred to office audit or field audit.

It is also important to know that when you communicate with the IRS, they usually record your phone call or correspondence and note it in their system. That information is only visible to the accounts management employees in the Service Center and to the taxpayer service employees in the local offices and Automated Collection System employees wherever in the United States they are located.

Office auditors (tax compliance officers), field revenue officers, and field revenue agents do not have access to that system. These employees will often have no idea that you never responded to any of the letters. It does not make sense. We are just reporting how it is.

It is important to state at this point, Service Center audit and collection employees working your audit case cannot file liens against you, or levy (seize) your bank accounts or salary, wages or other income. That comes later.

The IRS conducts over 1.7 million correspondence (mail) audits every year and collects $9 billion from them; it is a good and efficient program for the IRS, but many taxpayers receiving these letters will just send a check instead of disputing the IRS information.

Service Center Accounts Management – Collection Cases

All cases at some point end up as either refunds, no change audits or there is a balance due. Balance due accounts are worked in Service Center collection. They will work your case for 26 to 105 weeks, depending on the dollar amount and other circumstances. If balance due cases are not resolved in the Service Center, then they can either be issued to the Queue for the Automated Collection System (ACS) or put into a Queue waiting to be issued to a field revenue officer. A Queue is a long waiting line and when ACS or field collection has enough free employees and resources then they will have a chance of working the case.

ACS will only hold cases in its inventory for 52 weeks and then they will transfer them to the Queue to be assigned to a field revenue officer.

Some higher balance or more difficult cases from Service Center accounts management or ACS go directly to a field revenue officer.

Millions of cases are in each of these queues and may never be worked, because the IRS does not have the employees or resources to work them.

An IRS collection field group manager in Dallas, Texas acknowledged that the Queue for his area had dozens of cases with balances over $1 million that would likely never be issued to a field revenue officer for collection, because he did not have enough employees to work those cases.

In Chapter 8, Collection, we will tell you the dollar amounts for installment agreements and tell you how much each IRS section can work dollar wise. This will give you the knowledge you need if you speak with the IRS. For instance, if you owe $300,000 then you should not be speaking to ACS at all. You should request your case be assigned to a field revenue officer. Do this in writing if you have to. But stop talking to the ACS person who can do nothing to resolve your case.

Collection Letters

There are fewer letters on the Collection side, but if you do not respond to those letters, you are at great risk of losing your money and possessions. The IRS loves to get what they call "levy sources", places where you have or earn money accounts, wages, salary and any other income that you have.

LT 11 **Final Notice of Intent to Levy and Notice of Your Right to a Hearing.** This notice and referenced publications explain how to request an appeal if you do not agree. You need to file a Form 12153, A Request for a Collection Due Process Hearing to the office at the address shown on your levy notice within **30 days** from the date of the letter to appeal the action with the IRS Office of Appeals.

CP 63 **We are Holding your Refund Because You Have Not Filed One or More Tax Returns and We Believe You Will Owe Tax.** This is a new change in IRS. Not filing will cause your other years' refunds to be held. You need to file those returns immediately, even if you do not believe that you will owe any tax.

CP 71 **Annual Letter to Remind You That You Still Have a Balance Due.** This letter is required to everyone who owes a tax balance every year. You do not have reply to it. If you have an installment agreement, offer in compromise pending or your case is declared as "currently not collectible" then this letter does not affect any of that. This letter generates tens of thousands of phone calls.

CP 77 **Alaska Permanent Fund Dividend Program.** This attaches to your annual payout from the state of Alaska. This notice and referenced publications explain how to request an appeal if you do not agree. You need to file a Form 12153, A Request for a Collection Due Process Hearing to the office at the address shown on your levy notice within **30 days** from the date of the letter to appeal the action with the IRS Office of Appeals.

CP 90 **Final Notice of Intent to Levy.** This letter is issued when the IRS is issuing a levy under the Federal Payment Levy Program (FPLP). This takes 15% of your Social Security, federal retirement benefit or other U.S. Government benefit that you receive. This letter notifies you of your unpaid taxes and that the IRS intends to levy to collect the amount owed. This notice and referenced publications explain how to request an appeal if you do not agree. You need to file a Form 12153, A Request for a Collection Due Process Hearing, to the office at the address shown on your levy notice within **30 days** from the date of the letter to appeal the action with the IRS Office of Appeals. **CP 297** is the same as this letter.

CP 92 **Notice of Levy upon Your State Tax Refund.** This notice and referenced publications explain how to request an appeal if you do not agree. You need to file a Form 12153, A Request for a Collection Due Process Hearing, to the office at the address shown on your levy notice within **30 days** from the date of the letter to appeal the action with the IRS Office of Appeals. **CP 242** is the same as this letter.

CP 242 **Notice of Levy upon Your State Tax Refund.** This notice and referenced publications explain how to request an appeal if you do not agree. You need to file a Form 12153, A Request for a Collection Due Process Hearing, to the office at the address shown on your levy notice within **30 days** from the date of the letter to appeal the action with the IRS Office of Appeals.

LT 501 **You Have a Balance Due on One of Your Tax Accounts.** This is the first notice you will receive from the IRS when you owe taxes. There are no appeals rights. You should get your financial records in order and prepare to either contest this tax or figure out how you can pay it.

LT 503 **We Have Not Heard from You and You Still Have an Unpaid Balance on One of Your Tax Accounts.** This is your second notice that you owe taxes. You should contact the IRS by phone or in writing to discuss, but read the Chapter 8 of this book first.

LT 504 **You Have an Unpaid Amount Due on Your Account. If You Do Not Pay the Amount Immediately, the IRS**

Will Seize (Levy) Your State Income Tax Refund and Apply it to Pay the Amount You Owe.

CP 523 **IMF Installment Agreement Default Notice.** This notice and referenced publications explain how to request an appeal if you do not agree. You need to file a Form 12153, A Request for a Collection Due Process Hearing, to the office at the address shown on your levy notice within **30 days** from the date of the letter to appeal the action with the IRS Office of Appeals.

LT 3172 **Notice of Federal Tax Lien.** This letter is sent after the Notice of Federal Tax Lien is filed. If you do not agree with the lien or it is causing you financial hardship, then you have **30 days** to file your appeal on Form 12153, Request for a Collection Due Process Hearing, and send it to the address shown on your lien notice within 30 days from the date of the letter in order to appeal the action to the IRS Office of Appeals.

The following letters are sent from the field collection department, by a revenue officer who is directly assigned to your case.

LT 1058 **Final Notice with Intent to Levy.** This notice explains how to request an appeal if you do not agree. You need to file a Form 12153, A Request for a Collection Due Process Hearing, to the office at the address shown on your levy notice within **30 days** from the date of the letter to appeal the action with the IRS Office of Appeals.

LT 1058E **Notice of Disqualified Employment Tax Levy.** This notice explains how to request an appeal if you do not agree. You need to file a Form 12153, A Request for a Collection Due Process Hearing, to the office at the address shown on your levy notice within **30 days** from the date of the letter to appeal the action with the IRS

Office of Appeals.

LT 1085 **30-Day Letter Proposed 6020(b) Assessment.** This notice explains how to request an appeal if you do not agree. You need to file a Form 12153, A Request for a Collection Due Process Hearing, to the office at the address shown on your levy notice within **30 days** from the date of the letter to appeal the action with the IRS Office of Appeals.

LT 1153 **Trust Funds Recovery Penalty Letter.** This notice explains how to request an appeal if you do not agree. You need to file a Form 12153, A Request for a Collection Due Process Hearing, to the office at the address shown on your levy notice within **30 days** from the date of the letter to appeal the action with the IRS Office of Appeals.

LT 3172 **Notice of Federal Tax Lien.** This letter is sent after the Notice of Federal Tax Lien is filed. If you do not agree with the lien or it is causing you financial hardship, then you have **30 days** to file your appeal on Form 12153, Request for a Collection Due Process Hearing, and send it to the address shown on your lien notice within **30 days** from the date of the letter in order to appeal the action to the IRS Office of Appeals.

Sometimes you don't get the right to file an appeal until the IRS has taken levy/seizure action or filed a federal tax lien.

Now you know about the most important letters you can receive from Service Center Accounts Management. You need to know that the Service Center Accounts Management does not issue levies or liens. Some levies may be issued by the computer system automatically with no IRS employee ever reviewing your case; like for the letters CP 77, CP 90, CP 92 and CP 242.

In the Collection Chapter, we will explain to you how to respond to the collection letters found in the Collection Chapter and what options are available to you to resolve your balance due case.

Chapter 6
Taxpayer Assistance and IRS Walk-In Offices

According to the IRS, the Taxpayer Assistance Centers (TAC-also known as Taxpayer Service) are located in 400 IRS offices across the United States and are supposed to provide face-to-face assistance to taxpayers who:

- Cannot resolve their problem through IRS online services, over the telephone, or by correspondence.
- Need a document issued to them in a reasonable period of time.
- Require or prefer face-to-face contact.
- Require multilingual assistance.
- Want to question the IRS bills and letters.
- Want to have their tax balances adjusted.
- Want to make payments or installment agreements.
- Need alien clearances/Sailing Permits (For non-citizens who want to leave the United States legally)
- (IRS - Departing Aliens and the Sailing Permit)
- Need to apply for a license to operate their trucks over highways. (Heavy Highway Vehicle Use Tax Form 2290)
- (Instructions for IRS Form 2290)
- Need to apply for Individual Taxpayer Identification Numbers (ITIN); this is for foreigners and non-English speakers.
- (General IRS ITIN Information)

How to Order Your IRS Tax Transcript

You have a choice of various types of transcripts; find out below what is needed for your business.

There are five types of transcripts. These can be used when you apply for a mortgage, student loans, state and local taxes, SBA loans, and FEMA/Disaster loans.

The transcripts are called:

- Tax Return Transcript – This is a line by line record of your tax return. If you want the record of your tax return with all penalty, interest and additional assessments, you want this transcript.
- Wage and Income - Best to order when you are trying to file your returns and are unsure what income was reported as being paid to you. These are not accurate and available until 13 months after the end of the tax year. For example, the 2015 tax information is not available until January, 2017. This is used for delinquent tax returns.
- Account Transcript – Best transcript if you have an audit or collection issue. It will tell you what your original tax was plus any additions to date.
- Record of Account – This shows that you have filed tax returns.
- Verification of Non-Filing is when you do not need to file a tax return, but a creditor needs to know that the IRS is aware of that and that is not an issue with the IRS.

How to Find Your Local IRS Office

To find an IRS office near you, use Google or Bing to search "Contact Your Local IRS Office". Most offices are open five days a week (M-F) from 8 or 8:30 a.m. to 4:30 p.m. They are rarely open on Saturdays during the filing season; they are never open on Sunday. When you locate an office near you, select it and find out exactly what they do at that office. Most offices are near major population centers. Some offices only see taxpayers by appointment. So if you have a long drive, call the number of that office first to make sure they still provide the services and hours posted. Some have changed their hours or closed altogether and have not updated the website.

In the past, these offices have been important because some taxpayers need information or forms- like "right now", when they applied for employment, mortgage loans, security clearances, college financial aid and are trying to get a license to drive their truck on the highways.

In the past, Taxpayer Service handled every aspect of tax law that walked in the front door of the IRS office. It was usually two gruff-speaking older folks who knew all the procedures and the answers to all the questions. They would help the elderly, the poor and the disabled prepare their tax returns. They would actually give anyone who asked any tax form that they desired. They answered technical tax law questions, and they were a vital part of the IRS - the first person that a taxpayer might meet. They were tough, and could be short with taxpayers, but it was worth it. They knew their stuff. Then over the last ten years these amazing workers started to retire. The newer workers were told to direct the taxpayer to call the IRS phone numbers or use the computer.

The IRS does have employees that speak over 150 languages, but it is difficult to find one in a local office. They usually utilize a contracted phone service for interpreters now. The interpreters are not IRS employees; however, they must not disclose any of your information to anyone else.

Many IRS offices now provide Facilitated Self Assistance (FSA), a self-assistance computer kiosk with an IRS employee located in another location who is available to assist you with navigating the irs.gov website. This is also known as Virtual Taxpayer Service. With FSA, you can access the irs.gov website to complete a number of IRS-related tasks or get more information on the following subjects:

- Free File program
- Forms & Publications
- Where's My Refund?
- Earned Income Tax Credit (EITC)
- Tax law questions
- Transcripts
- Online Employer Identification Number (EIN) Application
- Online Payment Agreement
- Electronic payments (Direct Pay and EFTPS)

Taxpayer assistance employees are also supposed to advise you of your rights and are supposed to help you prepare and file forms for Collection Due Process Appeals (CDP), Audit Appeals, Collection Appeal Rights (CAP), and Form 911, the form used to contact the taxpayer advocate (Request for Taxpayer Advocate Service). Many of the employees in local offices do not have the training to assist in all of those needs and they will tell you to go online. You have the right to ask to speak to a supervisor.

Some of the services you might need are easy to get online, especially to find out your refund status, get blank forms and to apply for an Employer Identification number. But you need to own or have access to a computer and know how to operate it. Millions of people do not have that. The IRS does not seem to care.

In fact, once we saw a taxpayer who was old and barely spoke English and he wanted a transcript of his past tax return. The taxpayer assistance worker told the old man to go to the computer located in the center of the office. He could not figure it out and no one would help him, until another taxpayer crammed in the booth with him and helped him to order the transcript.

Today's taxpayer assistance employees are told to do as little as possible in the office and to direct taxpayers to access alternative services online, such as Direct Pay, Get Transcript, Online Payment Agreement, or Return Preparation locations. They often tell taxpayers to just call the number on the letters they received.

What will happen if you go into an IRS office in 2016? You have to take your shoes, belt and jewelry off and will be searched upon entering the Federal building by armed guards who will x-ray you and your possessions. You cannot bring in your cell phone if it can take photographs. No knives, drugs, or anything that could be called a weapon. Go figure. This is a sorry example of where the government is right now - afraid of its own people.

After the search, you will be directed to the TAC office. You will know it in an instant, because there is usually a long line of other taxpayers just waiting to see the IRS also. Then you will see the receptionist who will ask what your reason is for coming into the office and then decide if they can help you or if you will need to see a TAC "specialist". You will be handed a number and you will wait 1-2 hours if you are lucky. Sometimes you can wait 8 hours and then be pushed out the door and told to come back the next business day.

While you are waiting in line, you might see a sign on the wall that tells you "Your Contact Will Be Recorded". This means that you will be subject to being tape recorded or videotaped. There is a small notice of this posted in the employee's booth, but most people are so stressed at this point that they do not notice.

You may also see a television screen beaming the following message to all the taxpayers waiting in line:

"Don't Wait in Line – Go Online"

If you are in line, you will see people who are elderly, disabled, a minority, and who appear desperate for the IRS to help them. Most are not computer literate.

When you first speak to an employee, they are required to tell you their name and employee identification number, like they are inmates at a large prison. Treating employees like numbers instead of as individuals is demoralizing to them.

There is very little privacy and everything one taxpayer says can be heard by the next five taxpayers in line.

The length of your visit will vary. Many offices have high volumes of people seeking help. They will issue you a ticket and then you wait. If they do not serve you, you will be sent home when the office closes. Sometimes they will post a sign that tells you 2 hours before the office closes that they are not issuing any more tickets.

In the National Taxpayer Advocate's report issued on January 14, 2015, National Taxpayer Advocate Nina E. Olson said that "Nearly 200 million Americans interact with the IRS each year, more than three times as many as any other federal agency." (Individuals file nearly 150 million returns, including 50 million joint returns.)

Because of the complexity of the tax code, large numbers of taxpayers turn to the IRS for assistance. The IRS typically receives more than 100 million telephone calls, 10 million letters and 5 million visits at its walk-in sites from taxpayers each year.

The National Taxpayer Advocate noted that in 2004, the IRS offered the best ever taxpayer assistance. It answered 87% of calls from taxpayers seeking to speak to an assistor and hold times averaged 2.5 minutes. The IRS responded to a wide range of tax law questions, both on its toll free lines and in its roughly 400 walk-in offices, they prepared 500,000 tax returns for taxpayers who requested help (particularly low income, elderly and disabled taxpayers) and maintained a robust outreach and education program that touched an estimated 72 million taxpayers.

During the 2015 tax filing season, the IRS answered an average of 40% of all incoming calls, but for three weeks at the busiest part of the season, the IRS only answered 10% of the calls, with an average hold time of 59 minutes.

Surveys have found that while no one likes paying taxes, 61% of taxpayers trust the IRS to fairly enforce the tax laws. The IRS Oversight Board showed in its survey that taxpayers believe more funding should be directed to answering the phone. In fact, in the 2016 budget an additional $290 million was allocated for this purpose. We will see what impact that has. The Oversight Board Chairman Paul Cherecwich, Jr. said that "Taxpayer satisfaction with IRS customer service has fallen to its lowest level in more than a decade. This is directly tied to deep cuts in IRS funding which has only served to punish honest American taxpayers who must endure long wait times over the IRS toll-free telephone lines and at walk-in centers."

As the IRS restructures the TAC, offices will close and taxpayer frustration will result. The IRS continues to close or reduce the size of all of the IRS offices. Taxpayers can only expect more of the same in the future. More hassle, more frustration and more abuse.

Under this new plan there might only be one office left open for a whole state. All the other offices would have what is called "IRS Virtual Services." This is where a taxpayer goes into the office and speaks through a computer screen with a TAC employee who is located somewhere in the United States. The only office to continue to handle taxpayers who have valid appointments would be located in a major city in each state. Low population states will feel the effect even more.

The IRS claims that this plan makes good business sense. But the National Taxpayer Advocate said "The "Pay to Play System", where only those with money get access to the information needed to prepare their taxes, is wrong. The Advocate said, "Those who can afford to pay for tax advice will receive personal service, while others will be left struggling for themselves".

Remember that the taxpayers who are calling in for help are trying to comply with the tax laws or want to make an installment agreement. It is abusive to send out letters and then not answer the phone when taxpayers call. National Taxpayer Advocate Nina Olson stated that in 2016 and beyond, the IRS is moving towards their "Future State Plan". This plan is supposed "to offer taxpayers online taxpayer accounts through which taxpayers will be able to obtain information and interact with the IRS." This is a little late in coming; it was supposed to have been delivered as required by law in 1999, according to National

Taxpayer Advocate Olson.

The IRS issued a statement that "The IRS remains fully committed to personal service to taxpayers, and the IRS believes that increasing the availability of self-service interaction frees up in-person resources for taxpayers who truly need them, including those who are not comfortable online or don't have personal access to a computer."

We will let you, the taxpayer, decide how this works out when you cannot get in touch with the IRS.

One Congressman, Kevin Brady, R-Texas, said that "When Americans contact the IRS, they need serious help – not another layer of bureaucracy. This 'Future State Plan' raises serious questions about the agency's commitment to making it easier for people to do their taxes. IRS employees' main priority should be to deliver excellent customer service to hardworking taxpayers who fund our government and pay their salaries."

"Taxpayer rights are central to voluntary compliance," the National Taxpayer Advocate report says. "If taxpayers believe they are being treated, or can be treated, in an arbitrary and capricious manner, they will mistrust the system and be less likely to comply of their own volition. By contrast, taxpayers will be more likely to comply if they have confidence in the fairness and integrity of the system."

As John Q. Public might say: "I think, in a nutshell, everybody should pay their taxes, including the other underground economy, including anybody who purchases things; they should pay a small amount of tax on the items purchased. Say, you're a drug dealer and if you buy a Cadillac with cash, you pay the same taxes as the guy who is not a drug dealer."

In the past, the local IRS office was staffed and charged with providing tax returns, accepting cash tax payments, answering tax law questions, assisting people in preparing their tax returns, assisting the disabled and elderly with their tax matters, and was the public face of the IRS. Now they don't do any of those things, due to budget cuts and reduced numbers of employees.

Mostly they work Examination notices and Collection notices up to a certain dollar amount. They generally work cases with a balance of $50,000 or less. They can offer excellent assistance if you are lucky enough to be sent to an IRS employee who knows the system.

Nina Olson, the IRS National Tax Advocate said that "the IRS continues to view itself primarily as an enforcer, envisioning a future that rests on the 'mistaken assumption' that it can save money and end direct contact with taxpayers by automating assistance service. It should be emphasized that more than 98% of all tax revenue collected by the IRS is paid voluntarily and timely," said Olson, who estimated that less than 2 % is collected through enforcement actions. "Thus, increasing enforced collection would be a hollow victory if voluntary compliance declines because of decreasing taxpayer service and the attendant loss of good will."

Some offices only take appointments, so you can go and wait and then find out that you cannot get an answer even to a simple question. IRS offices no longer carry the IRS tax forms; they tell you to print them on your own computer or they will mail you a form in 2-3 weeks from some distant service center.

Now, the new policy of IRS taxpayer service/walk-in office assistance is to refuse to accept your cash. That's right – the Internal Revenue Service will not accept your cash as legal tender to satisfy your tax balance. They want checks or money orders. They do not accept credit cards in the office. There is even a new service being tested where you could make a cash payment to the IRS at a 7-11 convenience store!

One of the primary functions for TAC now is not to aid and assist taxpayers, or educate them or prepare tax returns for those in need. Mostly what they do is answer questions about the letters from the service centers. As we have seen, those letters are about information on the tax returns, or about proposed changes on the tax returns or about balances due.

It is important to know that the TAC does not have an inventory of cases, and does not have the authority to bind any of the other IRS units with their advice or information.

National Taxpayer Advocate Olson stated that "Having written a tax code so widely and rightly criticized for its complexity, the government has a practical and moral obligation to help taxpayers comply." She said that "existing taxpayer service should not be withdrawn to the point where taxpayers have to incur additional compliance costs just to file their returns and pay their taxes."

Taxpayer Assistance does record the fact that you visited them on the same system that Service Center Collection and the Automated Collection System use. Unless you have an emergency situation where the IRS is harming you, we suggest you bypass the IRS TAC, because it seems like they just don't want to see you.

Chapter 7
Examination Audit Process

So, it happened to you – you received that dreaded letter saying that you are being audited by the Internal Revenue Service. This chapter will take you through the audit process for both audits done in an IRS office as well as audits done at your home or place of business. Take a deep breath, grab a cup of coffee and let's get started!

The first thing you might ask is "Why me?" The answer could be that you had a couple of red flags pop up because of the type of business you are in or perhaps someone reported paying you money that you didn't report as income. You also may have been selected for audit as part of that unlucky few included in the IRS National Research Program (NRP) study used to determine the audit plan for each fiscal year. NRP returns are usually selected randomly, sometimes as part of a specific industry or type of return (1040, Partnership, Corporation).

Every tax return is compared with other similar tax returns and those that are variations from the mean are given a secret computer score called the Discriminant Index Function, (DIF). The higher your score, the more likely your tax return will be audited. The way this works is all the tax returns are processed and then categorized by the industry, type of business and similarities with other taxpayers in your same income level. Then the computer comes up with what it sees as similarities and differences and arrives at a standard mean. They may look at returns that were filed by a certain tax preparer, or that were prepared by hand or by those with the same address.

The program is very secretive and very subjective. Every year it focuses on a new group of taxpayers and businesses. DIF examiners do not know why a case has been pulled for review, so they use their experience and judgment to subjectively decide what issues will be covered in the audit and for how many years. Many of the leads prove to be unproductive.

The Treasury Inspector General for Tax Administration reports that more than 62% of all audits selected from the Discriminate Index Function (DIF) were closed with no change in tax at all. Audits on all individual income tax returns selected for audit (from the DIF and other IRS programs) show no tax changes or increased refunds in 20% of the cases according to the IRS. This is a waste of government resources. Clearly the IRS needs a better formula to determine where fraud and abuse is in the tax returns it audits. Audits create a lot of fear with taxpayers; that is why we believe taxpayers have the right to know their DIF score in the same way they know their credit score. This would remove a lot of fear from the system.

Other audit selections systems are called the National Research Project (NRP) and special return projects. The NRP uses a statistical draw of a number of returns. The draw is done using Social Security numbers and employer identification numbers. These audits can be very intrusive.

NRP audits are usually "line by line" and can involve cases that are partnerships, sole proprietorships, corporations and high income individuals. Or they can look at a certain item on the tax return - like interest, or employee expenses or home office deduction. The cases can also be selected by type of industry or type of business, like doctors, realtors, butchers, truckers or construction companies. These yield a higher rate of increased tax assessment than DIF cases alone. Usually in these cases 80% of the audits result in increased tax assessments.

Some of this comes from the Market Segment Specialization

Program (MSSP) and the Industry Specialization Program (ISP); this tracks all the statistics on a return divided up by the code listed on the form as to the type of business. Both programs accumulate statistics and come up with a mathematical equation of what is the standard deviation above or below the mean. Cases that do not fit this model will trigger an audit inquiry. Some can be easily explained with an audit letter and proof of the questioned expense.

The National Research Program (NRP) is a comprehensive effort by the IRS to measure compliance for different types of taxes and various sets of taxpayers. It establishes a sample tax return for each type of tax that it claims is representative of the whole taxpayer population.

Two other special programs are the High Income Fast Track Initiative (HIRTI) and another is called the High Income Under-Reported Income Program (HURI); both of which select certain types of cases to be worked as priority cases by the IRS. Both have a high potential for a lot of additional tax and for potential fraud case development.

There is also the secret Unreported Income Discriminant Function System, (UIDIF). This is a system that analyses tax returns in comparison with data from other returns and makes statistical comparisons as to the likelihood that there is unreported income. This could be more accurate if the IRS would share information with other agencies like county assessors and to compare the taxes paid and value of real estate, but they do not.

The National Research Project (NRP) also separates cases as "Abusive Tax Schemes and Transactions." This is for taxpayers or tax preparers who appear to be committing fraud.

The NRP segregates "High Income High Wealth" taxpayers, and "High Income Non-Filers." Some of these cases are worked by Special Enforcement Program (SEP) agents. These employees are not to be taken lightly. They sometimes do not even make contact with the people they are investigating and just start issuing summons to collect data and issue levies to seize whatever they find. Return Preparer Audit Projects (RPAP) are audits that the IRS uses to determine how much of what is filed is accurate and is a statistical project that gives the IRS data as to who files and if what they file is accurate. It targets a certain group of taxpayers and businesses.

We have worked on one of these audit projects. We had sixteen IRS employees who targeted an eight block area in Chicago. We went door to door and in every business and every house, we stopped everyone, and asked them their name, address and Social Security number or employer identification number. We wrote down their information. We wrote down license plate numbers of all the cars on the street and around the business. We were told by IRS management that if someone was not home or did not reply to us, we should return with a summons requiring them to come to our office and provide detailed information. We were looking for people who had never filed, who had underreported income, and people who were not in the system at all. We looked at their homes, apartments, and circumstances to determine that they were appropriate for their reported income levels. These audits required that you prove everything on your tax return: birth certificate, Social Security card, marriage certificate, death certificate, divorce decree, driver's license, and military discharge papers, rent receipts, mortgage papers, school records and immunization shots for your children and proof for every expense. If you did not have it, the auditors raised your tax balances on the spot. This happened years ago and is now prohibited since 1998.

In those days it was still possible to not have a Social Security number and be self-employed.

Back to you, dear reader, and the IRS letter in your hand. No matter the reason for your audit selection, the letter has been received and we are going to help you prepare for the days ahead. We will tell you what to expect, what we suggest you do, and, most importantly, what we suggest you not do while dealing with an IRS audit.

Small comfort to you at this moment, but according to IRS Commissioner John Koskinen, the audit rate will continue to shrink in upcoming years, due largely to the lack of revenue agents (RA) and tax compliance officers (TCO). The IRS has not hired large groups of new employees in over 6 years and seasoned agents and TCOs are leaving the Service in droves due to retirement or better offers.

The audit rate for 2016 is projected to be less than 1% of all individual returns filed. A projection for total individual returns filed approaches 150,000,000, so a 1% translates to less than 1,500,000. When you scale these returns over the types of audits performed, you will see that "playing the audit lottery" puts the odds in your favor against a full scale audit. In 2015 individual taxpayers with higher incomes suffered higher audit rates. Taxpayers with income over $200,000 face an audit rate of 2.61%. Those who earn over $1 million face an audit risk of 9.55%, partnerships and S-Corporations enjoy a much smaller audit rate, again due to a lack of trained revenue agents. Also if IRS opens an audit on one partner it is obliged to open on all partners and that is cumbersome.

How Long You Have to Worry about Being Audited

The IRS has three to six years to audit tax returns. The six-year statute comes into play when a taxpayer has not reported 25% or more of their income. If there is actual tax fraud- the audit risk never ends.

How Long Should I Keep My Tax Records?

We suggest that if you are self-employed, own real estate, or own stock, bonds, or retirement accounts, that you keep your tax records, including tax returns, for at least ten years, just to be on the safe side. Because some types of receipts fade or disappear in a year, we also recommend that you photocopy all your receipts, or you may have no legible receipts if you are ever audited.

Types of Audits

There are three types of audits that you might face. The first, and most common, is referred to as a correspondence audit. You will receive a letter in the mail informing you that a possible error has been identified by the IRS. The correspondence examination technician is a lower-paid employee working in an IRS Service Center. This employee may work part time or be a seasonal employee who has been specifically trained on relatively simple issues that can be resolved by the return of documents to substantiate the income or expense issue being questioned. Documents such as W-2s and 1099s filed with the IRS are matched with what is reported on your return and any discrepancies are usually handled via a correspondence audit.

The first audit letters you receive asking for information may be numbered differently but could include: Letter 566, Letter 566-D, Letter 566-E, CP 75, CP 75A, CP 75D, and CP 06. Usually, Letter 566(CG) signals a correspondence audit. When you receive any of these letters, look at your tax return and go through all the numbers. Compare what the IRS is showing in your letter to what you put on your return. Pull out all your receipts and records that support what you put on your tax return. Chapter 5 covers additional correspondence you may receive from the IRS Service Centers, so please refer to that chapter if you receive other requests.

When you receive letters referring to an audit or an examination, you should make copies of everything requested to send to the IRS. Do not ever send original documents and only send what is requested – nothing else. If you have questions, there should be a toll free number you can call. Be sure and note who you talked to, when you talked to them and what was said and keep that information.

Important - if you think the IRS letter may be fake or if it asks that you send money, bank account information, credit card information or your Social Security number, you should call the toll-free number – 1-800-829-1040. The IRS will not contact you for an audit and demand money at the same time. The IRS knows your Social Security number, so requests for this information should be reported immediately. Additionally, the IRS currently does not contact taxpayers by email for audit appointments or collection actions. Unless regulations change, any e-mails you receive purporting to be from the IRS are fake! More about Identity Fraud can be found in Chapter 15 of this book.

The next type of audit you might experience will be an in-office audit with a Tax Compliance Officer (TCO). TCOs, often called tax auditors or office auditors, are highly trained to work 1040 returns and will examine such items as income, employee business expenses, itemized deductions on Schedule A, dividends and interest on Schedule B, investments and capital gains on Schedule D, business income and expenses on a Schedule C and some Schedule E or F issues, depending on complexity. Employee business expenses should be reasonable compared to occupation and income. The Internal Revenue Manual states that cases are to be reviewed with "heavy reliance on discretion, judgment and experience." But it is important to remember that the government cannot actually tell you how to run your business. It cannot penalize you if you make bad business choices and end up losing money.

Most in-office audits last 2-4 hours, although some audits of Schedule C (sole proprietorship) businesses can last one full day and you could get called back again.

During an in-office audit, you should bring everything you are asked for, but nothing more. You should answer every question asked of you, but do not volunteer extra information. Do not bring big unorganized boxes of information. Never allow the IRS to sort through your box. The TCO will generally have 2-4 issues they have been assigned to audit, and you do not want to give them any ideas for new issues to examine!

Years ago, a TCO in training was auditing a small nursery business. The taxpayer grew trees and supposedly sold them for profit. He also had a full time job at a government agency, as did his wife. There was no store front, no posted hours, and no indication that the taxpayer was actually doing business. Because he claimed a loss on his Schedule C, the auditor focused on the seemingly non-existent business. During the audit, the taxpayer was rude and uncooperative with the auditor. He would not hand her the receipts but instead held them in front of the auditor, not allowing her to touch them. He claimed his dog food and veterinary bills as expenses, as he said the dogs guarded the trees during the day. Because of his uncooperativeness and refusal to answer questions, his tax returns for three years were sent to a revenue agent for audit, where it was determined that his unreported income was high enough to warrant a referral to Criminal Investigation. Had he simply cooperated with the auditor and let her look at the receipts, his business loss would have been disallowed and he would have paid a relatively small amount of tax, interest and penalty. The moral is – follow the instructions and answer the initial questions. You do not want a tax compliance officer or revenue agent to dig any deeper!

When you appear at an audit, whether in an IRS office or in your own business, you should dress professionally for your business, but do not "overdress" or wear showy jewelry or have expensive accessories. From the moment an auditor or agent first sets eyes on you, you are being audited – even before you open your mouth! Don't dress like a homeless person, unless you are, but do remember that your ability to pay is being assessed as much as any other aspect of your return. We will discuss more examples of "lifestyle/income audits" later in this chapter.

The third type of audit done on individuals is from a revenue agent, which is also known as a field audit. The revenue agent will come to your home or place of business, or may work in your tax professional's office, if you have retained a representative with power of attorney.

Revenue agents (RA) have a degree in accounting or accountancy and are trained to handle the most complex tax issues. Some may be certified public accountants (CPAs) or some may have masters or doctorate degrees. The complexity of the cases, however, is dependent not on the education of the revenue agent, but on that employee's pay grade and/or experience.

RAs may start the audit with only a few issues, but are allowed to "expand" the audit should they find other possible discrepancies. They may look at your bank statements and other books and records. If you don't cooperate with them and provide the initial requested documents, they will issue a summons and look at everything in your life. Again – give them everything they have asked for, but nothing extra.

Many new audits could be stopped and the cases closed using a method called "Survey without Taxpayer Contact." This can occur when a taxpayer is known to be in bankruptcy, when a taxpayer has suffered extreme hardship or illness or the taxpayer is deceased. The decision to survey a case is based on the professional judgment of the examiner. The IRS does not use normal industry standard practices for case building, which allows it to waste government resources auditing people and companies that should not be audited. That is why cases are closed as audited but "no change," (meaning that the return is accepted as filed by the taxpayer) or audited with an increased refund due to the taxpayer. Twenty percent of all cases are "no change" or give the taxpayer more money back. All cases can be surveyed (put on the shelf and never worked) based on the professional judgment of the examiner. If they just had access to more information, it would make the system operate better.

The IRS can manage its inventory if they used this "survey a case" option. They currently use it to close cases without action because of resource limitations (i.e. no money or employees to work the cases).

The RA will do some background analysis on you as a taxpayer. This may include the search as to your filing requirements and returns filed over the past three to five years. Also carefully scrutinized will be a comparison of the information documents sent to the IRS from others that affect your return, such as W-2s for wages and salaries, 1099s for interest income, dividend income and other items reported on the form 1099. The RA will review the computer information from your returns, perform a real estate check as to property owned, and an internet search as to a web page or other information you have made available for the public to see. In general, a thorough review of your life style will be made before you are contacted by the RA. The RA will know a lot about you before you even know your return has ever been selected for audit.

Tax compliance officers and revenue agents are trained to notice your style of living and your manner of dress. This is true, also, for revenue officers who are collecting tax. A shiny diamond ring or a flashy Rolex will tell an IRS employee that you have assets and, obviously, income.

A field agent will not only visit your business; they will also visit your house. They will look in county records for other property in your name, your business name or even in the name of other family members in your household. Even if you've retained a representative, the agent can still drive by your home or other property and find out a lot about your style of living.

In the 1990s and up until 2000, the IRS was vigorously conducting audits which were known as lifestyle/financial status audits and they matched up your living circumstances to what income you reported. For instance, if you have two houses, three cars and live an affluent lifestyle and report income of only $100,000 a year it raises serious questions about how you can afford to do that. Authors of this book worked on projects where we pulled information on high dollar real estate transactions that were paid for in cash or with large cash down payments; we also summoned car dealerships to get records on individuals who paid all cash for their cars. An offshoot of that was the car dealerships were not reporting this, and that led to charges against them as well. When people are living beyond their visible means it can trigger an audit.

Sometimes their own jealous friends, family and neighbors will turn them in. We have witnessed many audits where a taxpayer will show business losses of $80,000 but show no income. Or show mortgage interest paid on a million-dollar house of $76,000 and car payments on luxury cars of $35,000 a year and then reported income of $40,000. The auditor would ask how they did that and they would be confused. Some would start talking and the story they told was always interesting. Some reported that they spent as much as they took in so they did not have to even file income tax returns. We always counsel anyone to report all of their income as required by law. But to be smart, at least report the amount of your expenses. If the IRS can track you spending $15,300 a month, then you need to have income of $15,300 a month that is taxable. Be smart, not greedy.

Many revenue agents will request your bank statements and then look at every expense and every deposit and then figure out what your income actually is, and you better hope that that was the same figure that you reported on your tax return. Sometimes, you will have to explain loans, credit card advances or purchases or money you inherited to explain where your income came from. You need to know that by law, all income, legal or illegal, is taxable.

These audits were very effective and large tax assessments were made. That is apparently why Congress killed the idea in its RRA 98 legislation. This helps the wealthy and those who derive their income from the underground economy. Despite RRA 98 legislation, however, the way you live and how you spend your money is still considered as part of a field audit, and it is legal.

Here's how a "lifestyle audit" can affect your tax audit. For example, say your tax return indicates a business loss and an income at or below zero, but you have an RV or a large boat parked at your residence in an expensive area of town and your tax records online show you paid property tax on a house worth $400,000. Bumper stickers on your late model vehicles may show that your children go to a private school. Your spouse may stay at home and collect antiques. All of these things indicate that you have income, despite the numbers on your tax return. These factors will likely be used to determine you owe additional tax and guess what? The IRS is allowed to assess that tax based on a determination that you had enough money to live in the manner in which you've become accustomed!

A curious revenue agent may look at your social media to see what types of hobbies you have. It is important to note – a revenue agent or auditor is not allowed to access social media such as Facebook, Twitter or Instagram by using a government computer. The system will actually stop them from doing so. However, many agents have their own accounts on personal devices and although they are not supposed to use their personal accounts to look up taxpayers that have been assigned to them, many do so anyway. Here is where you can protect yourself – lock down your profiles on Facebook or other social media so that only your friends can see your posts!

You will, of course, be able to refute the notion of additional tax owed if you have kept records to show that past income or even inheritances allowed you to purchase these assets prior to the year being audited. It is important that you maintain records to prove that you are living within your income or even that you are in debt up to your ears. In this case, showing debt is good for your case.

There is hope for you yet. Because the IRS ranks have thinned so much in the past decade, RAs as well as TCOs are stressed out over the rising case inventories they carry. Most agents want to get in, look at the pre-classified issues and get out. Like their co-workers the TCOs, RAs will ask you a series of pre-developed questions and will request you provide certain documents to substantiate your income and expenses. Again – answer all of the questions and nothing more. RAs are trained to look at your body language and listen to the tone of your voice. If you are too "chatty" or act nervous, the RA (and TCO) will wonder what you are hiding. Try to relax, if you can, and simply answer the questions to the best of your ability. If you don't know or can't remember the answer, then say so – do not try and guess.

One trick that many revenue agents do is using the premise that "nature abhors a vacuum" and it works like this. The RA will ask you an open-ended question such as "Tell me about your day to day business operations". You should come back with a matter of fact, rough outline of what you do as the business owner. The RA will likely nod, smile or maybe say "Oh, really?" It is human nature to talk about your "baby" (your business), so, you will continue to talk. The RA will let you babble merrily; all the while taking notes and listening for tiny nuances that might open the door to adjustments to your tax return that will cost you money!

What should you do? Don't fill the silence! Answer briefly and then look at the RA/TCO and let them be the next one to talk. Practice this technique with a friend or spouse if you think it will be difficult for you. In this case – silence is golden and a lot less expensive.

As an example to illustrate the power of your words – a revenue agent was auditing a small bar in a rural area. This agent was friendly and lived in the same town, so he knew the owner was also a bartender at his own bar. (Keep in mind – RAs are trained to be friendly, because they want to encourage you to talk!)

The revenue agent asked the owner/bartender how many nights a week he tended bar and was told six nights. Then the RA asked – "Do you ever have a beer while working?" to which the owner replied – "Sure, 5 or 6 a night, usually".

Remember – the cost of beer would be a cost of goods sold (inventory) and an expense of the business; however, the cost of the owner's personally consumed beer is not an allowable expense. This bar owner's answer to a seemingly benign question resulted in several thousand dollars of a disallowed expense and more tax assessed!

The RA will look around your business and make note of any assets. He or she will ask you about vehicles and employees of your business. The RA will possibly want to interview your key employees, such as a bookkeeper or office manager. In order to do this, you have to give your permission, otherwise it is disclosure and that is a serious offense to an IRS employee. All of these things are normal as part of a field audit, so it should not make you particularly worried.

IRS employees are human beings and many are very nice people. Some can be real jerks. If you treat your TCO or RA with respect, chances are good that your audit will be a better experience. If you are mean, curse, rant and rave about how much you hate the IRS or are just generally disagreeable, the TCO or RA may decide to make life a bit more difficult. It's a normal human reaction to lash back when someone treats you poorly.

Your Rights During an Audit

When you receive your audit letter, you will also receive a copy of Publication 1, Taxpayer Rights. These rights include:

- A right to professional and courteous treatment by IRS employees.
- A right to privacy and confidentiality about tax matters.
- A right to know why the IRS is asking for information, how the IRS will use it and what will happen if the requested information is not provided.
- A right to representation, by oneself or an authorized representative.
- A right to appeal disagreements, both within the IRS and before the courts.

Your audit letter will tell you what is being audited, where the audit will be and what documents or other information will be needed. You may receive a separate Information Document Request (IDR) with a detailed listing of specific documents required to be presented. The name of the person doing the audit and their telephone number will be provided. If the audit is being done in an IRS office by a TCO, the appointment time and date will also be provided. If the audit will be done by a revenue agent, you will be asked to call within a few days to schedule an audit appointment. The revenue agent audit may last one to 3 days initially and could include follow up days to complete. The

TCO audit (in the IRS office) will probably last 2-4 hours but a follow up appointment may be scheduled.

Your right to have a tax representative means you may hire someone to speak for you and represent you before the IRS. You will need to sign a Form 2848 Power of Attorney, granting your power of attorney (POA) for tax matters to your representative. You do not have to show up for the audit or respond to the RA again, as long as your representative continues to provide the information requested and responds to the RA or TCO in a timely manner. Often the RA will try to insist on an interview with you, but you do not have to attend as long as your representative is working with the RA to resolve the audit. The RA will request a tour of the business if the return is a business return. For that, you also do not have to be present as long the representative is there. If you do agree to an interview, have the representative there to assist with answering any questions. In general, be polite, but quiet. Let the representative handle the audit. If the representative does not respond to the RA and in general is difficult, the RA can initial procedures to bypass your representative and deal directly with you.

Allowing a revenue agent into your home is not advisable. They may see papers, or assets that show you have an affluent lifestyle and this usually ends up badly for you. You can suggest that you meet them at their IRS office, because you have elderly or sick family living in your house, or you are in the middle of a redecorating project.

Once the power of attorney is in place, the RA should not contact you by phone unless the bypass procedures have been followed. A copy of all correspondence with your representative will be sent to keep you informed as to the progress and if you want to, you can contact the RA, but this in not advisable. It is best to let your representative handle the audit. Actually, it is good advice to secure a representative right away. Your representative must be licensed to practice before the IRS in order to take your place and act on your behalf. If you just want to have a friend at your audit for moral support, they may not act on your behalf or speak for you during the audit unless they are licensed.

Rules regarding tax representatives can be found in the instructions for Form 2848 or in Circular 230, both found on the IRS website. We do not suggest bringing a friend to an audit; sometimes they can say things that will cause the agent to investigate you further and that might result in an increased tax for you.

The more information you provide at or before the initial appointment, the faster the audit will proceed and the sooner it will be over. Despite what you might be told by tax representatives or other advisors, you do not want to purposely drag out the audit and think the IRS will give up and go away. It won't happen! What could happen is that the RA or TCO will become suspicious and open up more returns for different years or even related returns such as employment or partnership returns, which will cost you a lot more in terms of time or paying someone to represent you.

What Happens During the Audit?

In office audit, we would routinely hear taxpayers yelling and arguing. Many taxpayers were so afraid to be audited. Some would self-medicate and come into the audit drunk or high. Some were angry and belligerent. Some taxpayers slurred their words and had an unbalanced gait as they walked down the hall to their audit. We remember one taxpayer, a middle-aged man who had suffered a heart attack during his audit and was lying on the floor. He died right in front of us. His face turned black from lack of oxygen. We all stood there staring at that man. Some of the other auditors tried to hurry up and complete their audits before they released other poor taxpayers who were being audited.

During a TCO (in office) audit, you will sit across from the auditor during the entire time. You may ask for breaks as needed and if you are uncomfortable, you should say so. The auditor is expected to work quickly, so he/she may type out reports or other information while you are sitting there. This is normal – TCOs have very strict deadlines and try to finish the audit during the first appointment if possible. Keep your answers to the topic and try not to chatter nervously. You don't want to annoy the auditor or worse – give the TCO another issue to raise their curiosity!

A good auditor looks for financial connections. For example, if you are caught cheating on your taxes and your friends or family are also involved in that business, then they can open up their audit and start looking at them also.

A revenue agent has a bit more time to complete an audit, as they are required to look at more items. They will look at your previous and subsequent year (if any) tax returns. They will ask you for any 1099s issued by or received by you. They must check to make sure you filed all required returns. Just because they look at another return does not mean they are auditing it. A revenue agent will inform you if they plan to open another tax return under your control. TCOs and RAs will open another return (previous year or related) if they find a large number of adjustments in the return initially selected for audit.

Once the revenue agent goes through his/her interview questions and receives all of your requested documents, you will be free to step away or, if the audit is being held at your tax professional's office, you may be allowed to leave. In general, a revenue agent is supposed to work at your place of business or wherever the books and records are maintained. Arrangements can be made for an RA to work at your accountant's office if your accountant has been given your power of attorney (POA) and if all of the books, records and documents have been provided. Even if you are working at the accountant's office though, you will still be asked to give the RA a tour of your business. As stated above – as long as you have a representative with a signed power of attorney, you will not have to be present for any of these steps. A cooperative, experienced representative is worth his/her weight in gold when it comes to protecting you and your assets from an unwanted separation!

Concluding the Audit

An audit can be concluded in four ways:

- No change: an audit in which you have substantiated all of the items being reviewed and results in no changes.
- Change/No change: the audit resulted in changes to your income or expenses but not enough to change the tax you owe. Sometimes, you or your representative may find additional items that had not been claimed originally that could help you wipe out additional tax.
- Agreed: an audit where the IRS proposed changes and you and/or your representative understand and agree with the changes. This could be additional tax or even a refund.
- Disagreed: an audit where the IRS has proposed changes and you and/or your representative understand but disagree with the changes.

Your TCO or RA will provide you with a written report that explains each line item change. There may be many attachments to the report that will usually include the reasons for disallowing an expense or adding an income item. He/she will go over it with you and/or your accountant thoroughly and answer all of your questions. Sometimes, the audit will find that nothing needs to be changed or, even better; the changes are in your favor and you will receive a refund!

If you agree with the report, you will be asked to sign and date it. At that time, you may make a payment if you wish. Because interest continues to be charged on the unpaid balance, you can stop the interest by paying in full immediately.

If you do not agree with all or part of the proposed adjustments, you have informal and formal appeal rights. You may ask to talk to the auditor's supervisor. Say, for instance, you agree with the additional tax but not a penalty. You can often ask the manager to remove the penalty if you can give her/him a good reason for the error. If they will not do so informally, you can request Reasonable Cause relief, discussed in Chapter 14. We saw one case where a taxpayer owed $3 million and was facing a penalty for fraud of $700,000, and a clever tax attorney was able to agree to the tax and then the IRS did not assess the penalty.

If you don't agree with any of the adjustments and the supervisor denies any changes, you have the right to request a less formal Appeals mediation or file a formal appeal. You will receive a Letter 950, also called a 30-day letter. Attached will be detailed explanations of each adjustment. You will have 30 days to prepare a request to go to the Office of Appeals. We strongly suggest that if you are not working with an accountant, you consider hiring one at this time. An enrolled agent (EA), certified public accountant (CPA), or tax law attorney can assist you in your appeal and will likely be worth the fees you pay to him/her.

This process of working with an appeals officer is discussed in Chapter 10.

If you do not respond to the Letter 950 (also known as a 30 day letter) and do not prepare a request to go to the Office of Appeals, your case will be sent to Examination Technical Services. There, a statutory notice of deficiency will be prepared and mailed to you via certified mail.

A notice of deficiency, also called a "statutory notice of deficiency" or "90 day letter," is a legal notice in which the Commissioner determines the taxpayer's tax deficiency. The notice of deficiency is a legal determination that is presumptively correct and consists of the following:

- A letter explaining the purpose of the notice, the amount of the deficiency, and the taxpayer's options
- A waiver to allow the taxpayer to agree to the additional tax liability
- A statement showing how the deficiency was computed
- An explanation of the adjustments

The purpose of a notice of deficiency is as follows:

- To ensure the taxpayer is formally notified of the IRS's intention to assess a tax deficiency.
- To inform the taxpayer of the opportunity and right to petition the U.S. Tax Court to dispute the proposed adjustments.

A notice of deficiency is issued for unagreed deficiencies of income, estate, or gift tax liabilities as well as for certain excise taxes. Letter 531 is the most common letter used for the notice of deficiency for income tax cases.

Once you receive a notice of deficiency, this is your opportunity to have your case heard in tax court. If you do not have a representative, now is definitely the time to find one to assist you, represent you and prepare the petition to tax court.

You have 90 days to prepare and file this petition to tax court. There is no "wiggle" room here – if you miss the deadline, you will have an assessment made and will be expected to pay your tax deficiency immediately.

All is not lost, however. Once you have filed your petition to tax court and extended your statute of limitation by signing the proper forms, your case will be sent through the Office of Appeals before being put on the tax court docket. An appeals officer will contact you and/or your representative to see if there is a possibility of settlement.

You can use Google or Bing to look for Internal Revenue Manual Examination Processing, to see all of the processes that are in place for opening, conducting and closing your audit. Some of the reading is a great cure for insomnia; however, you will also see the behind the scenes look at why and how the IRS does what they do to audit your tax returns.

Hopefully, we have de-mystified the examination audit process for you. If you feel that an audit will bring up complex tax issues or will simply stress you out, you do have the right to have a representative during the audit.

IRS Form 2848 Power of Attorney will have to be filled out and signed in order to authorize an individual to represent you before the IRS. The individual you authorize must be a person eligible to practice before the IRS. You may authorize a student who works in a qualified Low Income Taxpayer Clinic (LITC) or Student Tax Clinic Program (STCP) to represent you under a special appearance authorization issued by the Taxpayer Advocate Service. Your authorization of a qualifying representative will also allow that individual to receive and inspect your confidential tax information. The IRS will not talk to your representative unless you have this form on file for each tax period under examination or in collection status. You can list more than one year on the form.

IRS Form 8821 can be used to authorize any individual, corporation, firm, organization, or partnership you designate to inspect and/or receive your confidential information verbally or in writing for the type of tax and the years or periods listed on the form. It can also be used to delete or revoke prior tax information authorizations.

Form 8821 cannot be used to authorize your appointee to speak on your behalf, to execute a request to allow disclosure of return or return information to another third party, to advocate your position with respect to federal tax laws, to execute waivers, consents, closing agreements, or to represent you in any other manner before the IRS. Only Form 2848 can be used for those reasons.

The authors of this book, all former IRS employees from various jobs, highly recommend you consider appointing a power of attorney to represent you during an audit, particularly if you feel uncomfortable with tax laws or did not prepare your own tax return. Revenue agents and tax compliance officers are skilled in the art of getting you to "spill the beans" regarding the way you did business. Although we do not advocate that anyone should cheat on his/her taxes, we do believe taxpayers should use tax law to their advantage to pay the least amount of tax. A skilled enrolled agent or certified public accountant can make sure you take advantage of all the reductions in tax available and can represent you during the dreaded audit. If, however, you feel like you can go it alone, please do go online to and Google or Bing search - Publication 556, Examination of Returns, Appeal Rights and Claims for Refund.

The good news about all of the process is – your chances of getting audited have decreased significantly, thanks to a severely underfunded IRS budget. The down side is that the federal government receives 95% of total funding from taxes collected through the Internal Revenue Service. As fewer taxes are collected, less funding is available for critical government programs and needs such as infrastructure, military and national security.

Paying taxes is a fact of life. Paying more than you should is not.

The IRS Can't Tell You How to Do Business

Many taxpayers think that the Internal Revenue Code says that you cannot deduct expenses from "hobbies." If you conduct your business like a real business, devote a certain amount of hours to it a week, and are "profit motivated," and you keep good records, then you will probably be able to defend the business expenses in an audit. One myth is that you need to make a profit in three out of five years in business. This is not true. The government cannot tell you how to run your business. If you are formally conducting your business as advised by a tax professional, then maybe it will take you longer to make a profit. If you spend more money in the early years, you may be establishing yourself in your market. It is important to know that we have observed many tax professionals who are so conservative with their tax advice that they are doing a disservice to their clients. If you have a legitimate business expense put it on the tax return. The chance of you being questioned about are only 1% (chance of an audit) but now due to a declining work force the IRS will not even be able to keep up with that low number.

You Must Always File Your Change of Address Directly with the IRS

Worse are the audits that happen because the taxpayer never received notice and had no chance to appeal an audit. The auditor really has no incentive to actually find you and talk to you and get information. He sends notices to your old address and then of course you do not respond. Because you were never found and notified, he can close his case faster. This is an old auditor's trick.

Say you were audited for 2008. In 2009 the IRS received 19.3 million pieces of mail that were undeliverable - many of them audit notices. You thought everything was fine for that year; you remember getting a refund. You have moved several times but always file a return. But the IRS sent the notice to your 2009 address and the mail was not forwarded. So they went ahead and assessed you $20,000 in new tax for that year. You have moved and only were told by the IRS to keep your records for 3 years. So you throw out those records in 2012. Now you find a Notice of Federal Tax Lien is showing up on your name filed in some far away county. You are in so much trouble; you just don't know it yet. Constructing those old records is next to impossible and this is the first you heard of it in 2014. This is a common nightmare we have seen many times.

The chief reason for this is that when you move you cannot change your address over the phone with the IRS. The IRS does not allow this; you cannot change your address over the internet or on the phone. It must be in writing using Form 8822. Most people assume the IRS knows where they are because they still file every year. But that is not the fact. We hope that you are never audited, but know that sharing this information will go a long way to protect your rights.

Chapter 8
Collection

—⁂—

The collection of taxes is big business to the IRS. Every year they collect $3.3 trillion. But some taxpayers do not pay. In fact, there are more and more non-payers every year and now the IRS is owed $380 billion. There are currently 5.1 million cases in IRS Collection case inventory. IRS Collection is effective and efficient in tax collection. They collect about $48 billion a year. For every $1 spent to collect these delinquent taxes, they bring back $6. The problem is that the unpaid tax balance has risen about 21% over the past five years, and this is due to the fact that the number of collection employees has declined by 23%.

The IRS issues 1,995,000 levies/seizures every year and 535,000 Notices of Federal Tax Lien. These are quite damaging to the 2,530,000 taxpayers who receive this type of IRS "enforced collection." Because there are fewer IRS Collection employees, 37% fewer levies and liens were issued from 2012-2014. This will be little comfort to you if the IRS issues one of these against you.

Most of the individual balances due are for less than $50,000. In fact, 66% of the balance due cases are for $5,000 or less. The Treasury Inspector General for Tax Administration reported that the IRS is very effective at collecting balances under $5,000 but not as effective collecting balances over $25,000.

The IRS Master File computer is instrumental in this collection effort, because it issues automatic levies of state refunds, IRS refunds and Social Security payments. It also issues Backup Withholding Orders which require that 28% of your income be sent to the IRS instead of being paid to you. So as long as the IRS computer is capable of spitting out levies, taxpayers stand the chance of getting hurt.

At some point you may respond to the IRS, in a letter, phone call or in person. This chapter tells you who you might be talking to and how you should handle the contact.

If you have been receiving letters from one of the IRS service centers and place a call to them, you will speak to Service Center Accounts Management. If it is a collection case, they will transfer your call to Service Center Collection. If you are able to get through on the telephone they will tell you how much you owe and demand that you pay it today. Each level of collection has dollar limits as to the type of accounts and the type of taxes that you owe. Income taxes have different dollar limits than employment/business taxes do.

We caution you; if you owe the IRS, you should try to do everything that you can to borrow and fully pay the taxes you owe. Because the IRS is the most dangerous creditor in the world, the IRS can seize your cash, bank accounts, autos, business and most of your wages - all without ever once going to court and getting a formal judgement against you.

When you contact the IRS, you might just be inquiring as to what your options are. You might barely be paying your expenses and you cannot pay anything more. During your conversation with the IRS employee, however, you may say the wrong things and get trapped into an installment agreement that you cannot afford. We have seen it hundreds of times. Accounts Management, Service Center Collection and ACS cannot help you if you owe more money than they can handle in their section. So if your balance exceeds the amounts shown later in this chapter, you should tell them that you do not have the information that they are asking for and that you want to speak to a tax professional. You should also tell them that you request that your case be transferred to a field revenue officer, and then end the call, because they can do nothing more for you. Follow the phone contact up with a letter to the address on your original letter to request the transfer to the revenue officer.

We suggest that you find out what the IRS is offering you first, with its automatic installment agreement and its online application for an installment agreement. Use Google or Bing to search Online Payment Agreement – IRS. The less you talk to the IRS, the better the deal you will receive.

Before we tell you the many options available to you, first you must file any tax returns that you have forgotten, neglected or refused to file.

The Goals of IRS Collection

All of IRS Collection is guided by the same principles - to collect as much money as quickly as possible with the least amount of expense to the government. "Balance due" cases are separated by the type of case, the number of quarters or years that you owe and the dollar amount owed. Their goal is to collect full payment from you today. If the IRS determines that is not possible, they will set up an installment agreement with you, or even declare your case to be "currently not collectible." This means that you still owe the money and penalties and interest will continue to be added on, but the IRS realizes that because of your financial circumstances you are not able to pay anything at all at that time. Your case then goes to inactive status and no one will take your bank account or wages for at least the next two years, unless your income rises significantly. Then the whole process begins again with new financials and the possibility of an installment agreement at that time.

Can You Represent Yourself Before IRS Collection?

Determining if you can represent yourself in a collection case is difficult. It depends on how much you owe, for how many years you owe and what kind of taxes that you owe. All of those factors affect how the IRS looks at your case and what options you have to resolve it. When you do not have much income or assets it makes it easier for you to work your case yourself. The trick is to learn the IRS system. Many people have huge tax balances - some in the hundreds of thousands of dollars - due to high income in the past or businesses where they were charged the Trust Fund Recovery Penalty. Those balances climb quickly, usually doubling every five years. So no matter how much they pay, they will never be able to pay off the taxes.

Many people that we have represented over the years are capable of representing themselves before the IRS, but do not do so, because they are too afraid, upset or so stressed out that they would rather pay us, as enrolled agents, than ever speak to the IRS.

For most people, the more they owe the IRS, the less likely they are to be able to pay it. Sixty-six percent of all collection cases are under $5,000; those you can handle yourself. Most people owe under $50,000. This is the same amount as you might spend for a really nice car. If you paid it off over 6 years, you would have high payments, but it is possible for you to pay the balance. That is possible as you will see later in this chapter, but the IRS always seems to have so many exceptions to every rule that it can be it very confusing.

This chapter should be read along with Chapter 12, where the financial statement (Form 433-A/B - personal and business financial statements) preparation is discussed and with Chapter 13, Offer-In-Compromise. These three chapters together will give you the maximum advantage in dealing with the IRS.

Your Goals in Dealing with the IRS Collection

If you are not challenging your tax balance as being incorrect, then your goal is to get your tax case resolved. This can be done by paying the tax or negotiating for an installment agreement or having your case declared "currently not collectible" (CNC) due to financial hardship. There are many types of collection arrangements. Your first goal should be the peace of mind that comes from having an accepted installment agreement or being told that your case was declared CNC. Finding out that your bank account has been seized can be a devastating surprise. The IRS rarely releases a bank levy and this leaves you having to explain to your creditors why their checks or direct debits bounced. Add on top of that the bad check charges which can run $30 each and you have a real mess on your hands. At least you can rest at night, knowing that the monster that the IRS can be will be sleeping for a while.

If you are unable to fully pay your taxes, then your primary goal is to make a reasonable agreement with the IRS or to have them declare your account "currently not collectible" due to hardship. But you must have all your ducks in a row. The easier your case is able to be worked by the revenue officer, the more likely you are to get more favorable terms. Don't kid yourself, this is not going to be a pleasant, uplifting experience; it is just going to be more fair and reasonable to you if you follow their rules just like they have to follow those same rules. We will tell you your options and then you can make wise choices in how to solve your IRS troubles.

What Kind of Deals Can You Make with IRS Collection?

There are many installment agreement options offered by the IRS:

- If you can pay within the next 120 days, you can get an online installment agreement and there is no service charge, no financial statement required and no Notice of Federal Tax Lien.

- The Automatic Guaranteed Installment Agreement is used for cases with balances of $10,000 or less (*excluding* penalties and interest) that can be paid within 36 months. There is no financial statement required and no Notice of Federal Tax Lien required. You can apply online and a service charge applies.
- Streamlined Installment Agreement for cases that owe $10,001 to $25,000. (*including* penalties and interest) The payments can be spread out over 72 months. This agreement is offered even if the taxpayer has the ability to fully pay today per IRM 5.14.5.2. You may need to share this with your collection employee. No financial statement and no Notice of Federal Tax Lien are required. The streamlined installment agreement is for personal income taxes and business income taxes under $25,000. A service charge applies.
- The Streamlined Installment Agreement is for cases where from $25,001 to $50,000 is owed. You will need to complete Form 433F or Form 433A- both Collection Financial Statements for Individuals; no Notice of Federal Tax lien required. A service charge applies.
- All other Installment Agreements apply to balances over $25,000 that cannot be full paid in 72 months or cannot be fully paid before the Collection Statue of Expiration expires. Form 433-F is required for ACS cases. 433-A, and Form 433-B is required for cases being worked by Field Collection. Federal Tax Lien optional up to $50,000, required over $50,000. Chapter 12 of this book will give you step by step instructions on completely these forms.

For cases in the range of $25,001 to $50,000, the IRS will allow you 72 months to pay under the Streamlined Installment Agreement option. The IRS will require you to submit either Collection Financial Statement Form 433-A or Form 433-F and they will make a determination about filing a lien against you. The IRS wants more financial information and you will need to provide a Collection Information

Statement, (CIS), and get the Notice of Federal Tax Lien, which are more intrusive in your life. Individuals and defunct businesses both can qualify for this agreement. This is much talked about on radio and television commercials which offer tax help and is called the "IRS Fresh Start Program". This was introduced in 2012 and raised the dollar amounts for installment agreements and offers in compromise. As usual, the IRS made it so complicated; it does not offer much benefit to most taxpayers. It is not much of a "Fresh Start"; it does not reduce the tax balance, or remove any penalties or interest.

For any of these categories, the taxpayer can make a lump sum payment to reduce their account to the amount within the IRS guidelines for types of agreements. For example, if you owe $30,000 and can pay $5,000, the installment agreement terms will be more favorable to you, not the IRS. This is an important change, because in the past, the IRS did not let you do this.

If you have an installment agreement on any amount over $10,001, which will not be full paid before the Collection Statute of Expirations time (ten years from the date the tax was assessed), this is called a Part Pay Installment Agreement (PPIA). A Notice of Federal Tax Lien is required to be filed.

Types of Business Taxes and How to Work with the IRS

- In-Business Trust Fund Taxes - these are taxes that a currently-operating business owes and these are for Form 941 (employment taxes) only. An Express Installment Agreement $10,000 or below is covered under Automatic Guaranteed Installment Agreement (see above) and offers 24 months to fully pay. A Notice of Federal Tax Lien may be filed, but it is unlikely if the balance is under $25,000.
- In-Business Trust Fund Taxes for amounts over $10,001 to $25,000 - must be paid within 24 months thru a Direct Debit

Installment Agreement (see later). No financial statement required. Notice of Federal Tax Lien is usually required to be filed.

- If you owe corporate income taxes or owe employment taxes on a corporation that is now out of business, you are not legally required to pay those taxes, because they are a debt of the corporation entity and not you personally. You are likely to be assessed the Trust Fund Recovery Penalty if you owe employment taxes. Once those are assessed against you, then they become your personal taxes, and are no longer business taxes.
- We have never seen a case where the Trust Fund Recovery Penalty is assessed for amounts under $10,000. We have heard revenue officers encourage delinquent taxpayers to pay down their business trust fund balance so that it is under $10,000.

If you continue to "pyramid" (owe more) new taxes or do not file future tax returns and make Federal Tax Deposits, then you will face continuing IRS enforced collection actions. If you are still in business, the IRS can seize the funds from your bank account every 30 days and can levy your credit card processing company every day and seize your daily receipts.

Service Charge for Installment Agreements

All installment agreements come with a service charge of $120 (for a regular installment agreement or with a Payroll Deduction Installment Agreement). If you are paying with a Direct Debit Installment Agreement the service charge is $52. Some people can get a reduced rate of $43. Use Google or Bing to search for Form 13844, Application for Reduced User Fee for Installment Agreements.

You need to know that even if you have an installment agreement, you are still charged the Failure to File Penalty and the Failure to Pay

Penalty. Both of these penalty rates are up to 25% of the balance, plus 3% interest, which is compounded daily and continues to be charged for the length of the agreement. The good part is that any payments that you make are applied to the tax first.

Service Center Collection works cases up to $25,000 for business taxes and up to $50,000 for personal income taxes. Generally, if Service Center Collection is unable to resolve the case due to the amounts being above $50,000 it will transfer your case over to the ACS System.

ACS works cases up to $100,000. ACS sends high or medium risk cases to the Queue after 26 weeks. Low risk cases are not sent to the Queue, but are "shelved by National Office" after 104 weeks. The IRS prioritizes the cases by the income reported, the balance due or expected balance due in the case of non-filers and other factors; for example if the case is for an individual or a business. If ACS is unable to contact you or work with you, depending on the type of case it is, they will transfer your case directly to a field revenue officer or to the queue for field collection. This is based on the priorities that the IRS establishes. One priority is a business that is in operation, has employees and is not paying in the money that was withheld from the employees' checks. The IRS takes this very seriously.

All cases over $100,000 are transferred to the Queue where they wait to be issued to a field revenue officer. Some are transferred directly to a field revenue officer.

Types of Installment Agreements

There are three types of agreements. One is the **Standard Installment Agreement**, where you send a check or make a payment using EFTPS every month. The second is called a **Direct Debit Installment Agreement (DDIA).** This is where the IRS takes the money out of your checking account every month. This type of agreement is impossible to stop. We suggest that you open a checking account at a different bank and use that account solely for making the installment agreement payments. This advice is given because things happen in your personal and financial life every day and you need to be in the best position to handle that. For example, if you are now unemployed and barely able to pay bills, a normal IRS DDIA would just keep drawing the money out of your account. After you are in an installment agreement, you can expect little or no customer service, because the employee you are talking to has no control over your case. The IRS is not flexible or accommodating.

If you choose a DDIA, it can take the IRS 2-4 months just to input it on their system. So you may need to make manual payments in the meantime.

If the IRS has already filed a lien against you, and if you are in a DDIA, they will consider withdrawing the Notice of Federal Tax Lien after you have made two months' payments. Use Google or Bing to search Form 12277 – Application for Withdrawal of Filed Form 668 (Y), Notice of Federal Tax Lien. The problem is that the lien is already showing on your credit report. This is just stating that the IRS is pulling back its lien, not that you don't still owe the money. The IRS may also withdraw the lien if it will help you pay your taxes more quickly. A Federal Tax Lien will cause any credit that you are still able to get to come with high interest rates since you are a credit risk. Potential lenders will think of it this way – "This person did not pay the IRS; why would they pay me back either?" Liens can cause people to lose their existing jobs, lose their ability to be licensed, bonded and insured, lose their security clearance, and cause future employers to shy away from hiring them.

Even if you have a lien against your home, it can be "discharged" or "subordinated". That means that the IRS will take the equity in your home and then allow you to sell it. Or if you are trying to refinance your mortgage, the IRS may allow a new mortgage to jump ahead of it in line, and take priority over the Federal Tax Lien. This is usually because it will allow the taxpayer to pay more money to the IRS. See more lien information later in this chapter.

There is a third type of agreement called a **Payroll Deduction Installment Agreement**. Never agree to this. It is extra work for your employer and presents many problems. It could lead to you losing your job. Besides, it makes no sense to let your employer in on your private business. The IRS cannot force this type of agreement on you.

In all types of installment agreements, you need to know that any future tax refunds that you have will automatically be held by the IRS and applied to your back taxes. If this causes you a hardship, you can file a new W-9 Form claiming more exemptions or changing your filing status. This will reduce your refund and give you more income throughout the year, which can be used to pay your agreement.

Form 9465 Applying for an Installment Agreement

To apply for an installment agreement, use Google or Bing to search for Form 9465. You can print and mail it in or you can apply online. This is for a streamlined installment agreement that provides up to 72 months for you to pay your taxes, penalties and interest. The IRS will let you know within 60 days if they approve your agreement proposal or not.

If you have had an installment agreement in the past and defaulted on it, or if you owe more than $25,000 but less than $50,000, you must agree to either a DDIA or Payroll Deduction Plan.

If you owe more than $50,000, you must complete Form 433-F. This is a Collection Information Statement that is not as detailed as Form 433-A, Form 433-A (OIC) and the Form 433-B. This form is only used by Service Center Collection and ACS. Revenue officers will not accept it. Conversely, the Service Center and ACS will not accept the more complete Form 433-A either.

We advise throughout this book that you complete Form 433-A, and make sure that you get credit for all of your expenses, because the Form 433-F does not give you that knowledge or opportunity. So do Form 433-A first and then take what you need out of it to complete the Form 433-F. It will save you big money.

If you do not agree to pay by direct debit or payroll deduction, you must complete Form 433-F and file it with this form.

If the balance of taxes for all years is not more than $50,000, you do not need to file Form 9465; you can just complete the installment agreement online.

If it seems like the IRS makes it so complicated to make an installment agreement, you will soon learn that nothing is ever simple in the IRS.

When choosing a date for your installment agreement, we always suggest you start it two months after the date of application, because it really does take the IRS time to look at your request and approve it. They can always say no, but at least you will have asked for those terms. So if today is June 10th, then make your payment date proposal August 15. You can only choose any payment date from the 1st to the 28th of the month.

Never double up on your payments. Don't do this because the IRS computer does not understand. The computer expects a payment from you every month by a certain date. If you make 2-3 payments all at once, it does not care; you still need to make the payment on time next month. If you do make additional payments, it will help you, but don't count on the idea of pre-paying your installment agreement.

If you are unable to make your payment, you need to know a secret that the IRS does not tell you. The installment agreement system has a onetime automatic skip payment built into it. It will not default your agreement. This is very important if you are under financial stress. You do not need to call. But you can send a letter saying you missed the payment and why, and plan to resume the payments next month. Send this letter to the IRS and keep a copy yourself.

If the IRS is Not Calling You, Then Why Are You Calling Them?

You need to know that when the IRS Master File computer reflects that your case goes into installment agreement status 60, currently not collectible status 53, bankruptcy or litigation status 72, appeals status 72 or has been shelved or surveyed, it is not assigned to any IRS Collection section. No one will have direct access to your case. If you call, no record will be made of the call. No one can help you. You are under the IDRS Master Computer. That computer is impossible to communicate with; it only understands actions. If you do not pay, it understands that you are starting to default your agreement and will send you a terse warning letter.

What You Expect from the Service Center

If you call Service Center Collection, they will first verify who you are, where you work, and where you bank. They have very structured interviews and will ask if you have your monthly income and expense information. For most people, this is a shock, because they were not thinking that far into the future. They were just calling to see what could be done about the back taxes. They did not expect to be launched into making an installment agreement. They usually don't know or do not remember all the expenses they have every month. So they end up agreeing to an installment agreement for a much higher amount than they can afford.

Service Center Collection cannot issue levies to seize anything, but they do make notes on their system regarding the fact that you called, what you said, and how you acted. That record will determine how you will be treated in the future. If you are rude or disrespectful it will come back to bite you later. Make sure you watch your mouth and be respectful.

All of these things are why you need to complete Form 433-A

before you call. That will allow you the time to research what the IRS really allows you for all of your monthly expenses. This is the secret to gaining maximum advantage in your IRS negotiations, because some months you will have expenses that change, car repairs, medical expenses, life's emergencies, etc.

If the IRS employee that you are speaking to is rude, intimidating or makes you uncomfortable or stressed out and the interview is not going in your favor, then just hang up. No need to explain or give notice. For the IRS, it is another lost call, no big deal. Then you can get yourself together and call back. The Collection Roulette will offer you another employee. If you are better prepared, then maybe you will get lucky the second time and be able to negotiate a better payment plan. But first, you need to remember what we already addressed earlier in the book. You must be calm, patient, and respectful. You must be ready to tell your story and make the IRS come around to your way of thinking. You must not be rude, belligerent, use swear words, or ask for something that the IRS simply cannot give you. That is why you are reading this book - to find out your options.

Service Center Collection is not known for having a big heart. In fact, their Internal Revenue Manual advises its employees, "If the taxpayer states that they are having financial difficulty, ask them if they can make a minimum payment of $25 a month and increase it over time." Wait, what? You just established you don't have any money and still they want money? Now you are beginning to see what you are up against. The best IRS employees do what they are told to do and in Service Center Collection and ACS, there are boilerplate scripts for them to use in questioning taxpayers. These do not allow for the human factor to play much part in their case decisions.

What You Can Expect from ACS

This next part can get confusing. If you owe over $50,000 in income taxes, then Service Center Collection may not be able to help you, so they will transfer the case to the Queue (the holding place) leading into Automated Collection System (ACS). It might take some time for you to be contacted. In all the phases of collection, high tax dollar balances always go to the head of the line. You can still send in payments even without an agreement. Just put your Social Security Number on the face of the check and the tax year where you want it applied. The IRS must post the check where you want it to go.

ACS generally will work cases from $25,000 to $100,000. That is for income taxes. Employment taxes (Form 941) have lower dollar thresholds, because they are due every quarter. This means that they can rapidly pyramid (increase) into large balances and thus they receive more immediate attention. Employment tax cases over $25,000 usually will be assigned to a field revenue officer.

Form 433-F - Collection Information Statement - is the only form that ACS and the Service Center Collection use. It seems silly, but that is how they were trained. The problem with that statement is that it does not explain your rights to claim full credit for the National Allowable Expenses that are approved for your area. We have advised many people how to do that in our practice. Because the IRS will allow your car payments and rent expenses higher than you may have, it makes sense to buy a new car or upgrade your living arrangements. For example, if you owe taxes and are living in your parent's basement and not paying rent, the IRS will not allow you credit for rent. If you have a lease with your parents which includes utilities, then the IRS will allow it. It might be in your best interest to rent an apartment and have the IRS allow you that expense plus utilities, especially in cases where it is unlikely that you will ever be able to pay the taxes in full. Everything you just read for Service Center Collection applies double here, because the person in ACS has their finger on the LEVY BUTTON. If you get them irritated, they will end the interview and send all the right letters so that they can take your bank account, wages, salary and any other income that you have.

The cases in ACS are never assigned to an individual employee.

Employees just work whatever calls come in. If you are well prepared with your financial data, they may ask you to send in some verification to their secret "eFax" telephone number. There is no master list, even within the IRS, of these phone numbers. If you are able to get the information to them either by mail or using the eFax, the same person will review it and then make a decision on your tax matter. This is where you send a fax and it goes directly into the IRS employee's email. Remember that the IRS does not use email for collection cases, so this is the only way you can get a message directly to the person with whom you spoke. This information might include copies of bills that seem high to the IRS, or copies of your last three months' bank statements. Then they will tell you if your installment agreement is approved and its terms.

ACS transfers 23% of its cases, valued at $14.5 billion, to the queue for the field revenue officer. It closes 16% of its cases as "shelved by National Office", mostly for people who owe $5,000 or less. Those lucky taxpayers will lose future refunds, but will not be worked in active collection.

What You Can Expect from Field Collection

The last place that your case can end up is with a field revenue officer. Many stories have been told about these employees, involving their officious behavior, and abuse to taxpayers. Many of the stories are probably true. One of the authors of this book, Richard M. Schickel, shares many such stories in his book "*IRS Whistleblower*" (available on Amazon). These are definitely the IRS employees who can destroy your life, just by their signature. They can and have seized everything a person owns, except for some small amounts that the law allows people to keep. (Use Google or Bing to find - Property Exempt from IRS Levy) It takes a long time for a revenue officer to be assigned to your case, no matter how urgently you want to resolve it. Then when they are assigned, they seem to want everything "right now" (usually in 10 days to 4 weeks). After you submit the information, you might wait up to a year to hear back from them again, depending on the complexity of the case. With all the runaround that you will feel you have experienced if you have tried to call the IRS, you will be happy to be assigned to a revenue officer – a person who will be your sole contact on your case and someone you with speak with personally. You will be happy for a minute. Then the endless questions, judgments and evaluations will start. The IRS will comb through your bank statements and your credit report; they will see if you have used your passport for travel, and they will tell you how your future lifestyle will look like.

The first time you meet your revenue officer in person is when they come knocking on your front door unannounced. They will judge you - how you talk, act, and look. They will evaluate your lifestyle, the jewelry that you are wearing, including watches or anything else that might indicate a more elaborate lifestyle. Bling especially catches their eye. This is a good reason not to let them into your home to interview you. The revenue officer wants to see what you own. They will also note if you are cooperative and want to pay and willingly work with them. Since only one revenue officer comes to your door, they have their own "good cop – bad cop", routine where they talk one way to you sometimes and another way at other times, depending on what they want you to do and how fast they want it done. If you are cooperative, you should have a good experience, except when your case is being reviewed by their manager or when your case is over a year old. Then they become very aggressive and if you do not do everything that they want, they start levying your income and assets. You cannot just refuse to speak to your revenue officer.

You may want to hire a tax professional to speak for you. You also have rights. You have the Collection Appeals Program and the Collection Due Process Appeal right. You can also open a case with the IRS National Taxpayer Advocate. You can also contact your

Congressperson, Senator or the White House and ask them to advocate for you. That is free and if you have a good argument for what you want, they can help you. But you need to know and understand all of these rights first, and how and when to use them. You have rights that are explained in bureaucratic detail in (Google or Bing search) The IRS Collection Process Publication 594 and also in Publication 1 Your Rights as a Taxpayer. These publications discuss the collection process, payment options, federal tax liens, appeals rights and summons. A summons is used by the IRS when you do not cooperate or provide information that they require to verify your financial condition. A summons legally compels you or some third party - like your bank or credit card company - to meet with the IRS and provide information, documents and/or testimony. These are used to force you to provide the Collection Information Statements, Form 433-A or Form 433-B. If you cannot attend, you must respond to the IRS in writing to request a new time to appear. If you do not appear, the IRS can go to Federal District Court and sue you to comply with the summons. We have known dozens of tax resistors who refused, so the judge jailed them for contempt of court. We remember one man who was in jail for over 2 years for failing to provide a Collection Information Statement to the Court.

Changing, Adding to or Ending Your Installment Agreement

You can call or write the IRS to try to change your agreement. We have never seen this work. If you need to change the agreement, you will have to default and send them a letter saying that due to unemployment or some other circumstance you can no longer pay the agreement. If you have additional tax balances which should never happen, you should try to pay them off. Always try to leave the original agreement intact.

If it is later in the year, and you should have been making estimated tax payments, but you were not able to, you can try this. Just consider the current year another lost year and throw it on the pile with the other years you owe for; those can all then be included in an installment agreement.

This is important. The IRS demands that you be in full filing and paying compliance before it gives you an installment agreement. So we are telling you how to give yourself a break today. Put as much money together as you can and deposit it into the next tax year in January. You can use the EFTPS System to make your deposits. That way you can start the new tax year and be in compliance with the law. We suggest making monthly tax deposits, instead of quarterly tax deposits. The quarterly system gets too many people in trouble. For instance, if you owe $3,000 a quarter, it is hard to come up with that at one time; it is easier to come up with $1,000. We suggest that you voluntarily make monthly estimated tax deposits. Then you know the money is there and that you will not get into trouble with the IRS in the future.

This way you have also budgeted for the new higher tax deposits and figured that in when you negotiated your installment agreement with the IRS.

How to Get Your Case Closed as Currently Not Collectible

When the IRS has researched your financial situation, it can temporarily put your case on the shelf. It still collects penalties and interest, but it is no longer actively being worked in Collection. That means no threat of losing bank accounts or other income.

Service Center Collection has the ability to close your case if you are current with filing new taxes, you owe under $25,000 and you are:

- In jail
- Living solely on unemployment, disability, welfare or Social Security

- Suffering from a terminal illness
- Paying excessive medical bills
- Losing your home to foreclosure or have had a foreclosure in the past
- Unemployed with no income
- A graduate of the Bankruptcy Court
- Unable to locate
- Unable to contact

As we explain your collection options, you have to change your way of thinking to understand how the IRS thinks. This may sound strange, but the worse off that you are in your life, the better off you will be in negotiations with the IRS. If you have lost everything and are sick, unemployed, underemployed or old, you get maximum bonus points. The reason is that the IRS wants two things from you. They want you to get current with filing all tax returns that should be filed and second they want you to keep filing and paying taxes year after year into the future. At the same time, they also want to get money for the back taxes. When you show them that you are not worth much of anything, and they look at your projected future income situation, they might see that you will be more likely to go from bad to worse rather than the other way around. So your poverty, pain and illness actually have meaning and value in negotiating with the IRS. Sometimes in addition to declaring your case as "currently not collectible", the IRS employee will also suggest that you should file an Offer in Compromise to settle the debt forever.

We remember working with one taxpayer (while a revenue officer) who had not filed a tax return for many years. He had made a lot of money from investments. He lived in a small rundown house, his wife of 50 years had died recently, and he was sick and dying. He was on oxygen and smoked cigarettes throughout the interview. He wanted to get things straightened up with the IRS before he died. He wanted the IRS to help him prepare his tax returns, but IRS employees are not able to do that, nor can they recommend any tax preparers. He was old and sick and confused. So we spotted a telephone book and opened it to a page for CPAs. He called and was able to file eight years of returns with us a few weeks later. When we had calculated all the penalties and interest, he owed $375,000, which we collected on the spot.

Remember earlier where we said you must link your story together and carefully share it with the IRS? It is that sequence of events that will make the IRS appreciate your situation. For example, you had a business, your bookkeeper embezzled from you, the economy crashed and you lost your business, you started having trouble at home, you started self-medicating (alcohol, drugs) and your spouse left you. Now you are working for $10 an hour at Home Depot, part time. You lost everything but your tax debt.

If your case is assigned to ACS or Field Collection you can use these same circumstances (your story) combined with your financial statement, to establish that you do not have enough income to make any installment agreement payments. Remember it will be your story combined with your ability to live within the National Allowable Expenses that will make your case.

The collection employee is trained to establish a sense of urgency about your delinquent taxes. You will not feel that the IRS is very worried about the situation if you are making current tax payments. But that is important to you. You cannot make an agreement if you have no W-2 withholdings or paid-in estimated tax deposits for the current year. You should adjust your tax withholdings during the time you are negotiating your installment agreement. You can always decrease it later. It is better to have all your estimated tax payments in for the current year, than to make an agreement and then next April, find that you owe one more year of taxes that you still cannot pay. We have found it almost impossible to amend your installment agreement once it begins. But when you talk to the IRS, they will say you have an extension to file your return or it is not due yet. That does you no good when it is due, because then when you file it you will have a new balance due and that will default your old agreement.

CSED Expiration: Will I Owe These Taxes Forever?

No, your tax balance will expire ten years from the date of assessment. It is important to find out what your Collection Statute of Expiration (CSED) date is, because it will give you hope and knowledge that on that day, you will no longer owe the unpaid taxes. You can ask the IRS what that date is, or you can request a transcript. See IRS Get Transcript. We say this because many people get depressed and even despondent because they have tax balances. With that knowledge, then you can prepare yourself for the road ahead. Remember that if you file an appeal, bankruptcy, or an offer in compromise, these will all extend the CSED by 6 months plus the time you that your case is being worked by these functions.

Resolving Your Collection Case through Bankruptcy

This subject could be a book in itself. So we will just touch on the high points. The filing of a Notice of Federal Tax Lien is reported on your credit report. So is a bankruptcy. In our experience they both have the same impact on the taxpayer.

Chapter 7 Bankruptcy is a liquidation bankruptcy. All of the debtor's non-exempt property is sold and distributed to creditors. This might be a good option for a person who has no assets, just debt, and has income under an amount that the courts find to be reasonable. Use Google or Bing to search Bankruptcy Chapter 7 Means Test. Then all debts are discharged (cancelled) forever.

Chapter 11 Bankruptcy is a reorganization bankruptcy usually involving a business or an individual. This is where the debt is divided into different classes and a payment plan begins to pay at all creditors, at least in part. In this bankruptcy some or all of the IRS penalties can be removed by the bankruptcy court.

Chapter 13 Bankruptcy allows an individual to consolidate their debt and make payments over a three-to-five-year period. Some of the debt is extinguished in the process and the debtor has the ability to retain some or all of their property if they comply with the plan. Any individual, whether employed or self-employed, may seek Chapter 13 protection so long as the individual's unsecured debts are less than $383,175 and secured debts are less than $1,149,525. Many people are unaware of this type of bankruptcy. In a bankruptcy situation, if it is filed before an IRS lien, a taxpayer who has higher income may benefit. A Bankruptcy Court Trustee will monitor their case.

In all three types of bankruptcies, the U.S. Bankruptcy Court has allowable monthly living standards and expenses, similar to the IRS National Allowable Monthly Expenses.

Income taxes but not Trust Fund Recovery Penalty assessments can be discharged in the following circumstances:

- If the tax debt is related to a tax return that was due at least three years before the taxpayer files for bankruptcy.
- The tax debt must be related to a tax return that was filed at least two years before the taxpayer files for bankruptcy.
- The tax assessment must be at least 240 days before the bankruptcy filing.
- The tax return was not frivolous or fraudulent.
- The taxpayer was not guilty of tax evasion.
- You will need to consult with a qualified bankruptcy attorney regarding your case.

We have seen many cases over the years where the taxpayer had gone through bankruptcy and their attorney did not seek to get the old taxes discharged. This is sad. You can't go back. You will need to bring this up specifically if you go this route. We saw one case where a bankruptcy attorney did inform the taxpayer that if he could just wait 74 more days an $87,000 tax debt would have been wiped out. But the client foolishly chose to file the bankruptcy petition too early. Good tax planning is always about getting good advice and having the right timing.

Filing bankruptcy automatically stops any IRS collection actions. None of the bankruptcies are an easy out. They will cause change in people's lives and finances, sometimes painful and unwanted change, but it can beat working with the IRS.

Your Tax Balance and the Notice of Federal Tax Lien (NFTL)

If you agree with the balance due, it is always better to pay it, or borrow the money, instead of being in an installment agreement with the IRS. That is because in cases where over $50,000 is owed, the IRS will file a Notice of Federal Tax Lien which is a lien against you, your name, your real estate, your automobile, and any other assets or income that you have or come into in the future. In cases where Notices of Federal Tax Liens are filed, 21% of taxpayers have never talked to the IRS and there has been no review of their finances or circumstances. The NFTL is a public notice that you owe money, and that is scary. Friends, relatives, neighbors, creditors, co-workers and anyone else will be able to look into your financial affairs and talk about you and your taxes. Worse yet, right after the lien is filed you will receive dozens of letters and phones calls from predatory tax firms who will claim to represent you and will charge you a lot of money to do that. We suggest that you find a local tax professional to talk to who can represent you, and especially be available to you.

If a Notice of Federal Tax Lien is filed by ACS or Field Collection you will receive a copy of it and a copy of Letter 3172 – Notice of Federal Lien and Right to Collection Due Process Hearing.

If you miss the 30-day deadline, you can still file a CDP for an Equivalent Hearing, however this does not freeze any pending collection actions.

In both cases you also have the right to file a Collection Appeals Request (CAP), which is basically the right to talk to the manager of the employee taking the action against you. If you cannot reach agreement with their manager, then your case will be forwarded to Appeals for their review. Use Google or Bing to search for Form 1660 - Hearing Available Under Collection Appeals Program. We have never found those to be very productive, because the manager is just another employee who used to do collection work, so is likely to share the same attitudes as the employee. You have the right to file a CAP before or after a lien or levy is filed, or after a seizure has taken place, when your installment agreement has been denied or terminated. This temporarily stops collection. Use Form 9423 Collection Appeal Request to start this process.

Special Circumstances

The Trust Fund Recovery Penalty (TFRP) is not a penalty at all. It comes as a result of your actively participating in a company that did not pay its payroll taxes. You may have been a corporate officer, a signer on the bank account or a person that the IRS determined to have the power and authority to direct the company's money. At some point, you decided to use the money for something other than paying the IRS. You may have done this to try to save a failing business. We will not address this further in this book. If you have been contacted by the IRS and scheduled for a Trust Fund Recovery Penalty Interview - run; don't walk to a tax professional for advice relevant to your particular case. Trust fund taxes are like student loans, never forgiven and you cannot discharge them in a bankruptcy. Trust fund assessments against you personally can be resolved in the Offer in Compromise process. In any event, you need a legal strategy for dealing with the TFRP process. Any tax professional with experience in this can help you.

Inheritances

We have seen some taxpayers who inherit money and put it in their bank accounts. We have seen the IRS levy those bank accounts and take all the money. In one case a woman lost $82,000 and in another case $134,000. Don't let this happen to you. You should talk to the lawyer for the estate. You can turn down the inheritance and the money can be divided about remaining heirs. Please hire a tax professional to help you with this, because it is a shame for the person who left you the money to have sweated and saved all those years only to have all the money go to the IRS. That is why we always advocate trust and estate planning while you are still able to do it.

Bad Things Can Happen to You if You Don't Do What the IRS Wants

If you don't file your tax returns, you can go to jail. Strangely, not paying your taxes is not something that leads to jail, although for the ten years when you do owe the tax, you might wish you could hide out there. If you do not file, the IRS will prepare tax returns for you with its Substitute for Return Program (SFR). This will label you as either single or married filing separately, and not give you any deductions and will only give credit for yourself; none for your dependents. These returns always show a high tax balance due. You should never accept these returns. SFR tax assessments are never dischargeable in bankruptcy. To change them, you must file Form 1040X- Amended Income Tax Return.

However, the IRS will ask you for returns going back 8-10 years if you have not filed for a long time. You do not need to file returns going back more than 6 years unless it is in your best interest. This would include if you need the 40 quarters/ten years' credit to get a Social Security benefit. Another secret that the IRS does not share with you is that they are only supposed to ask you for the last six years of tax returns. Do not file any more than that. This is based on their own procedural guide. The Internal Revenue Manual states in IRM 1.2.14.1.18 and Policy Statement P-5-133, that the collection enforcement period will not be more than 6 years, unless fraud can be established. You don't need to argue with the IRS over this, just quote them this section.

If you do not pay, you can expect the IRS to levy/seize your:

- Bank accounts
- Wages, salary and any other income
- Your house, vacation house, rental house
- Cars, trucks boats, RV's, campers
- Stocks, bonds, dividends
- Rental income
- Business income
- Current and future tax refunds
- Social Security or disability check
- Inheritances
- Interests in corporations, partnerships, trusts or estates
- Lawsuit proceeds
- Business equipment not otherwise exempt
- Retirement accounts which include 401(k), IRS, Keogh, SEP
- Pensions and profit sharing plans. The IRS cannot force you to withdraw money from your pension plan. It cannot assign a value to something that you cannot withdraw or are not old enough to qualify for a benefit from
- If you close an IRA to pay your taxes, you pay tax on that, but also a 10% penalty. If the IRS seizes the IRA, there is no penalty. You can encourage the IRS to issue a levy
- Anything else you own
- You can also lose your passport if you owe tax, penalties and interest of more than $50,000.

We worked one case where a couple was getting divorced and they had not filed for the last two years. They fought all the time. Finally, the IRS levied for the other years where they owed taxes, and because they could not get together to file their tax returns, the husband suffered four months of lost real estate broker commissions from his sole proprietorship. His wife was also levied on, but she was protected from levy by a Limited Liability Company (LLC). The IRS cannot levy directly on an LLC; it can only get a "charging order" that allows it to take any money being paid out from the LLC. So this gives some protection to a self-employed taxpayer in an LLC, but rarely does so.

What We Would Like the IRS to Offer Delinquent Taxpayers

The problem with the IRS system is that the IRS has no place for you to go online so that you can check in and describe what is happening in your life that contributes to the unfiled returns or unpaid tax. When you call the IRS at 1-800-829-1040 they may not have your case, it might have been transferred or closed. If the case was closed as uncollectible, no record is made of the call. So as much as we advocate calling the IRS, sometimes it is best to just be still and keep your head down and not attract attention to your case. This is always the case when you receive a CP 71 (Annual Reminder Letter).

In a perfect world, we think that the IRS would be wise to offer anyone who owes $50,000 or less, seven years to fully pay their tax balances. This arrangement would not require a Collection Information Statement (financial statement) or Notice of Federal Tax Lien. This type of agreement would require a Direct Debit Installment Agreement.

This would be the most cost effective way to raise billions of dollars in taxes with a minimum cost. Then the IRS could concentrate on businesses that are not paying in their employee withholding taxes and on investigating the underground economy that fails to pay about $700 billion a year in taxes, according to government estimates. A final word to the wise regarding bribing an IRS employee. Don't even go there – because this is the kind of case that the IRS loves to prosecute and you will be convicted and go to prison. Enough said.

Chapter 9
Criminal Investigation

The IRS Criminal Investigation (CI) website says, "Some people bend the tax law, others break it. Criminal Investigation's job is to pursue the lawbreakers". One of the informal mottos of CI is "Greed follows prosperity and we follow greed."

The IRS CI does not have the time or resources to locate and punish all the taxpayers that are deliberately cheating on their taxes, so they look for those cases that they think have the best chance for prosecution. The IRS CI gets convictions on 80% of all their cases; they have the highest conviction rates of all federal agencies.

The IRS Criminal Investigation completed 3,853 investigations in 2015 - down 25% from 2013. Of these investigations, 2,879 people were convicted and sent to prison.

There is a lack of staff and resources that forces criminal investigators to set high dollar amounts before they will even review a tax evasion case. The number of criminal agents is at an all-time low; it is projected to drop down to 2,139 in 2016, down 36% from 1995.

The IRS Criminal Investigation Division prosecutes many financial-related crimes, not just tax evasion. Almost 40% of their cases are for money laundering, human trafficking, mail and wire fraud, or are drug related, as well as any other fraud activity. Of the 3,853 in convictions for 2015, 1,541 were for actual non-tax-related criminals.

Narcotics-related cases made up 955 of the total number. Many IRS CI agents work with the FBI, DEA, ATF, ICE and Customs and other federal law enforcement agencies. This reduces the number of agents that could be working on a case against you. Regular convictions for tax fraud in 2015 were 60% or 2,312 for income or employment tax fraud or evasion. This is significant because it reduces your potential risk of being investigated by IRS Criminal investigators.

A very interesting site we found for this information is www.trac.syr.edu. It has a wealth of IRS statistics. These reports tell you which states have the highest risk of a tax conviction. The top states are Arizona, Florida, eastern Michigan, western Pennsylvania, Virginia, Connecticut, New York, Oregon, Rhode Island, and Tennessee.

The TRAC (Transactional Records Access Clearinghouse) data is so specific that it also tells which federal judges have the highest conviction rates. When you combine this information with the IRS "tax free zones", where tax audits and collections are almost non-existent due to low populations and few IRS employees, you will see that you have a very low risk of a criminal investigation in your case unless you are so flagrant, egregious and noteworthy as to almost demand IRS attention. If you use Google or Bing to search– "IRS Wants You to Know About Scams and Cons", you will learn about many taxpayers who got caught by IRS CI.

The major factor being looked at in evaluating an IRS case is whether there are any patterns in the individual's filing of tax returns. Did you have a plan to not pay the taxes and exercise it over 2-3 years or more?

The IRS does not prosecute its own cases. The IRS is required to work with and pay the Department of Justice attorneys to fly in from Washington D.C. to prosecute their cases. This causes the IRS to forego further investigation and to reach plea bargains in many cases. The IRS does have attorneys that are also Special Assistant U.S. Attorneys but they only answer legal questions that are technical in nature and they appear in bankruptcy court proceedings where the taxpayer owes the IRS money.

Who is Criminal Investigation Interested In?

Usually Criminal Investigation is not interested in cases involving complex business fraud, items a jury cannot understand, or old or sick people, no matter what they have done. This is because some defense attorneys have brought their clients to court in wheelchairs on oxygen and even with make up to make them look older and sicker than they actually are. A jury is unlikely to convict a person in that condition for tax crimes. The IRS CI is interested in people that are highly educated, prominent, notorious, outspoken about the tax system or critical of the government.

In determining if they should prosecute, the IRS will try to look not only at health, age, mental condition, education and also economic status; they will also try to determine the intent the taxpayer had at the time of the alleged offense. Then they will determine if the taxpayer has changed their thinking in the present day. It seems that being remorseful is helpful, when the IRS has evidence that you broke the law.

All CI agents are accountants or CPAs; many are former IRS revenue agents. Our experience with them showed us that most of them don't really like tax cases as much as they like big flashy mob-related cases, money laundering cases, drug cases, human trafficking or sex/slave/prostitution cases.

There are so many other suspicious cases that could be investigated and prosecuted if only the IRS had the resources. The IRS has dollar limits for criminal referrals and that limits the number of cases that can be referred to them. CI is very picky about which cases it chooses to investigate and prosecute. They love to pin perjury (lying) charges on people. These are people who sign tax documents that swear that nothing they signed is false. This is called the *jurat* statement written just above the signatures where you swear to the accuracy of your tax return. They strive for felony charges but also will charge some people with misdemeanors if they can be sure of a conviction. Some offices will try to pin both on you.

Local IRS CI offices get more credit from the IRS CI National Office for the felony convictions than for misdemeanor convictions.

A friend, who was a criminal agent for many years, told me he knows within the first hour of questioning someone about alleged tax crimes if he can make a case or not - depending on how fast they crack and start spilling information without an attorney being present and before they explain your Miranda rights protection. This method is used throughout the IRS in Criminal, Audit, and Collection. It is known as the 80/20 Rule. The IRS employee will get 80% of the most important facts in your case in the first 20 minutes of talking with the taxpayer. Then they can decide what to do with the case.

Criminal agents normally have only one or two cases, so they have the time and resources to devote a lot of attention to you.

The burden of proof in a fraud case is on the IRS. They must prove and provide evidence of the taxpayer's criminal intent at the time the tax evasion occurred. They must prove that the taxpayer knowingly, willfully and intentionally sought to evade taxes. This includes admissions or false statements of the taxpayer. It includes interviews with third parties, and examining the taxpayer's books, records and bank statements. The IRS will also look at the taxpayer's education and employment history, and look at the taxpayer's lifestyle. They look for the Badges of Fraud. These are the secrets of what the IRS is looking for when they interview a taxpayer. They are far-reaching and very subjective. To give you a clear view of what the IRS regards as the Badges of Fraud see the IRS Fraud Handbook. IRM 25.1.2. which will show you those IRS "secrets".

What Happens if CI Doesn't Get Who They Want

The IRS has models of who they would like to prosecute. If you are one of those cases they identified but they were unable to find enough information to use to indict you, watch out, because they will make sure that you are audited and the IRS takes the hardest line with your case. If CI works with the Examination Division, they will make sure that you will feel the pain of a civil federal case.

Undercover Criminal Agent

Sometimes criminal investigation special agents like to play pretend. They go out and pretend they are businessmen involved in whatever business you are in. They drive up in a flashy car, previously seized by the IRS, with a Rolex and other expensive jewelry on them that came from criminal forfeiture seizures from someone else. They will have government money to wine and dine you. Then they will ask to buy your business and want to see your books, so then you will show them the books that you would show the IRS if you were audited. Then they ask for the "real books," to show how much you really make. Once they see those books and where you keep them, the potential seller is told that they will pay huge amounts for their business. Actually in many cases the seller of the business is also lying and wants to inflate the potential sales price of his business. But this is what really happens: the IRS undercover agent goes back to his office with his notes. Normally he would have been recording you and if he was able, had you in a location where you were being filmed or at least photographed.

This does not sound like fair play, does it? It sounds like entrapment to us. The courts have consistently upheld this sort of behavior. The undercover agent will go to all your customers and banks and creditors and issue summonses to collect data. By then it is too late to do anything but plan for some time off in a federal prison.

Civil Forfeiture

In 2012, the IRS criminal investigation agents did civil forfeiture seizures 639 times, with only 20% of the cases being prosecuted. CI keeps a portion of the money and goods seized. The person losing the money has the burden of proof on them to demonstrate the cash, cars and other assets were not tied to criminal activity. Most people don't have the money to fight the IRS in court so they just lose what was seized.

The IRS does not explain why they are doing the forfeiture and in most cases does not accuse the taxpayer of money laundering, tax evasion or criminal activity. They just take the money. The original law was designed to catch terrorists, money launderers and drug lords who deposited less than $10,000 in an effort to evade the federal bank reporting requirement. But it has harmed many innocent taxpayers who have lost everything that they owned, even if tax evasion was never proven, and they were never charged.

CI also enforces the Treasury Forfeiture Fund and not only does a lot of work enforcing the Internal Revenue Code, but also other financial crimes. Then CI comes up with criminal charges and tax assessments over the next few years. CI can seize money or assets based on the belief that they have been illegally obtained or no income tax has been paid on them. They do their seizures (forfeitures) without any legal tax assessments being made. The greatest benefit to the government is that the seizure is against the property, not against a person. This clouds the rights that a person has in the case. How can a million dollars represent itself? These are also called jeopardy assessments when they are initiated on non-criminal cases.

We remember one family-run business had $447,000 seized from its accounts because of a pattern of cash deposits under $10,000 which were legitimate and based on the knowledge of the law that the family-run business had of the banking system. They were told by their CPA that if they made deposits over $10,000, they would get in trouble with the government. That is not true. After holding the money for two years, where no federal criminal charges were filed, their lives and business were destroyed. Recently the Justice Department decided that the seizure was wrong and that the money should be returned. The IRS offered no explanation, no apology, no damages or other compensation for damages to the business or the family's reputation. The return of the money was just too little, too late.

The IRS only stopped this practice recently after the New York Times ran an article that pointed the spotlight on this dubious legal practice.

Suspicious Activity Report

IRS Criminal investigation agents and revenue agents have access to a secret list called the Suspicious Activity Report (SAR). This is where banks or individuals related to the financial industry make reports, some factual, some subjective and without substance. They are in effect snitching on other people. The SAR is used by "anyone who knows, suspects or has reason to suspect that a transaction or pattern of transactions is suspicious and involves more than $2,000." This report gives them ideas about where to look for criminals who commit financial/white collar crimes. This list is ripe, because it also includes all the people who have made cash transactions for more than $10,000. If you pay $20,000 cash for a car, the dealer is required to report it. If you deposit more than $10,000 cash in a bank account, the bank is required to report it. Big Brother is watching everything you do. And you never hear about it. The bank and the Treasury Department/IRS can also track your currency from the serial numbers and the magnetic coding on each bill. We have read many creative reports on SAR documents – that were not true when investigated, but some people want to get other people in trouble with the IRS.

The IRS receives millions of these reports every year and it is impossible to investigate them all. Some reports are made stating that a person may have come into a bank and put $6,000 cash into one account and $6,000 into another account. The bank teller thinks they are doing it to avoid reporting a transaction over $10,000 so they file a report. Banks reported many outlandish things in the reports we saw.

Criminal cases can come from many sources. We knew one agent who used to watch HGTV, a network that specializes in real estate sales and renovations. He got information that could provide case leads to investigate. The program tells the names of the program participants and how much they have available to pay for new homes. This information is easily searched to determine if owners have reported that amount to the IRS. This information can also come from the acquisition of luxury cars, vacations homes or a high spending lifestyle without any apparent means to pay for it. At one time, revenue officers and revenue agents could initiate their own case work and investigations, based on leads that they had personally developed.

After the tax laws changed in 1998, IRS employees had to write up any information they obtained in their investigations of underreporting tax and send the facts to the Information Leads Center to be evaluated. Then the IRS could decide if they wanted to pursue that taxpayer.

Informants and Whistleblowers

Informants are people who turn in information to the IRS on spouses, relatives, ex-employees, ex-employers, co-workers, neighbors, friends and small businesses that they believe violated the tax laws. Whistleblowers are people who are reporting on government agencies, large businesses and individuals. An informant fills out Form 211-Application for Reward for Original Information. In 2014, claimants received $53 million in rewards but the IRS collected $367 million more in taxes because of it. There is a formal network used to collect information from people who want to turn in their neighbor or boss. The IRS pays out great rewards for such information. An informant/

whistleblower can get 15-30% of what taxes are collected, based on the information provided. A few years ago, the IRS paid one informant $104 million after he provided foreign banking secrets. Sometimes the information is already known by the IRS from various reporting sources, so what a whistleblower may give is just verification of that, but they will not receive an award for information that the IRS already knows.

Informants come from the IRS, local states attorneys, State Attorney Generals, Members of Congress and the White House. We have worked investigations on leads from all of these sources. It never occurred to us at the time that the IRS could be used as a political tool. We just did what the case required. Every case in the IRS is coded as to the source of information. As you can imagine, if an employee gets a case that has a code that said the case was from the White House or Congress that would get top priority in an agent's inventory.

We have found it to be amazing how quickly some people will turn in their family, friends, co-workers and neighbors.

Parallel Investigations are where an audit or collection case is being worked civilly by a revenue agent or revenue officer, but is secretly being directed by a criminal agent.

Owing money to the IRS is not a crime. When you have actively and purposefully evaded taxes, then you have committed a crime.

If you do not file your tax returns, that is also a crime, a misdemeanor or in some circumstances, a felony. If you are found guilty of that, it is punishable by up to one year in prison (per count) and up to $25,000 fine for each year or period that you did not file.

One clue that you are being evaluated for referral to IRS CI is if you have not filed tax returns and the IRS revenue agent or revenue officer does not ask you to file the returns or does not seek to prepare them for you. Failing to file tax returns is tax evasion. It is a federal crime.

There are also cases where some fraud appears to be evident to the revenue officer or revenue agent. Those employees, with managerial consent, can then go to Criminal Investigation with the evidence. This is where it can get very tricky. CI will review the case and will either accept the information and develop it as a criminal case or they will go back to the original employee and say that there is not enough information for a criminal case, yet. The Criminal Investigator will then tell the enforcement agent what is needed and how to get it.

This becomes a parallel investigation when the taxpayer provides more and more information and data, thinking they will be able to get the audit over with or the collection case closed. In fact, they are only tightening the noose around their own neck.

Now this is the part where you need to pay close attention. You, as a taxpayer have the right to ask if your case is being worked as a parallel investigation or if the information that you are providing is being used to build a criminal case. IRM 5.1.5.6 instructs the enforcement officer to say "information provided by you can be shared" with IRS Criminal Investigation. According to IRM 5.1.5.8, all information must be shared with IRS Criminal Investigation.

You should ask "Is my case being worked as a parallel investigation with Audit/Collection or Criminal?" Then, write down or record their answer. The IRS enforcement employees are instructed to be silent if asked this question and to never confirm or deny if Criminal Investigation is involved. So if the IRS employee is silent or refuses to answer, then you know that you need to stop the interview and seek out a competent criminal tax attorney.

What to Do if You are Contacted by an IRS CI Special Agent

You will be contacted by your assigned special agent in a place where they feel it is most secure for them to be. They do not call ahead to set an appointment and you are usually caught off guard. They like the advantage this gives them. You are surprised or even shocked and this may cause you to say or do things that will help them develop a criminal case against you. Your special agent will show you their badge and credentials. You will probably notice that they are also armed. They have the power to arrest you, right on the spot, if you threaten or assault them. Next they will tell you that you are "the subject of a criminal investigation for violations of the Internal Revenue Code." They will explain that you have a Constitutional right to not say anything and that anything you do say can be used against you. Then they will start to ask you questions. Our advice to you is for you to take their card and tell them that you want to talk to an attorney first. Then ask them to leave. Then shut your mouth!

We have seen cases where taxpayers have inadvertently incriminated themselves right at the first interview.

You need to know that they already knew a great deal about you before they contacted you. They might have been listening to your telephone calls, monitoring your mail, going through your bank statements, credit card statements, and mortgage applications. They might even have gone through your garbage looking for other financial records.

Do not talk to friends or family about this at all. You need to contact a Criminal Tax Attorney. You can Google or Bing that term to get you started. The only person you can trust at this point is your lawyer who has attorney-client privilege with you and cannot repeat what you tell him or her.

This might sound paranoid, but we have worked many cases where friends, family or ex-employees have turned the taxpayer in. So until you determine who you can trust, trust no one except your attorney.

Criminal tax attorneys charge a lot of money. If you know that you did break the law, tax or other laws, don't worry about how much it might cost to hire that attorney. What price is your freedom? You need the best legal mind available to you. If you are innocent, and can prove it, you still need a great attorney to protect you, because the IRS CI is coming after you and they won't stop until they get what they want.

You need to know that at this point, you don't know what they are even investigating. The key words are "We are investigating you for a criminal tax violation." When you hear those words, don't say another word about the case.

If they are contacting you based on an investigation they are doing on someone else, they may be seeking information that you know about that person. We still advise you to speak to a lawyer first, so that you do not accidentally self-incriminate yourself.

We have seen criminal cases that prove that tax fraud and tax evasion have occurred and we have seen those taxpayers who come to the realization that they have done something wrong and perhaps have broken the law. At this point, they realized that they were probably headed for jail. Suddenly they woke up, acknowledged their guilt and together with their attorney made a plea agreement. This is where the IRS gets a win in court and while there might be some tax restitution, penalties and maybe even jail time, they fared better than those taxpayers who fought the IRS every step along the way.

At this point, all we can do is tell you Good Luck!

Chapter 10
Office of Appeals and U.S. Tax Court

IRS Office of Appeals is an independent organization within the IRS but separate from the enforcement divisions. When you receive a letter that tells you that you have the right to appeal something, you should take that opportunity. (See Chapter 5 – Service Center Processing). You may still be able to resolve your case with a revenue agent or revenue officer for a few weeks after you receive your letter with appeal rights. But if that does not go well, then the appeal is ready to be processed by the IRS. Remember - all letters that contain appeal rights are time-sensitive, and you have to count the days correctly or you lose that appeal right.

The Office of Appeals is interested in resolving tax problems before taxpayers go to tax court (or district court if you pay the disputed tax in full). IRS Appeals officers (AO) work audit cases and Settlement officers (SO) work collection cases. They have broad powers to settle issues you raise in your case as well as to abate penalties or even change tax amounts. The Office of Appeals has the ability to "do the right thing" in your case.

One thing that appeals officers will consider is called the "hazards of litigation." This means that if the case the IRS is presenting is not strongly supported in facts, law and conclusion, then the Office of Appeals is likely to modify the government's position and make some settlement with you. The thought behind this is that if you take your case to court, the IRS is not certain if it will win or not.

Also we have seen many lower dollar cases (under $25,000) settled in the Office of Appeals. One appeals officer said this is because taxpayers who may have not provided information during their tax audit finally pull their records together and prove what they put on the tax return. He also said that Appeals works every case without regard to the dollar amount. So a $300 tax case receives the same balanced consideration as a $30,000 tax case. He said that if there are factual issues that the taxpayer did not have an opportunity to present before the IRS, then IRS Appeals will consider the matter.

The Mission of the Office of Appeals is:

> To resolve tax controversies, without litigation, on a basis which is fair and impartial to both the Government and the taxpayer in a manner that will enhance voluntary compliance and public confidence in the integrity and efficiency of the service

When you have your case worked in Appeals, you will get an objective, impartial and neutral review. If you lose in Appeals, you can still go to tax court.

The big difference between the Office of Appeals and tax court is that Appeals is about doing the right thing for you and for the United States Government.

In part, this happens when you have your story well developed and written in a clear and concise manner. You should record what happened to you to cause the tax balance, why it happened and what you did when you discovered it. You are able to present information, records and evidence to support your tax argument. The better prepared you are for your Appeals conference, the more pleasant will be your experience.

Appeals/settlement officers are often considered the cream of the crop of IRS employees; they are extensively trained, have years of collective experience in tax law review and have a mandate to try to settle case outside of tax court. This happens because tax court costs the IRS a lot of money; it is more cost effective to settle cases at lower levels.

Appeals officers make decisions that affect only your case - their decisions are not something that becomes precedent, like a court case would.

The Office of Appeals will work a case by looking at it as if it is a brand new case. The appeals officer will review the facts and circumstances and the legal issues in dispute. They might make determinations in your favor based on the law that the revenue agent, auditor or revenue officer did not know or consider during your audit or collection action.

Your story is very important and the appeals officer is very interested in your financial hardships, emotional, and/or physical issues that you may suffer from may be relevant in deciding what the IRS should do regarding collections.

In audit cases, you will need evidence to prove what happened. Books, records and receipts will help to prove your deductions and expenses. Having marriage certificates, birth certificates, or other information will allow you to clear up your filing status, dependents and exemptions.

If there is a legal or tax citation that you feel applies to your case, this is the place and now is the time to present it.

You will receive a letter from the IRS Office of Appeals confirming that they have received your case and they will set a meeting time. You can be present in their office or the meeting can be over the phone. We do not think it makes a difference either way. We have heard some appeals officers say that they prefer to do phone interviews, but if you have something that would help to "sell" your story to the appeals officer, you should go to their office. Appeals cases are often assigned all over the United States, so you can file an appeal in Arizona, and find your case assigned to San Francisco, or Las Vegas.

In our dealings with appeals officers, we have found some of the same personality types that one finds in the IRS, because the appeals officers are all ex-revenue agents or ex-revenue officers. They were brought up in the same environment of putting the IRS first. Now they are like Administrative Law Judges - they have the power and many are willing to use it for the good of the government, and often in a good and reasonable settlement for you.

In the Office of Appeals, they also have the goal of closing their cases quickly and with a minimum of time and expense. They will follow the intent of the tax law, not the IRS goals of auditing certain issues. Too often the IRS tries to "draw a line in the sand" in taxpayers' cases by trying to prove some obscure point of the tax law. Appeals officers provide a balance to that.

Your case will be accepted for review by the Office of Appeals if ALL of the following apply:

- You received a letter from the IRS explaining your right to appeal the IRS's decision.
- You agree to extend the statute of limitations, if necessary.
- You do not agree with the IRS's decision.
- You have not and will not sign an IRS agreement form that was sent to you.

Appeals will not accept your case if ANY of the following applies:

- The correspondence you received from the IRS was a bill and there was no mention of appeal rights.
- You did not provide all information to support your position to the IRS during the audit or collection action.
- Your only concern is that you cannot afford to pay the amount you owe.
- You have moral, religious, political, constitutional, conscientious or similar arguments about the legality of the tax system or other laws.

A case may be taken directly to tax court if the taxpayer does not want to appeal within the IRS.

Appeal within the IRS

The tax decision reached by the examiner may be appealed to a local appeals office, which is separate and independent of the IRS enforcement employees who conducted the examination. The Appeals office is the only level of appeal within the IRS. Conferences with appeals office personnel may be conducted in person, through correspondence, or by telephone with the taxpayer or their authorized representative.

Instructions for requesting a conference with an appeals officer are provided in the letter of proposed tax adjustment. The Letter 950 is generally used to propose adjustments to various taxes, including income as well as employment taxes. The letter states that to request a conference with an appeals officer, the taxpayer will need to file either a small case request or a formal written protest with the contact person named in the letter. Whether you file a small case request or a formal written protest depends on several factors. Recently, the IRS has switched to a form that will be furnished during the closing conference for unagreed cases. This is Form 12203 Request for Appeals Review (Form found in appendix). It is simple to complete and often used for cases with a tax amount under $25,000.

If a conference is requested, the examiner will send the conference request letter to the Office of Appeals to arrange for a conference at a convenient time and place. The taxpayer or their qualified representative should be prepared to discuss all disputed issues at the conference. Most differences are settled at this level.

Only attorneys, certified public accountants or enrolled agents are allowed to represent a taxpayer before the Office of Appeals. An unenrolled preparer may be a witness at the conference, but not a representative.

Making a Small Case Request

A small case request is appropriate if the total amount of tax, penalties, and interest for each tax period involved is $25,000 or less. If more than one tax period is involved and any tax period exceeds the $25,000 threshold, a formal written protest for all periods involved must be filed. The total amount includes the proposed increase or decrease in tax and penalties or claimed refund.

To make a small case request, the instructions in the letter of proposed tax adjustment provide that the taxpayer should send a brief written statement requesting an appeals conference and indicate the changes with which it does not agree and the reasons it does not agree with them.

Be sure to send the protest within the time limit specified in the letter you received, which is generally 30 days.

Filing a Formal Protest

When a formal protest is required, it should be sent within the time limit specified in the letter. The following should be provided in the protest:

- Taxpayer's name and address, and a daytime telephone number.
- A statement that taxpayer wants to appeal the IRS findings to the Office of Appeals
- A copy of the letter with the proposed tax adjustment.
- The tax periods or years involved.
- A list of the changes that the taxpayer does not agree with, and reason for disagreement.
- The facts supporting the taxpayer's position on any issue that it does not agree with.
- The law or authority, if any, on which the taxpayer is relying.
- The taxpayer must sign the written protest, stating that it is true, under the penalties of perjury as follows:

    - "Under the penalties of perjury, I declare that I examined the facts stated in this protest, including any accompanying documents, and, to the best of my knowledge and belief, they are true, correct, and complete."
- If the taxpayer's representative prepares and signs the protest for the taxpayer, he or she must substitute a declaration stating:
    - That he or she submitted the protest and accompanying documents and;
    - Whether he or she knows personally that the facts stated in the protest and accompanying documents are true and correct.

Additional information about the appeals process may be found in Publication 5, Your Appeal Rights and How to Prepare a Protest if you Don't Agree.

We have included more specific information about preparing your appeal in the Appendix of this book.

This is Not "Let's Make a Deal"!

There is no place in the IRS where you can play "Let's Make a Deal." But many reasonable compromises are made in Appeals when one learns how to present the facts they have.

This is where it is difficult to counsel you as to what to do in your case. If the balance due is $25,000 or less, you can try appeals. However, if you have hidden or lied about the facts of your case and it affects more than one year, then you might settle the one year before appeals, but the other years will come out as new tax assessments. This can happen with cases in which the IRS is saying that you do not have self-employed contractors working for you, and instead they should be treated as employees. That can affect your business for years into the future.

If you want to do a consultation with a tax professional, it would be worth it at this point and could save you hours of frustration as well as a lot of money.

We have seen cases where the appeals officer overruled both collection actions and audit-proposed assessments. We cannot stress enough how important it is to tell your story fully and completely.

Appeals officers want to resolve taxpayers' cases to avoid court proceedings. If your case is rejected by the Office of Appeals, and you later file a petition in tax court at the same time you file, a new case is also opened in the Office of Appeals. This is mandatory. That is how much pressure both tax court and the Office of Appeals are under to resolve cases at the lowest level.

You can use Google or Bing to search the following terms Publication 5, Your Appeal Rights and How to Prepare a Protest if You Don't Agree, and Publication 556, Examination of Returns, Appeal Rights and Claims for Refund. Also search the term Preparing a Request for Appeals and Publication 1660, Collection Appeal Rights.

United States Tax Court

If you do not win your case in the IRS Office of Appeals, you can file a petition in the U.S. Tax Court. If you have paid your entire balance due, you can file in the U.S. District Court or U.S. Court of Claims. You are most likely to win a tax case in tax court, if you have a good argument and the law supports it.

You can represent yourself in tax court. You can also represent yourself if you are charged with murder. The question is what is best for you? Sometimes taxpayers have won in tax court without legal counsel, but that is rare.

The tax court has a user friendly website. Use Google or Bing to search the term United States Tax Court. (www.ustaxcourt.gov)

To get into tax court, you must file a petition in response to a deficiency or notice of determination. You are the petitioner and the IRS is the respondent.

The tax court website recommends that if you are unable to afford legal advice, you could seek help from the tax clinics located across the United States that participate in the Tax Court's Clinical Program or Low Income Taxpayer Clinics. These help low income taxpayers represent themselves in tax court.

There is also a tax court program called "Calendar Call" where tax practitioners volunteer their time to assist unrepresented low income taxpayers. Neither of these is associated with the IRS or the tax court.

You may also be represented in tax court by an attorney. In our experience this can cost $5,000 just to begin the case and quickly rise to $20,000 to $30,000. The more you owe and the more years that you owe for makes this a costly option.

Sometimes taxpayers will think the IRS decided their case one way only to learn that they have received a statutory notice of deficiency. In that case, you are under a time deadline, so you should file your tax court petition, which protects your right to a court hearing. You can continue to try to talk to the IRS and find out what is going on. Sometimes the IRS has deadlines they have to meet also.

You can file a Small Case Tax Court suit. This is done for amounts under $25,000 or less for each year in dispute. In a collection action case, the total unpaid tax (including interest and penalties) for all years cannot exceed $50,000. This proceeding is faster and easier to understand than the full tax court trial. Google or Bing Form 2, Petition Simplified Form.

You need the education, ability to read, and follow directions and be fluent in the English language in order to be able to represent yourself.

There are many remedies that you can obtain from the tax court. If the IRS has disputed your filing status, your right to claim your dependent children or has disallowed your Earned Income Credit, you can fight that in tax court. You will need to present your own proof that you had the right to claim what you did. This might include items such as the children's birth certificates, copy of a divorce decree or shared custody agreement, school attendance records and records of the children in other activities like sports to establish where they lived and who was paying for their expenses.

In a collection case, where the IRS may have issued a continuous wage levy, a taxpayer can contest it claiming that it presents a hardship and the case should be resolved as an installment agreement or found to be "currently not collectible."

Many of the remedies that a taxpayer might seek from tax court can be uncovered by talking with the IRS employee's manager, by filing an appeal or with the help of the Local Taxpayer Advocate. A taxpayer might also call or write to the President or a member of Congress asking that official to advocate for them.

The important thing to remember is that the law is very strict about how many days you have to file a tax court petition. All the actions by the IRS start on the date of the letter on a notice of deficiency (you owe money) or on a notice of determination. This date is when the IRS has decided that something you were doing was illegal and telling you to change it.

In a notice of deficiency case your petition must be filed by the 90th day from the date of mailing of the notice (or the 150th day if the notice is address to a person outside the United States). In a collection action, the petition must be filed within 30 days of the mailing of the notice of determination. The tax court cannot extend the time for filing a petition.

As we have stated, this automatically opens an appeals case so this is a good time to begin negotiating with the IRS again. Appeals officers usually want to settle the case, but you need to give them good reasons to do so.

You will also have to send all your information directly to the IRS attorney who will work the case and he/she may also propose a settlement.

We have seen many tax protestors go to tax court and have their cases thrown out. They then have heavy penalties placed on them because they filed a frivolous tax court petition.

Chapter 11
The Taxpayer Advocate Service

The Taxpayer Advocate Service (TAS) was created after years of IRS mistreatment of taxpayers who were trying to resolve their cases and were unable to do so.

When you disagree with the IRS, your first right to appeal the Collection revenue officer case decision is by filing the Collection Appeals Request (CAP) Form 9423 Collection Appeals Request with the RO Group Manager. If you do not succeed with the group manager, who usually was a collection employee before they became manager, we suggest that you file the more formal Collection Due Process Right (CDP) Form 12153 Request for Collection Due Process or Equivalent Hearing. Then an appeals officer can review your case; they are independent of the IRS enforcement employees.

When you have called or written to the IRS more than once and have not gotten through on the phone or received a call back or letter addressing your issues, then you can call the Taxpayer Advocate Service.

First, you need to determine exactly who is working your case. Remember that the IRS "Pipeline" is like a train that just keeps going forward with your case. It does no good to signal the conductor that you want to get off the train, if it has already passed your station. Replying to the last place you knew that you case was, does not often help you at all, because your case has already moved forward.

So you need to figure out if your case is in Service Center submission processing "The Pipeline" or Service Center exam or collection or if it is assigned to Automated Collection System (ACS) or has been assigned to a field revenue officer. If it is an audit case, it might have been assigned to a local office for an office audit or to a field revenue agent for a field audit.

Or you may have received a letter and then the IRS suddenly decided that your case was not worth working so they "surveyed" or "shelved" your case. That means they do not have the time or resources to pursue you right now and maybe never will.

If you speak to one person at the IRS 800 number you called, you will never again speak to that same person - that is how the system is designed. This is very frustrating to taxpayers, who have to repeat their story over and over. That is why we advise you to write a letter instead.

This applies to your dealings with any collection or audit employees; don't let them pressure you and bully you. If you do, then you are unlikely to be happy with the result of it. That is usually why you are contacting the TAS.

The criteria for getting your case opened by the taxpayer advocate office are that you have been unable to resolve your case after following normal IRS procedures. The second part is that you have been unable to resolve your case within the date promised by IRS.

The TAS is short staffed and its employees (who are independent of IRS enforcement divisions) are also overworked, and overwhelmed by the sheer volume of cases that they have assigned to them. TAS employees were usually in Taxpayer Assistance or Automated Collection (ACS) jobs prior to their jobs as advocates. Some will be sympathetic to your plight; some will take the IRS position.

The advantage of having the TAS involved in your case is that you speak to the same employee each time until your case is resolved. They will tell you about IRS procedures and rights that you may not know that you have. They will attempt to collect information that will help to bring your case to a reasonable resolution. However, the IRS is still involved in your case. The IRS makes the decisions about what will happen in your case.

But the TAS actually does "advocate" for you and attempts to find a middle ground where the IRS can agree to resolve your case in the fairest way possible.

We have seen many times where the IRS was being unreasonable and even when the TAS got involved it still did nothing to change how the case was worked.

That being said, we have also seen many cases that were being worked by the TAS close with very favorable installment agreement terms, or by being declared "currently not collectible". Or in audit cases they are successful in finding new opportunities for you to present the case data that will help you win your audit. They are also skilled in directing you on audit reconsiderations.

You have the right to file a Form 911 Request for Taxpayer Advocate Service Assistance when you meet the criteria outlined below. This is where you explain why you think your case should be worked by them instead of the IRS. There is room on the form to explain what your situation is; this is the best opportunity that you will have to get your case opened by the TAS. Whatever your story or as we said before your "chain of events" that caused the problems and left you exposed to the IRS actions will show up here.

More information is better than less. The TAS case worker is more like a social worker who is at least willing to listen and then see how the IRS system can be applied to your situation more fairly. Now they just need a good story from you. Sob stories are not useful; just record the facts and also acknowledge when you did something wrong or just plain dumb and how you are past that point now. If they open your case, you need to know that they are usually located in each state and once your case is assigned it will stay with that same person the whole time.

The TAS will open a case if you are able to prove that one of these events is happening to you:

- Taxpayer is experiencing economic harm or is about to suffer economic hardship.
- Taxpayer is facing immediate threat of levy, seizure or lien action.
- Taxpayer will incur significant costs for professional representation if the issue is not resolved now.
- Taxpayer will suffer irreparable injury or long term adverse effect if the case is not resolved now.

A taxpayer qualifies for the program if:

- They have experienced a delay of 30 days or more in getting case resolved
- If their case cannot be resolved in the same day.
- If taxpayer did not receive a response or resolution to their problem or inquiry by the date promised by the IRS.
- An IRS system or procedure failed to resolve the taxpayer's problem. This might be because the IRS did not pick up the phone when you called at different time over several days, or did not resolve your case when you spoke to them on the phone.

Google or Bing search IRS Taxpayer Advocate Official Site and it will bring you to their website and provide you with instructions on how to get their assistance. You can download the Form 911 there also. Their telephone number is 1-877-777-4778 for the National Office TAS. We have had some bad experiences using that number. Instead you can Google or Bing search "Contact Your Local Taxpayer Advocate", to reach your local office.

Every year, the Taxpayer Advocate Service helps thousands of people with tax problems. When working with the TAS, each individual or business is assigned to an advocate who listens to the problem and helps the taxpayer understand what needs to be done to fix it. TAS advocates will usually do everything they can to get the problems resolved and stay with the taxpayers every step of the way.

They are a great alternative to working with the IRS enforcement division.

Chapter 12
How to Prepare a Collection Financial Statement

This chapter will explain how to complete Collection Information Statements, (CIS) which include the following forms: Form 433-F, Form 433-A, 433-B, and Form 433-A (OIC) or 433-B (OIC). (Examples of forms are in the appendix.) The IRS uses these forms to determine how much you can pay towards your back taxes in an installment agreement or in an offer in compromise (OIC) situation. These forms also determine if your case will be declared as "currently not collectible". If you haven't read Chapter 8 of this book, it would be a good idea to refer to it while reading this chapter, as they do work together to answer questions about collection actions.

The Collection Information Statements are used in cases requiring financial analysis to determine a taxpayer's ability to pay. Most cases are Streamlined Installment Agreements, which require little or no financial analysis and no substantiation of expenses.

These are financial statements that you complete for the IRS to begin its research into your life and finances. Information will apply to these forms if you are seeking an installment agreement, "currently not collectible" status, or pursuing an OIC. There is a simple financial statement - Form 433-F, but it is only useful for the simplest cases where you owe less than $50,000. This form does not allow you get maximum credit for your expenses.

We advise you to complete the Form 433-A Collection Information Statement for Individuals and, if you have a business, the Form 433-B Collection Information Statement for Business, both forms which are required in all collection cases. Then you can draw the information from those forms and put it on the Form 433-F if you are working with IRS Service Center Collection or ACS. All Collection Information Statements are good for 12 months; after which the IRS may ask you to provide new information.

You must complete the Form 433-A (OIC) and/or the Form 433-B (OIC) if you are submitting an offer – read this chapter first and then Chapter 13 regarding OIC cases, for our best advice on how to prepare your financial statements to your benefit.

The IRS allows you to claim only a certain amount of money for your housing, utilities, food, transportation, clothing, medical and life insurance. For many people this means financial belt tightening; something they do not gladly embrace.

The IRS does not allow for credit card repayments, unsecured debt, church tithing and many other expenses that are a normal part of a taxpayer's life. One notable item missing from the list is for the costs of having, feeding and providing grooming and medical care to their pets. Most people do not understand that it is not the expenses, sometimes, but the way that you list the expense on the IRS form. The way that you categorize the expense will determine if the expense will be allowed or not. For instance, some people have mental, physical or emotional problems and are comforted or monitored by pets that help them live day to day. We have seen that some taxpayers have registered their animals as "emotional support animals", or "service or therapy dogs." You might consider this in your own case. Because these animals are protected by law, they are legitimate expenses. See www.USDogRegistry.org.

This is an example that shows that it is not what you list on the form; it is how you tie it in with your story and why that expense is important for your life. When expenses are listed in a certain way, then they become allowable. Sometimes there are other ways to make then allowable – see the Six Year Rule below – which takes away this scrutiny of expenses if the balance will be full paid in six years.

The IRS has been known to allow tithing of 10% if the taxpayer is required to make that charitable contribution according to an employment contract that they have that requires such contributions. A minister would be an example of this. Tithing is also allowed if it meets the necessary expense test. In some States we have seen tithing routinely allowed, especially in Utah.

The IRS does not allow luxury items, which are expenses that they do not think are "reasonable and necessary for you to live." The IRS disregards "the style to which you have been accustomed". The IRS will decide what your life will look like. This will not include luxury autos or trucks, boats, RV's, Campers, Quads, jet skis, valuable jewelry, fur coats, or items purchased at a luxury store. For instance, the IRS classifies a Mercedes, BMW, Lexus, Porsche, Jaguar, Bentley, Rolls Royce, Maserati, Range Rover, Land Rover and even some Saabs and Volvos as luxury vehicles. They expect you to downsize and sell what you have, buy a lower cost car and turn over the excess to the IRS. For example, if the car payment was $797 per month, the IRS would only allow $471 of the payment.

If having a flashy car is important to business, such as for realtors, the full payment may be allowed, because it is used for production of income.

The IRS can find any of your treasures that you do not report, because they order credit bureau reports, and have access to your mortgage or bank loan application forms, and auto credit applications. The IRS sometimes researches your bank statements and then finds out who your insurance agent is and sends them a summons. The IRS is looking for any items that you have insurance on, over the basic household insurance. This could include artwork, antique furniture, jewelry, furs, stamp collections, gun collections, antique autos, baseball card collections and any other items that are of value in your home.

Following is a summary of the IRS National Standards and Allowable Expenses. These are called the National Standard Allowable Expenses and they are customized for the county, state or region where you live. The standards are composed of:

- National Standard: Food, clothing and other items;
- Local Standards: Housing and Utilities
- Local Standards: Transportation
- National Standards: Out-of-Pocket Health Care

These are dollar allowances that the IRS believes are sufficient for a taxpayer to live in a style that the IRS deems acceptable. Most taxpayers have complained that these amounts do not allow them to meet current daily expenses because of the areas where they live. The allowable expenses do not take into account the differences on food costs, utility expenses, state and local taxes, and the real cost of living in different parts of the United States. They are very limiting in what they will allow to even be called an expense.

National Standards: Food, Clothing and Other items

National Standards have been established for five necessary expenses: food, housekeeping supplies, apparel and services, personal care products and services, and miscellaneous.

The standards are derived from the Bureau of Labor Statistics (BLS) Consumer Expenditure Survey (CES) and defined as follows:

- Food includes food at home and food away from home. Food at home refers to the total expenditures for food from grocery stores or other food stores. It excludes the purchase of nonfood items. Food away from home includes all meals and snacks, including tips, fast food, take out, delivery and full-service restaurants.
- Housekeeping supplies includes laundry and cleaning supplies, stationery supplies, postage, delivery services, miscellaneous

household products, and lawn and garden supplies.

- Apparel and services includes clothing, footwear, material, patterns and notions for making clothes, alterations and repairs, clothing rental, clothing storage, dry cleaning and sent-out laundry, watches, jewelry and repairs to watches and jewelry.
- Personal care products and services includes products for the hair, oral hygiene products, shaving needs, cosmetics and bath products, electric personal care appliances, and other personal care products.
- The miscellaneous allowance is for expenses taxpayers may incur that are not included in any other allowable living expense items, or for any portion of expenses that exceed the Collection Financial Standards and are not allowed under a deviation. Taxpayers can use the miscellaneous allowance to pay for expenses that exceed the standards, or for other expenses such as credit card payments, bank fees and charges, reading material and school supplies.

Taxpayers are allowed the total National Standards amount monthly for their family size, without the IRS questioning the amounts that they actually spend. If the amount claimed is more than the total allowed by the National Standards for food, housekeeping supplies, apparel and services, and personal care products and services, the taxpayer must provide documentation to substantiate that those expenses are necessary living expenses. Deviations from the standard amount are not allowed for miscellaneous expenses. Generally, the total number of persons allowed for National Standards should be the same as those allowed as exemptions on the taxpayer's most recent year income tax return.

A one-person household gets credit for $570.

A two-person household gets credit for $1,083.

A three-person household gets credit for $1,249.

A four-person household gets credit for $1,509.

Each additional person gets credit for $341.

The IRS is required to give you this full credit amount and cannot challenge it.

In practice, if you can establish that you spend more on food or one of the other categories, because of medical needs, you can document that and ask the IRS to allow more than the allowed amount. This also includes any special needs that you have due to food allergies, illness or disability.

But here is where you need to be careful also. If you have a relative living with you and you claim credit for that person, they must be also listed as a dependent on your tax return. A trap that many people fall into is that they will claim an aged parent and then the IRS will ask if that parent has Social Security or pension income. It seems like a simple question, but it is not. Next thing you know, the IRS will include that person's whole income in with your monthly income. If you fight that, the IRS will come up with a reasonable amount that your parent should be charged for rent and food. That will increase your income and cause you to have a higher installment agreement amount.

You need to be prepared for what is not important to the IRS, expense wise. The IRS does not allow you money:

- to loan to relatives,
- to take care of friends and relatives
- to pay for your super cable TV package or extra high speed internet
- for your hobbies
- for your charities
- for your pets or your veterinarian,
- for your new nails or your weekly manicure and pedicure
- for buying presents, toys, gifts
- for increasing your gun, coin, stamp or other collection
- for going out to eat, dance, have fun
- for going on vacations

We have already discussed tithing. The IRS wants you to pay them the maximum amount of money that you can and they decide how much that is. So be prepared to minimize your life style. The best thing that you can do for yourself if you owe the IRS is to swallow your pride and borrow money from anyone who will loan it to you.

The IRS is careful to not disallow these expenses; they say that they can be covered from the National Standard Allowable Expenses and that you can choose how you want to spend that money anyway that you want. That way they don't have to quibble about individual expenses.

When you are speaking to the IRS Service Center Collection or ACS, the IRS employees does not inform you of your rights to the National Standard Allowable Expenses and the amounts that are acceptable for those expenses.

National Standards: Out-of-Pocket Health Care

The IRS allows every person in your household under the age of 65 $54 a month for out-of-pocket health care expenses. This includes medical services, prescription drugs, medical supplies (e.g. eyeglasses, contact lenses, etc.) Elective procedures such as plastic surgery or elective dental work are not usually allowed. dental braces for yourself or your family are allowed if they are to correct physical or social issues.

Health care insurance is allowed also, but is listed in the expenses section of the form.

If you are over age 65, you and your spouse and elderly dependents are allowed $130 a month per person for out of pocket health care expenses.

Any health-related expenses can be listed. Out of pocket health care expenses include treatment for any special medical conditions. You would be able to be approved for much larger monthly expenses for out of pocket medical as long as you have documentation to support your claims. Do not be afraid to list what you need to maintain your health and this can include chiropractors, therapeutic massages, acupuncture, naturopath or other alternative medical practitioners. The IRS cannot question or decide on what medical treatments are appropriate for you.

Taxpayers are allowed the expenses of the $60 per person or $144 per person, without the IRS questioning the amount actually spent. This is not made clear on the Form 433-F.

Anyone who is facing health challenges knows that these amounts are not enough to cover much. If you have to pay a caregiver or a service to come and be with a family member who is sick so that you can work, you have to provide documentation. There is no limit on what you can claim. You might have one or more family members in various therapies and between your co-pays and deductibles you are spending a lot of money. Maybe that is also part of your story about how the tax balances arose.

When you are speaking to the IRS, they do not usually mention or offer to include these expenses on your financial statement. So you must sit down first and figure out where your money is being spent and then document it.

Local Standards: Transportation

Public Transportation: If you take public transportation, you are allowed $185 a month, unless you can prove that your expenses are higher. If you have to drive to the train and pay for parking and then pay for the train and then when you get where you are headed also take a bus, all those expenses add up. This becomes part of your story. If your expenses are higher than this, list them on your financial statement. The IRS has to allow you the full amount and cannot question it. These are all so that you can produce income.

Your expenses may not conform to what the IRS has; if they are different, or unusual in some way, then you must be prepared to prove them and tell why the expense is important to your life. These can include having higher insurance coverage than is normal, perhaps due to flood or hurricane protection. Or if you have high utilities, explain why. Maybe your septic field requires monthly service, or your house is slipping off its foundation due to floods or strong winds. Many people have different circumstances that affect their finances. The IRS must consider these and also mold abatement expenses as necessary additions to what you normally would list. The expenses can always be up to 5% more than the allowable amount, and that is acceptable to the IRS if you can prove why. But if you can establish why your expenses are greater than that, put them on the form and be ready to defend them.

Expenses for automobile ownership are divided into two sections. There is a **National Standard for Automobile Ownership Costs**. A single person could get credit for one car payment of $471. A couple would get credit for two car payments of $942. We have advised many clients to buy a new car to take advantage of this. Some collection employees will not allow payments for a second car if the spouse is not working. This is an issue that you can get decided in your favor. You can claim that you need that second car, to pick up your children from school, care for sick or elderly relatives, go to medical appointments, go to church services or other needs.

We have guided many taxpayers to the fact that they are driving old cars and on their financial statements, it appears that they can pay the IRS $500 a month. We point out to them that the IRS will allow a car payment of $471 a month for up to 72 months and that it only makes sense for their safety and continuing ability to go to work to be able have a newer, safer car. Many of our clients have purchased new cars. It is true that they usually face higher car payments, due to the tax lien, but it is worth it. Otherwise if you are in an IRS installment agreement and your transmission goes out and you need $2,000 to repair the car, you are out of luck, unless you default on your IRS agreement. This idea is just recognizing that without a car, you cannot get to work and without going to work, you cannot continue to be paying your current taxes.

We knew one commercial real estate broker whose job it was to take prospective renters around to offices for rent. She had been borrowing a friend's car to use for work. She asked the IRS for expenses for the friend's car and she was told that she would only receive credit for public transportation. The IRS told her that she could take her clients around town in a taxi cab or on the bus. Sometimes the IRS employee can be ignorant and that hurt this broker's ability to earn money.

With our help, she was able to buy a good used car and now receives the allowable expenses for transportation.

Sometimes the IRS will allow the expense of an auto and a motorcycle. If you are not sure, just list it on the financial statement and see what happens.

The second part of Transportation is **Automobile Operating Costs.** This varies by what region you are in. The United States is divided into 4 regions and 22 high cost cities. The IRS will allow between $173 in Seattle to $312 a month in Miami. To locate what they allow in your region search – IRS Local Standards: Transportation.

Operating expense is supposed to cover the actual amount spent monthly for operating costs, or the reference table shown at that link above.

If you use your vehicle for business, your expenses are likely to be much higher for fuel and maintenance. Some sections of the United States have very high insurance rates; others have toll roads, or high parking costs.

There is a part that is very confusing to most taxpayers who are completing their financial statements. On Form 433-A, and Form 433-F you are just allowed the car payment and the operating expense. But on the Form 433-A (OIC) which is used for Offer in Compromises, you are allowed these expenses, but if you have a car that is over six years old or has mileage of over 75,000 miles, then the IRS OIC officer will allow an additional monthly operating expense of $200 a month per vehicle. Please note that most Service Center Collection Employees, ACS and field revenue officers have never heard of this provision. That is because it is not in their Internal Revenue Manual. That is why we suggest that you purchase a new vehicle to take advantage of the monthly automobile payment allowance of $471 per vehicle.

The IRS does not usually give you credit for vehicles if you own more than two. It does not matter if your children drive those vehicles to go to work or school. Unless you can provide evidence why you need that vehicle, you will not receive that allowable expense.

You want to make sure to list all expenses related to child care also. If you have children in day care, and then also have bus costs and an additional babysitter so they are not alone until you get home from work, list all of these expenses on "other expenses."

For example, if you have a wheelchair-bound person in your house that needs a special vehicle to transport them to medical appointments, that fact should justify the additional expense.

The IRS will usually expect that you sell vehicles like RV's, campers, trailers, and off-the-road vehicles that have a fair market value of $2,000 or more. If you have old vehicles or inoperative vehicles, then you should sell them and that solves that problem. This can also help you to make monthly payments, because your insurance expense would also drop.

You need to know that the IRS will allow any of your expenses for your vehicle as long as they are related to your health & welfare or for the production of income.

We suggest that you write a letter to go along with your financial statement to explain any expenses that are not ordinary and allowed on the form. This can include your health conditions, and other expenses that you can document.

The IRS can allow extraordinary expenses if you can prove why they are necessary in your life. Sometimes you will need to pay for uniforms or tools so that you can continue to work. Any expenses that are related to your producing income can be on top of your other expenses. If you have a long commute to work and the monthly allowable amount is less than what it costs to operate your car and pay the payment, keep documentation and claim it. If you have a medical marijuana card in your state, this is not likely an item that the IRS would approve as it is illegal to use marijuana under federal law. However, if you have a doctor's note claim it and then if they deny it you can go to appeals and explain that it is doctor prescribed for your health conditions. Then see what happens.

Any expenses that are for your health and welfare should be listed on the financial statement. All expenses related to you producing income are reasonable and allowable expenses. That is because you producing income is good for the IRS in two ways - it means you will be able to pay your past due taxes and also your current income taxes.

There is no mystery in how the IRS comes up with the numbers when they tell you what will be an acceptable installment payment or acceptable offer in compromise payment from you. We will explain. Almost all the information will come from your Collection Information Statement.

The Allowable Expense standards were revised on April 14, 2016 and those numbers are lower than what the IRS allowed in the past. The amounts can change every year.

Six-Year Rule for Repayment of the Tax Liability

In cases where taxpayers cannot full pay and do not meet the criteria for a streamline agreement, they may still qualify for the Six-Year Rule. The Six-Year Rule allows for living expenses that exceed the Collection Financial Standards, and allows for other expenses, such as minimum payments on student loans and credit cards, as long as the tax liability can be full paid in six years. Taxpayers are required to provide financial information in these cases, but do not have to provide substantiation of reasonable expenses for balances under $50,000.

Actually the IRS will usually allow you to make your full required student loan payments as long as you can prove that you are actually making them. This is in your best interest to pay student loans off, because they can never legally be extinguished.

Form 433-F Collection Information Statement

This form is used by Service Center Collection and the Automated Collection System. It is easy to understand but gives you no information about how much the IRS will actually allow you in your expenses in accordance with the National Allowable expenses, so most taxpayers do not get credit for their real expenses and end up in installment agreements that are hard for them to pay. The good part of this form is that it does not ask a lot of questions that would lead to the IRS poking and probing into other areas of your financial life.

A secret about this form is that the Internal Revenue Manual 5.15.1.1 (3) states that revenue officers may use the Form 433-F if you owe less than $250,000 in income taxes, or less than $100,000 from the Trust Fund Recovery Penalty (and are a wage earner). But they do not, because another part of the IRM says that they must use the Form 433-A and Form 433-B. So don't try to fight City Hall on this issue. You need to save your strength for fighting for what you put on the financial statement. We suggest that you fill out the financial sections of the Form 433-A first and then take what you need and switch it over to the Form 433-F. This will make sure you get maximum credit for your expenses.

You need to be aware that the employee that is reviewing your Form 433-F in the service center or in ACS is not as highly trained, or educated and may not understand the need for the expenses that you are presenting. That is all right because if you have to file you case with the IRS Office of Appeals, then you will be prepared in advance. You will find a more sympathetic ear in an appeal.

In **Section 1- Personal Information**, the form asks about information for other people living in your house or who you claim as dependent. They will track these people down and check to see if they have income and if so, are they paying you rent, or for the utilities or food. So when you answer the question on the form "Contributed to household income" – think carefully. This question can help you if you have a relative living with you with no income and you are primarily supporting him/her as a relative or dependent. If he/she is an elderly relative, they are likely to have a pension or Social Security check and then you would need to include that in your income every month also. But if they are working, the IRS will expect them to pay a portion of the rent, utilities and their own food to you and then that is included in your income.

Section 2 - Employment Information for Wage Earners, seeks the name of your employer. It also asks if it is ok with your employer if the IRS contacts you at work. Never say yes, because it is upsetting to people at your place of work to pick up a call from the IRS, even if it is not for them.

Section 3 - Other Financial Information is when the IRS asks you questions about your past and future. You may be asked if you have given away or sold assets for less than full value in the last 10 years. They also ask about lawsuits and if you are going to inherit any money. Answer truthfully, but if you don't know something, just mark the box "no".

Section 4 – Personal Asset Information for All Individuals, is about your cash, lines of credit, real estate, autos and other investments. If you show $20,000 in a bank account, they will count that $20,000 as money that you could pay to the IRS today. We worked with one woman who had $100,000 in her bank account and she owed $150,000. We advised her to pay that money to the IRS. She disagreed saying that she like the feeling of security that she got knowing that that money was in the bank. A few months later, the IRS levied her bank account and ended that fantasy.

Then the IRS will look at stocks or bonds that you have and value them at 80% of fair market value. So if you have $10,000 in stocks, the IRS will say that the stock has an immediate cash sales value of $8,000 and that you should sell it to satisfy your tax debt.

The IRS asks about any retirement account that you may own, such as a 401(k), IRA or other. This is important for you to think about. If you have $10,000 in an IRA, but you are young and not able to withdraw it without penalty, the IRS will allow for the 10% penalty associated with closing out your IRA and having to include it on your income tax. Be very careful here if you owe taxes and have money in a 401k or IRA. If your retirement savings plan cannot be borrowed on or liquidated until you leave your employment and you have no vested interest, then the plan has no Reasonable Collection Potential (RCP) to the IRS. It is worth nothing to you and that makes it worth nothing to the IRS.

An example of this with a government benefit such as Social Security is that you have paid money in but cannot claim any benefit until age 62. Those assets will quietly grow until you no longer owe the taxes, so why put them out in full view? You are better off with an installment agreement or trying to get your case declared "currently not collectible".

Section 4 Line 16a is looking for any cash value that you have in your whole life insurance policy. The IRS will expect you to take that money and pay it towards your taxes. We have seen some taxpayers faced with this to convert their whole life policy into a term policy that has no cash value and usually provides for more insurance.

The IRS asks for the value of your house, condo, co-op, time share or other property that you own or are buying. They expect you to come up with a value. We like to use www.Zillow.com to determine an approximate value. Next you take away any first or second mortgages or other liens against the property to come up with your net equity in the property. Now, add that onto the amount of what the IRS expects from you in your offer in compromise or installment agreement. If you have equity, the IRS expects you to borrow against that equity and pay the money towards your taxes. Timeshares have little or no value in the resale market. It is not what you paid for the timeshare- it is about how much you could sell it for today.

Vehicles are much the same; we prefer to use the Kelly Blue Book website (www.kbb.com) to determine the value of your vehicle. Choose the option for a car in fair condition. You do not want to overstate the value of your vehicle.

In the last part of Section 3, the IRS wants to know what else you own of value. This could include artwork, antiques, furniture, jewelry, gold, silver, other valuables such as guns, stamps or baseball cards or any items of value in safe deposit boxes. Remember you want the fair market value - that is how much you could get if you sold that asset today. In this section you would list a value for the furnishings in your house. Perhaps you spend $10,000 to buy furniture. The value today is not $10,000. It is whatever your old couch would get if it were accepted for sale at the Salvation Army resale store. So you may estimate all your furniture is worth $3,000.

We remember one case where we were working an offer in compromise investigation and it looked acceptable. When we went to interview the taxpayer at his home to check out his lifestyle, we admired an original Norman Rockwell work of art that his father had given him. In those days it was valued at $85,000. The taxpayer never thought of it as something of value, only a beloved gift from his deceased father. The man had fallen on hard times due to poor health. He only owed $46,000 in taxes. So we rejected his OIC and a few months later came back and seized that painting right off the wall and sold it at public auction to pay the taxes. The taxpayer did receive some money also, as the bidding rose above the amount that he owed the IRS. That is pretty standard for the IRS.

Section 5 – Monthly Income and Expenses is the place where you list all income and this includes distributions from businesses and child support and alimony. Some people forget to list these.

What is important here is that they do not tell you anything about the National Allowable Expense amounts that are available to you. (Another IRS Secret!) You have to go find them for yourself. Use Google or Bing to search for IRS National Allowable Expenses.

You should put down the maximum allowable expense that the IRS allows for the number of people in your household.

The next section is about your housing and utilities. This is divided up by state. Google or Bing this search term: Name of your state – IRS Local Standards: Housing and Utilities. For Example- California-IRS Local Standards: Housing and Utilities. Pick the category that applies to you based on the size of your household. For example, if you are a single person living in San Francisco you would be allowed $2,918 a month for housing and utilities. In Manhattan, $3,669 a month; in Chicago, $1,766; in Jackson County, Arkansas, only $792; and only $773 in Gilmer County, West Virginia. Trying to live on the amount that you are allowed can be difficult, depending on what your standard of living was in the past.

It is important to know that the IRS will allow you more than this amount by at least 5% if you can prove why that is necessary. If you live in a house that was bought when the real estate market was high, then you probably have little or no equity in your house and a mortgage and utilities much higher than the Local Standards table. If you are negotiating for an installment agreement, the IRS will allow you your full mortgage and utilities payment for 12 months (The One Year Rule) regardless of how high the amount. But the understanding is that you will sell the house or restructure the mortgage, seek a loan modification or even take in a boarder or roommate. Be aware that in the 13th month of your agreement, the IRS will raise your installment agreement by the difference between what you were paying and what you are allowed by the National Standards. The One Year Rule does not apply to corporations, partnerships, limited liability companies or business expenses. Sometimes the IRS will deny you this, so you must insist on speaking to a manager and demanding that the One Year Rule applies in your case.

Preparing Your Form 433-B Collection Information Statement for Business

The Form 433-B is very comprehensive, but most collection employees are not adequately trained in how to understand the information presented on the form.

There is a lot more freedom of interpretation as to the value of assets on this form, and the income and expenses, than there is on the Form 433-A. As you review the form you will see that it is similar to the Form 433-A, asking for information about who owns the business and what the business does to make money. It is important to understand that what you list in Section 1 – Line 2b will decide how the IRS can use this information. If you are completing this form because you owe taxes, but the business does not, then the most important part is how much income you get from the business. If you are in a partnership, you might have assets or income that you have a share in. But you do not own the whole partnership. The IRS cannot legally claim the assets of the partnership, it can only levy on your share of the partnership. The book value of that asset may look like a lot of money, but its fair market value is limited. It is important to know that the only people who would be likely to buy your partnership interests would be your other partners. Besides, if the IRS seized your share of the partnership, you probably would not want to work there anymore, so that greatly decreases the value of the partnership - or may even put it out of business.

This same information also applies to your ownership in a corporation. A corporation is like another independent person, you may own shares in it, but it is a stand-alone entity. The IRS can seize the stock you own in the corporation, but cannot attack the corporation itself or its assets. This also limits the value of the stock both to you and to the IRS - because if you fail to work for the corporation, maybe it cannot continue to stay in business.

A limited liability company (LLC) is given some of the protections of the corporate shield that a corporation would have, but it is not a corporation. The value of this is also limited to how much you own if it is a single member LLC or a multi-member LLC. If the IRS is threatening to seize your LLC interest, you need to speak to your CPA, enrolled agent or tax attorney. Generally, the IRS can only seize your distributions from the LLC, after it gets a "charging order." This is a very involved process. The IRS can also attack an LLC in court, and say that the LLC was only created to put assets beyond the reach of the IRS. Any IRS litigation is rare, unless large dollars are involved. Again you would want to seek the assistance of a tax professional. Tax consequences of a partnership or LLC are governed by the laws of your state, which makes it even more important to consult a tax professional.

Most businesses use a bookkeeping system that keeps track of income and expenses. When the tax year is over, they send this to their tax preparer and it shows up on their personal tax return. This is where the advantage of owning your own business comes into play. There are many items that are in full view on the Collection Information Statement that allow a business owner more room to operate financially than a W-2 employee.

Some businesses own equipment that is depreciating every year. This shows up as depreciation on their tax form; as an expense that is losing money. That is only an accounting term; there is not actual cash loss. There are many expenses that can be paid for by the business that will benefit the owners personally.

The biggest drawback to any self-employed income is that it is not regular. You have to work and work hard to produce income. If you don't work, the business does not make money. The IRS employees who get regular paychecks every two weeks have a hard time understanding this concept. They think that just because you made $10,000 last month in your business you will make that next month also. Nothing could be further from the truth. Business is variable.

The bottom line number that is important is found in Section 5 line 49 – Net Income. This is the number that carries over to your Form 433-A on line 23- net business income.

If your monthly income from your business is highly variable, then you should look at the last 6 months or the last year and average the amounts out and attach a letter to the Form 433-B explaining why they should consider this variable income in making any installment agreement. Likewise, if your business is seasonal, you should state that in your cover letter. A prime example would be a lawn care business or tax preparation business. Your income in the "high" months should be averaged in with low or no income months.

Whatever financial statement you are required to fill out will take some preparation and time, but if you do it accurately, it will save you money every month in whatever installment agreement arrangement you make with the IRS.

If you are having financial difficulties, then careful preparation of your financial statement will allow the IRS to declare your case as "currently not collectible" for at least the next two years. Anytime that you can get the IRS off your back, at least for a while, it is a good thing.

Chapter 13
The Truth about Offers in Compromise

—⁓—

Congress thought that it would be a good idea to allow taxpayers who had little or no money or assets to make a final settlement of their old tax bills. They thought that this would cause the taxpayers to seek money from friends or relatives, churches or other organizations; money that the IRS could not levy or have access to itself. This would allow old cases to be closed and new "fresh" money to be paid to settle old tax accounts. It was a darn good idea and it made good business sense. But the IRS does not share that opinion.

In fact, in 1998, Congress, through the Internal Revenue Service Restructuring and Reform Act of 1998 (RRA 1998), encouraged the IRS to make it easier for taxpayers to make offers and do more to educate the taxpaying public about their availability. Congress gave the IRS discretion over how this was to be implemented.

The result was that Congress inadvertently gave the IRS more power to not accept Offers in Compromise (OIC). It required that all offers be accompanied with a nonrefundable deposit and a payment plan. The amount offered must be fully paid in either 5 months or in installments over a 6 – 24 month period. The deposit money did not mean that an offer would be accepted; the money is non-refundable, but will be applied to the outstanding tax balance. But if the taxpayer borrows the money to fund the OIC and it is not accepted, it produces a "sour grapes response" from the lender.

Although, the IRS has the limitless authority to compromise or settle any delinquent tax balances, it has little desire to do so. Instead, the IRS used RRA 1998 to raise the bar on OICs to a level where few taxpayers would quality for them.

In fact, many OICs are rejected because the IRS claims that the taxpayer can pay the tax in full. According to IRS reports, however, the IRS does not coordinate this with the collection revenue officers, so most OIC rejected cases never have any money collected from the taxpayer. The IRS turns down funds that it should be accepting.

It is foolish to believe the persuasive sales people that advertise on television or radio claiming to be tax professionals who tell you that getting an OIC approved is either easy or likely. That is far from the truth, unless you are old, disabled, sick, have low income, have no equity in assets and have no future financial prospects of that changing.

"Accounts Receivable" refers to the amount of money owed to the IRS by delinquent taxpayers. This amount increases year after year.

Accounts receivable due to the IRS totaled $24 billion in 1983, $61 billion in 1989, and is estimated at over $600 billion as recently as 2014. About 30% of it consists of penalties and interest. About 70% of the delinquent tax balance due cases have been declared as "currently not collectible".

The "currently not collectible" status can be given for many reasons:

- The IRS is unable to locate or contact the taxpayer
- Personal, financial or other hardship of the taxpayer
- Taxpayer/corporation is out of business
- Taxpayer is dead
- Taxpayer is in bankruptcy

It would actually make sense if Congress would mandate that the Bankruptcy Court automatically discharge all existing IRS debts when a taxpayer completes a Chapter 7 - Liquidating Bankruptcy action. Unfortunately, Congress seldom enacts tax laws that make sense.

The remaining part of the accounts receivable is in the active inventory or the cases that are in the collection Queue waiting to be assigned for collection action. It makes sense for the IRS to entertain offers in compromise or settle the outstanding tax bills, (many of them can go back 10-20 years) because of actions like bankruptcy or filing an offer in compromise or leaving the country for extended periods. All of these extend the normal ten-year statute of collections which is the normal time that IRS has to collect a debt from a delinquent taxpayer.

The IRS has never in our experience endorsed any program that lets some taxpayers get away with not paying their taxes.

There are, however, other ways that are sometimes better. Paying a reasonable and small installment agreement is one way to keep the case out of active collection. If you are paying an installment agreement the IRS will usually leave your case alone for anywhere between 2 to 4 years. If you have a time when you can no longer pay, you will present your circumstances, both your life story and your financial picture, and show that you do not make enough money to continue paying an installment agreement or in fact making any payments at all. Bankruptcy is sometimes also a better option than an offer in compromise.

Having an installment agreement or being found to be "currently not collectible" allows the statute expiration date of collections to quietly tick off the days and years until you are finally free of the taxes - whether they are paid or unpaid at the end of the ten-year period.

The offer in compromise system is unbalanced and prejudiced against the very taxpayers that it was designed to help. The IRS system does not allow you to make an offer without you also paying for the offer up front or paying a percentage of the amount offered over a two-year period. This is no guarantee that what you offer will be accepted. And you don't get the money back if it is rejected. So really this is not a good faith way of dealing with the tax balances for you, but it is great for the IRS.

If you are lucky enough to get your offer accepted, that is not the end of it; you sign papers that state that you agree to lose future tax refunds for the next few years. And you also agree that if you fail to timely file or pay new taxes in the next five years, the offer is canceled and you will owe all the penalties and interest and tax that you originally owed. So this in effect extends the collection statute five years into the future.

It is for this reason that we advocate that you get a transcript of your account. Use Google or Bing to search this term: IRS Get Transcript. You can order online, over the phone or by mail. If you order by mail you use Form 4506-T Request for Transcript of Tax Return. You will need your prior year's tax information because the IRS will ask for your Adjusted Gross income (AGI) and the IRS may also ask you some questions from your credit report, like old addresses, phone numbers, or ask about loans you had or have. The type of transcript that you want to order is called the Tax Account Transcript. You are looking for transaction codes (TC) on the following dates: the date of assessment - TC150; additional tax assessment -TC290; or additional tax of deficiency assessment by examination - TC300. These are the legal dates of assessment for your taxes. The latest date applies and then you add ten years to that. The most important information that you need to know about an offer, is that you need your tax transcript so that you know how far away you are from the end of the ten years - when you will no longer owe the taxes and when the federal tax lien will automatically be lifted off your assets and credit.

There may be other codes on the transcript that extend the collection statute, because you were in litigation with the IRS, you filed an OIC, you were in bankruptcy, or you were out of the country for an extended period. If you cannot figure this out, you can call the IRS at 1-800-829-1040 and wait for an hour or more and just ask them what the Collection Statute Expiration Date (CSED) is for each year that you owe.

If you are within five years of that collection statute expiration date, you probably do not want to file an OIC, because it will extend that collection statute date by one year plus the time that the IRS takes to work the offer.

If you have less than five years left on your collection statute, there is no good reason to file an OIC.

We know that what you have just read directly contradicts what you have heard thousands of times on the radio and television about how the IRS wants to resolve your tax accounts for only pennies on the dollar. They do not. In fact, out of 1.6 million collection cases, only 40,000 offers are filed and only 20,000 are accepted. In 2016, due to the retirements of thousands of IRS employees, some of whom work OIC cases, it has been announced that the OIC cases will be worked mostly in the service centers and not by field revenue officers, which is expected to lower the OIC acceptance rate to about 20%.

You have a better chance of getting your OIC accepted if you hire the services of an enrolled agent; many are retired IRS employees who used to work OICs for the IRS.

Now, you need to know that there are many types of offers in compromise and we will tell you which you might attempt to apply for yourself and for which you will need a tax professional either consulting and guiding you or doing the whole job for you.

We have reviewed the many videos about OICs on www.YouTube.com. The one by the IRS is dated and no longer correct, and the rest are from tax professionals but all of them have flaws in their information or approach. Trust what you read from the IRS official site.

Before you submit an OIC, you must make sure that you put everything on your Form 433-A (OIC). This information includes all income, benefits like food stamps or welfare payments, medical insurance reimbursements, or pending law suits or inheritances that you might receive. This amount also includes any income from side jobs where you make money, gambling winnings or any money you get from people living with you. Think of it this way - you are putting yourself under the IRS microscope. They will find out if you have not reported money you received. If they discover that you lied to them even once, your credibility is shot. You can kiss the OIC good-bye.

Sometimes the OIC is returned, though not rejected, because you did not follow the rules. The whole process is about you doing everything exactly as the IRS wants it done. You must fit in their process - they don't need to fit in yours. If you did not sign the OIC, or failed to list all the periods you owe for, or did not pay the required non-refundable application fee (currently $186) or make the non-refundable payments required, they will send the offer back. You are supposed to send two separate checks when you apply for the offer, one for the application fee $186 and the other which is your first deposit payment. If you combine the checks, they return the offer to you also. You should do a Google or Bing search for; Form 656 booklet "Offer in Compromise" and read it carefully for additional information.

Offer in Compromise with Doubt as to Liability - this is the kind of case where you are not only saying you do not want to pay the tax, but that you also think the tax amount is not a legal and correct tax assessment. You should never work this type of case yourself. We recommend hiring a CPA and, if the amount is over $25,000 due to the cost and hazards of paying for litigation in either the IRS Office of Appeals or U.S. Tax Court, you should consider a tax attorney or even better - a tax attorney/CPA.

You cannot do this OIC yourself. If you are at the stage where you owe money because of an IRS audit, you have already lost important rights that you had to appeal the case. Don't make the same mistakes again. You really do have much to lose. Going to tax court with an attorney can start at $5,000 and quickly rise to $20,000. So you need to make sure you are following sound legal principles and tax law.

Offer in Compromise Due to Effective Tax Administration. This is where the taxpayer has to prove that if the IRS collected the tax liability, it would cause economic hardship, or as stated in the Internal Revenue Code "there are compelling public policy or equity considerations identified by the taxpayer that provide a sufficient basis for accepting less than full payment." What that means is subject to much debate and the IRS has been very resistant to accepting many ETA offers. Our research shows that about 1% (about 400 a year) of all offers in this category are accepted. This is the type of OIC that could greatly benefit some people, but you need the help of a CPA or attorney/CPA who can guide you through the process.

We are aware that many people are without funds to pay such an expert and are economically excluded from this type of OIC. This is regrettable. We suggest that you contact your state's CPA society or your state's bar association for free legal advice and ask if they offer help to the elderly, disabled, or poor, or to those who are working, but unable to pay for professional assistance. There are Low Income Tax Clinics (LITC) run by tax professionals who are also funded in part by the IRS and they may also be able to help you. Do not attempt to do this type of offer yourself. One of the most important items of knowledge is that if the IRS is working your OIC and tells you that they will accept a certain dollar amount and make a counter-proposal, you can accept it or appeal that number. You have 30 days from the date of the rejection letter to appeal. If the total liability is over $2,500, the appeal must be in writing. The IRS employee will tell you before they propose rejection what an acceptable amount would be, or you have the chance to amend your financial statement or better explain what is on it. This includes explaining why the value of your assets is not as high as the IRS thinks it is. If you want to file an appeal, you use Form 13711, Request for Appeal of Offer in Compromise. Use Google or Bing to search this term. You should also attach a letter that explains why you think the OIC should be accepted. You should list any information that supports your case. This includes items that you are disputing.

You do not have the right to appeal the OIC rejection in tax court.

If you did the OIC pre-qualifier, and it told you that you could probably get an OIC, then you should not have any problems. The more you own and the more income you have, the more problems you will have in collection and OIC cases.

The worse off that you are, the better you will look to the IRS as an

OIC candidate. Most importantly – complete all of the forms concerning your income and debts accurately. Be generous but not excessive in estimating your living expenses. The IRS offer specialists are trained to ferret out this information from many sources, so do not lie.

Sometimes it can be something arbitrary that will prevent the OIC from being accepted, like you offer a very small amount like $1 or $100 or even $1,000 and the IRS employee just thinks that is too low, no matter your other circumstances. Or an OIC can be rejected if you have a criminal history or you are being investigated for tax fraud or some other violation of law. The IRS will not tell you this, of course. But this is one of the reasons we have seen used to reject cases in the past. Just the fact that you are being investigated by the IRS or some other federal agency can cause this to trigger a rejection.

If you have been informed by the IRS that they are going to reject your OIC and you do not have a plan to appeal the decision, you should withdraw the OIC. A rejection is a black mark on your record and we have seen these rejections prejudice future OIC attempts. You write a letter to the IRS agent who is working your case and tell them that you want to withdraw your OIC. No need to give a reason. Tell what periods you are withdrawing, your name, SSN, address and then sign and date and send via certified mail to them.

Offer in Compromise due to Doubt as to Collectability. This is where the taxpayer has shown through their financial statements and credit reports and bank statements that they are unable to full pay or borrow money to pay their taxes. They may be making payments toward the tax, but the payment is not expected to full pay the taxes, ever. Or their case may have been found to be "currently not collectible".

This type of OIC is the most often submitted and the most often accepted. It would make sense for the IRS to want to receive some lump sum payment from money they would otherwise not have access in order to settle old accounts and get them off the books. The IRS is worried that doing this would look bad to the general public, as though some people are getting away with not paying their taxes. All accepted OICs are open for public inspection. The IRS always taught us as offer specialists that accepting OICs would give people the idea that they could get away with not paying their taxes. We were also taught that offer acceptance would lead other people to do the same thing.

That is the way it is with all the tax laws and the IRS; they presume that people do not pay their taxes on purpose (deliberate intent). But in our experience, most people just made mistakes, dumb business decisions or were affected by death, divorce, drugs, or depression and that left them short of money to pay their taxes.

It is important to note that the offer in compromise process is not a chance to "negotiate a deal" with the IRS. The IRS rarely negotiates; it usually tells you what it will accept and what you must do to get your offer accepted.

This is a problem that many taxpayers face; they hate having the tax debt that they can never fully pay hanging over their heads, year after year. It seems to quietly torture them. They just want to be done with the whole thing, and the IRS does not think that way at all. The IRS does not care if your case just sits there collecting more penalties and interest, year after year.

The problem that many people have with the OIC process is that it is very intrusive into their financial affairs and it can take up to two years before you get a decision. In the meantime you will have been paying money every month and cannot get it back. But you will get credit for the payments off your total tax bill.

Will I Qualify for an OIC?

Use Google or Bing with this search term: IRS OIC Pre-Qualifier. This is a handy tool to find out if you qualify for an OIC. This will tell you upfront if you can even get in the door with an offer.

You must:

- Not be in bankruptcy.
- Be current with filing all tax returns past and present.
- Be current with all your estimated tax payments and deposits.
- Be current in paying any payroll or other business taxes.

You should have all your financial information available before you go to the site: your payroll statements, and other income, your rent or mortgage and utilities and your expenses.

The one thing that you can never ever do, is to sell assets or transfer them to friends, family or other people during the time that you owe the taxes. If you do that, then the IRS can go after them and seize those assets back. If you sell anything, it should be for market value and an arm's length transaction. A "secret lien" arises when you have income and know that you are likely to owe the IRS taxes, and then when you file the return the lien continues. This is called the IRS statutory lien. As we saw in Chapter 8 – Collection, eventually the IRS files an actual Notice of Federal Tax Lien against you in the county where you live. If you do transfer assets in this way, you need to know that the IRS can and will follow those assets with its lien. We worked on a case like this once where a taxpayer with a failing business sold his company to an unsuspecting buyer for $25,000 cash. The buyer did not get an attorney or a title search and did not know about the IRS liens. So the buyer lost his $25,000 and the seller skipped town.

A situation like this is called a <u>transferee or nominee situation</u> and the IRS loves to find these fraudulent transfers. Needless to say this will prevent you from getting an installment agreement or offer in compromise approved. You can't try to hide assets from the IRS. That is tax fraud and evasion and depending on the value of the assets, you can be arrested and tried and face prison time for doing this, plus you lose the asset anyway. We repeat, never lie to the IRS and never put something on the tax return that you cannot prove.

We have worked many OICs that had strange circumstances, but we were still able to get them approved. One was a bank robber who had stolen $125,000. The IRS says that all income, legal or illegal, is taxable. The taxpayer owed income tax due to a particularly overzealous county prosecuting attorney who made sure that the IRS knew about it. The taxpayer went to jail for 3 years. Then he got out, was rehabilitated and became a minister. He had a small income and wanted to file an OIC to get right with the IRS and God (he said). He settled his tax debt of $37,500 for $4,000.

You will prepare the Form 433-A (OIC) in all cases where income taxes are due. If you are self-employed or you are seeking to compromise business taxes you will need to complete the Form 433-B (OIC), Collection Information for Businesses, also. These are the most comprehensive financial statements that the IRS requires. These can be found by searching the term IRS Form 433-A (OIC) and IRS Form 433-B (OIC) using Google or Bing.

Some of the information on the forms will come from your tax return; this includes filing status, dependents and exemptions. You should have your last three years' tax returns handy while completing this form. You should also have your last three months' bank statements to remind you of where all your money goes every month.

In **Section 1**, they ask about information for other people living in your house or who you claim as dependent. They will track these people down and check to see if they have income and if so, are they paying you rent, or for the utilities or food. So when you answer the question on the form "Contributed to household income" – think carefully. This question can help you if you have a relative living with you with no income and you are primarily supporting her as a relative or dependent. If he/she is an elderly relative, they are likely to have a pension or Social Security check and then you would need to include that in your income every month also. But if they are working, the IRS will expect them to pay a portion of the rent, utilities and their own food to you and then that is included in your income.

In **Section 2**, the IRS asks questions about your business and they will follow up on this with research. Many questions will arise from this information.

In **Section 3**, the IRS asks about your cash and investments. If you show $20,000 in a bank account, they will count that $20,000 as what you should pay towards your OIC.

Then they will look at stocks or bonds that you have and then value them at 90% of fair market value. So if you have $10,000 in stocks, the IRS will say that this amount has an immediate cash sales value of $8,000 and then add that on your OIC.

Then the IRS asks about any retirement account that you may own, a 401(k), IRA or other. They value this at 70% of the value of the account. This is important for you to think about. If you have $10,000 in an IRA, but you are young and not able to withdraw it without penalty, the IRS will allow for the 10% penalty associated with closing out your IRA and having to include it on your income tax. So this is where they come up with the 70%. Be very careful here. If you owe taxes and have money in a 401k or IRA, why would you make an OIC? The rule here is that if your plan may not be borrowed on or liquidated until you leave your employment and you have no vested interest, then the plan has no reasonable collection potential to the IRS. It is worth nothing to you and that makes it worth nothing to the IRS. An example of this with a government benefit such as Social Security is that you have paid money in but cannot claim any benefit until at least age 62. Those assets will quietly grow until you no longer owe the taxes, so why put them out in full view? You are better off with an installment agreement or trying to get your case declared "currently not collectible".

Section 3 asks for the cash value of any life insurance policy. Again, why give the IRS the chance to look at something that they hardly look at otherwise? You should convert this to a term policy and use your cash value to pay for it.

Then the IRS asks for the value of your house, condo, co-op, time share or other property that you own or are buying. They expect you to come up with a value. We like to use www.zillow.com to determine an approximate value. Then you multiply that by 80% and come up with a number. Next you take away any first or second mortgages or other liens against the property and come up with your net equity in the property. Now, they add that onto the amount of what they expect from you in your OIC.

Vehicles are much the same; we prefer to use Kelly Blue Book website (www.kbb.com) to determine the value of your vehicle. Multiply it by 80% and that is your net equity in the vehicle and that goes on the OIC as well.

In the last part of Section 3, the IRS wants to know what else you own. This could include artwork, antiques, jewelry, gold, silver, other valuables, a gun collection, a stamp collection, a baseball card collection, and items of value in safe deposit boxes.

We remember one case, where we were working an OIC investigation and it looked acceptable. When we went to interview the taxpayer at his home to check out his lifestyle, we admired an original Norman Rockwell work of art that his father had given him. In those days it was valued at $85,000. The taxpayer never thought of it as something of value, only a beloved gift from his deceased father. The man had fallen on hard times due to poor health. He only owed $46,000 in taxes. So we rejected his OIC and a few months later came back and seized that painting right off the wall and sold it at public auction to pay the taxes. The taxpayer did receive some money also, as the bidding rose above the amount that he owed the IRS. That is pretty standard for the IRS.

Section 4 asks about your self-employed information – the structure of your business, type of business and contact information,

Section 5 asks many of the same questions as Section 3 above, but only for your business assets. Here they value your goods at 80% of fair market value. Now what you need to know is that you have the right to keep some of this property as exempt from their valuation, because the IRS cannot take away what tools you need to conduct your business and try to make money. Review the article on this Cornell University website which is clearer than IRS information on this subject. (http://www.law.cornell.edu/uscode/text/26/6334)

The IRS will usually come up with high valuations of business assets; however, you can challenge them. You can get a business appraisal or real estate appraisal and those give you evidence that your property is worth less. For example, in the case of general or limited partnerships, they might be worth something, because you are there working every day, but if the IRS seized your portion of the partnership, you would probably stop coming to work and then your share would be worth far less or even little or nothing. No investor would buy a share in a partnership for any serious money. So the IRS almost always over appraises the value of business assets. Challenge this with your own appraisals. The IRS employee will not care; in fact, it gives them evidence that supports the offer so they are usually happy about it.

Assets held in corporations or LLC's are accorded a different status and value. They are difficult to value, but if the owner does not show up and work every day they have only the salvage value of the assets. Goodwill is worth nothing. Do not be afraid to challenge the IRS on this. If you have a complicated case, we suggest you have a tax professional advocate for you.

In Section 5, the IRS is asking about your business income and expenses. If you do have a business, the IRS usually has a hard time understanding that you do not always make the same amount of money month after month. Some months you have losses. An offer from a self-employed person is ripe for the pickings of the OIC reviewing officer.

In Section 6, the IRS is looking for your monthly business income and expense information for being self-employed.

Section 7 asks for your monthly income and expenses of your household. What is important here is that they do not tell you anything about the National Allowable Expense amounts that are available to you.

You should put down the maximum allowable expense that the IRS allows for the number of people in your household. Use Google or

Bing to search the term IRS National Standards: Food, Clothing and Other Items. If you have children or other relatives living with you a certain percentage of time, you may be able to include that percentage in the calculation also.

On Google or Bing, search: IRS National Standards: Out of Pocket Health Care and then figure out how much each person in your house would receive by their age and insert on the form.

The next section, you use the search term IRS Local Standards: Transportation. You will see that if you use public transportation you are allowed $185 a month, unless your commuting costs are higher. The national car ownership costs allowed is $471 for one car and $942 for two cars. That means that if you have a lower car payment, or a car that is more than 4 years old, you could buy a new car and the IRS would allow you to spend $471 a month for your car payment.

The next section deals with car operating expenses. This includes how much it costs you to run and maintain your car. If your expense for insurance or other operating expenses is higher, write it here and be prepared to prove it to the IRS.

Operating costs are different in different parts of the United States. Figure out which number applies to you and insert it on the form.

The next section is about your housing and utilities. This is divided up by state. Google or Bing this search term: Name of your state – IRS Local Standards: Housing and Utilities. For Example- California-IRS Local Standards: Housing and Utilities. Pick the category that applies to you based on the size of your household. For example, if you are a single person living in San Francisco you would be allowed $2,937 a month for housing and utilities. In Manhattan, New York $4,076 a month; in Chicago $1,824; yet you would go down to $816 a month in Jackson County, Arkansas and $789 in Gilmer County, West Virginia. Trying to live on the amount that you are allowed can be difficult, depending on what you standard of living was in the past.

It is important to know that the IRS will allow you more than this amount by at least 5% if you can prove why that is necessary. If you live in a house that was bought when the real estate market was high, then you probably have little or no equity in your house and a mortgage and utilities much higher than the Local Standards.

You need to be prepared for what is not important to the IRS, expense-wise. The IRS does not allow you money to loan to relatives, to take care of friends and relatives, your super cable TV package, your extra high speed internet, your hobbies, your charities, your pets, your veterinarian, getting new nails every two weeks, mani-pedis, or adding to your gun, coin, stamp or other collection. Gifts and presents, going out to eat or dance, going on vacations or buying more toys are all unallowable items.

We have already discussed tithing. The IRS wants you to pay them the maximum amount of money that you can and they decide how much that is. So be prepared to minimize your life style. The best thing that you can do for yourself if you owe the IRS is to swallow your pride and borrow money from anyone who will loan it to you.

The IRS is careful to not disallow these expenses, they say that they can be covered from the National Standard Allowable Expenses and that you can choose how you want to spend that money anyway that you want. That way they don't have to quibble about individual expenses.

Form 433-B (OIC) is similar to the Form 433-A (OIC), and it is easy to follow. This form asks you to determine the value of your assets and then put them down on the form. You are building a number which is how much you should offer.

In the real estate section, we suggest that you value your business property using www.zillow.com which the IRS is known to use and this is free. Otherwise you can get appraisals from local real estate agents or have a paid appraisal done. However you come to a number, you multiple this fair market value times 80% and come up with a number.

The same for your vehicles; you can use www.KBB.com for free to value your car, and then multiply it by 80%. Remember if you have a car or truck that is 6 years or older or has more than 75,000 miles you qualify for an extra $200 a month in auto operating expenses.

In doing your self-evaluations, you should lower them if the condition of your house is not perfect and the same for your car. Remember you are not trying to impress the IRS, you are trying to show them the real value and adding this information will help, like the furnace and air-conditioning are 20 years old, same for the roof, the driveway is full of potholes and the neighborhood is no longer safe. This gives you some room for negotiation. Remember whatever you put down, the IRS will usually challenge it. That is fine, then your case is ready for appeal.

Section 4, 5 and 6 are for self-employed taxpayers and follow the same rules as above, except some of your tools and equipment are exempt from levy so have no value. This is because if the IRS takes away your tools you cannot do your work. Usually the IRS will base the business value on the assets and income only. But if they pick some higher number, you need to challenge that. We remember one OIC case where a restaurant that had no assets and had suffered an embezzlement submitted an OIC. The IRS looked at their financial statement and saw that their gross receipts for the year were $146,517. So they listed that as an asset. That was income, not profit, so the IRS was wrong in doing that. Eventually an offer was accepted for $4,317 to compromise a $36,000 tax bill.

Section 7 is where the monthly income and expenses are listed and evaluated by the IRS. They will look for all income from whatever source. Like we said side jobs, cash income, loans, etc. will be reviewed. This is the most important section because you put whatever you can justify on the form as explained in Chapter 12 and then make sure that you research the IRS National Allowable Expenses charts to make sure that you get full credit for all of your expenses. You need to be thinking that the IRS will challenge every line on the form and act accordingly. You should plan on writing a one-page letter that will explain any circumstances that do not fit into the IRS cookie cutter expenses.

Note, we advise you to make installment agreements with your state taxing authority, before you go to the IRS, so that you have an installment agreement with the state. This is because states are usually owed smaller balances and are very aggressive in their collection efforts.

We also suggest that if you were not current with paying your student loans, that you start paying and update your agreement. The IRS will allow this monthly payment, and since it can never be discharged in bankruptcy and never expires, it should always be your first priority.

Section 8 calculates your offer amount. You cannot offer zero dollars. Even $100 is unlikely to be well received. There is also a processing fee of $186 just for submitting an offer. If your income is below the defined poverty rate for your area, then the filing fee can be waived. See Section 4 of Form 656 to see if you qualify. In figuring out what to offer, follow each IRS rule to the letter. Make a reasonable offer that they are likely to accept. Do not give the IRS reason and cause to reject your OIC out of hand because you failed to put information on the form, reported low asset values, or made a low ball offer. Remember this: you already took all the money that you owed for tax. Income tax is based on income after all. You had it in your hands and you chose to spend it somewhere else. So you have that money in your pocket or you did, so don't be cheap now. Paying for the right advice can save you big money.

You carry the Offer Amount over to Form 656, Offer in Compromise with Doubt as to Collectability.

Section 9 asks for more specific information on your assets and future income prospects.

Section 10 is where you sign and there is a checklist of all the documentation that you must send along with the OIC.

People who have the best chance of getting an OIC accepted are those who are filing a "Streamlined OIC". This is for wage earners, unemployed, and retired taxpayers. This is designed for cases where your total household income is $100,000 or less, and the amount that you owe is $50,000 (tax, penalties and interest) or less at the time you file the OIC.

OICs are subject to acceptance based on legal requirements. An offer in compromise is an agreement between a taxpayer and the IRS that settles the taxpayer's tax liabilities for less than the full amount owed. Generally, an offer will not be accepted if the IRS believes that the liability can be paid in full as a lump sum or through a payment agreement. The IRS looks at the taxpayer's income and assets to make a determination regarding the taxpayer's ability to pay.

How the IRS Reviews Your OIC

It all comes down to your circumstances, financially, and in the rest of your life.

If you have any of the following issues, they may seem bad to you, but they are good for your OIC case.

- You are age 60 or older.
- You have a family history of early death.
- You have mental health problems. (depression, bi-polar, diagnosed or undiagnosed.)
- You have physical health problems.
- Down turn in employment in your industry or profession.
- Your lack of job training or job skills.
- Your lack of education.
- Your loss of business contracts.
- Current or expected layoffs at your company.
- Your desire to quit working and retire due to health or age.
- You have a poor work history, or are unable to find and keep gainful employment.
- You or your spouse or close relatives are going through a crisis due to death, accident, trauma, bankruptcy, abuse and other personal problems.

- You have addiction problems: gambling, drugs (legal or illegal), alcohol, or sex that affects your ability to work. It does not matter if you are in rehabilitation for the issue. IRS does not have the right to judge you.
- You are caring for a severely ill or disabled family member and this is taking a toll on you.
- You have a terminal illness or are in a hospice program and trying to settle your financial affairs before you die.

All of these actually speak well for your OIC, as long as your numbers support this also.

The most important thing that you need to know about OICs is that there is no secret formula. There is no percentage, no best guess about what you should offer. The IRS clearly spells out what it expects and each OIC is tailored to the numbers on your financial statements. There is no magic or mystery to this process. The chief variable is in deciding how much your assets are worth. Never lie about anything you tell the IRS, because those lies usually turn up when the IRS employee is looking at all your financial transactions. You cannot cry poor, but have a busy credit card or many meals out on your debit card statements. The IRS employee is human and will keep it simple and ask you how you can afford whatever it is that you are spending your money on, based on the fact that you do not show that much income on your tax return. Remember this is not a tax amnesty, the IRS is not compelled to give you a break, unless it makes good business sense for the government to do so.

See Chapter 12 -How to Prepare Your Financial Statement for instructions on how to prepare your Collection Information Statement for Individuals, Form 433-A (OIC) and Collection Information Statement for Businesses, Form 433-B (OIC).

Chapter 14
How to Get Tax, Penalties and Interest Reduced or Eliminated

If you are reading this chapter, you are probably holding an IRS letter in your hand and are shocked to see that your unpaid tax carries with it many penalties and interest - sometimes as much as 60% of what the tax was.

Penalty assessment is big business at the IRS. Tens of billions of dollars in penalties are assessed each year. The IRS even admits it. The IRS assesses penalties which are subjective and punitive as a deterrent to stop behaviors it does not like, such as not filing taxes timely and paying taxes late. There is also a penalty called "Failure to Pay", which is assessed even when a taxpayer is actually paying on an installment plan.

There are more than 140 penalty provisions in the Internal Revenue Code. Part 20 of the Internal Revenue Manual (IRM) (found at https://www.irs.gov/irm/part20/index.html) will give you an overview of what an IRS employee must look at when determining whether to apply a penalty.

In 2013, the IRS assessed individual and employment penalties for inaccuracy, bad checks, late/non-filing, failure to make estimated tax payments, failure to pay penalty and fraud. These penalties were assessed against 37.9 million taxpayers.

In 2013 the IRS assessed taxpayers almost $26 billion in penalties, but they ended up losing $11,458,194 in penalties when taxpayers filed appeals. This is important - when the taxpayers challenged the penalties - the IRS backed down. From 1989 to 1993, one IRS study verified that the IRS removed penalties about 40% of the time, when the taxpayer filed a protest and asked for the case to go to the Appeals Office. This is another IRS secret. Never automatically accept and pay a notice or adjustment from the IRS. Never! The IRS might be wrong or back down if you protest.

The IRS has the power to take away penalties, but is very reluctant to do so.

The IRS Manual claims that:

"Penalties are to encourage voluntary compliance. Penalties should do the following:

- Be severe enough to deter noncompliance,
- Encourage noncompliant taxpayers to comply,
- Be objectively portioned to the offense, and
- Be used to educate taxpayers and encourage future compliance.
- The penalties are to be applied "*fairly, consistently and accurately*."

Penalties are not intended to be a punishment for taxpayers seeking to comply with the tax laws. The IRS goal is to get the delinquent taxpayer back on the tax rolls and know that they will "voluntarily" file and pay in future years.

Many taxpayers are told by IRS employees that penalties cannot be abated. In fact, some IRS employees are not even aware that these penalties can be removed routinely.

Sometimes the IRS will waive estimated tax penalties if the amount of tax due is under $1,000, where there was no tax liability the previous year, or the taxpayer is disabled or newly retired. This is found in the Internal Revenue Code Sec. 6654 (e).

IRC Section 7508 states no penalties will be assessed against a taxpayer who is serving in a combat zone.

An example of how large and how quickly penalties and interest can grow is shown in the following case. If you owe $10,000 for personal income tax and do not file the return for 6 months and do not pay for 4 years you will owe an additional $2,500 for **Failure to File Penalty (25%)**, $2,250 for **Failure to Pay Penalty (up to 25%)**, and interest compounded daily of 3-4%. If you don't pay it the balance will actually double every 6 years.

You realize that you made a mistake in not filing and paying in the first place. That is clear. But why such punishment from the IRS? Now your head is clear and you are at a point in life where you just want to settle up with the IRS and pay what you reasonably believe you owe with interest and then move on.

What do you do now? You have seen those ads on TV about settling your taxes for pennies on the dollar and as you found out in the last chapter that is not a system that will probably work for you.

So what do you do? This chapter will offer you ways that the IRS does not want you to know about to get the penalties and sometimes even the interest reduced or removed completely.

So that sounds like the IRS will dutifully slap you on the hand to gently correct your behavior and turn you around and get you back on the tax rolls. This is similar to getting stopped for a speeding ticket - you expect a fine or penalty and then you expect to get back on the road. But at the IRS, the fine lasts ten years into the future – because of the IRS Notice of Federal Tax Lien.

Congress provides for penalties and the IRS chooses to be very harsh in their application. The IRS has the authority to abate penalties; they just don't like to do so until persuaded with valid reasons. The doctrine of "Reasonable Cause" will be discussed throughout this chapter.

In your dealings with the IRS, it is likely that you will feel like you are just getting punished over and over. The balances continue to grow and you are unable to full pay or borrow the money, you just keep getting more penalties and interest.

The IRS Manual states that the IRS employee that you are working with, "May educate taxpayers and encourage future compliance by explaining the penalty, discussing the causes of your delinquency and listening to the reasons for noncompliance." IRS employees should be alert to information received in discussions with you that indicate possible reasons for abatement of penalties. (IRM 20.1.1.2)

What is Your Story?

First, you must get your story together. Every taxpayer has a story about why they failed to file or pay their taxes. Your story can save you money. Let's go back to the beginning of your tax issue with the IRS. What was the primary triggering event that caused you to not do something that the IRS required you to do? As so often happens, it is not usually just one thing that happened that caused your tax woes. There might have been a triggering event, but then other events compounded that event and continued long after the original event. This covers many areas.

The IRS will look at your filing history and see if you have had any problems in the last three years with filing or paying. This is not a stand-alone factor, just something that they keep in mind.

Second they will consider the length of time between the event cited as a reason for noncompliance and when you finally did file your tax return.

An example of this is that a few months before your tax return was due, a member of your family died. That would be a reason to take away the failure to file penalty, but if you did not file your tax return until the next year, then they would deny it on those grounds. Remember, and this is the important idea in this chapter, nothing stands alone. So in the time after the death, you may have been in mourning or had to move, take care of an elderly parent, change jobs or whatever else that death caused in your life. All that change might have caused you to become depressed, or use drugs or alcohol to self-medicate. That could change the focus to make the case qualify for penalty abatement. There usually are many factors involved in every transaction in life. The IRS employee is not a mind reader. You must give the IRS all of the facts and circumstances to have "reasonable cause" for abatement of penalties. Be prepared for follow up questions that might be asked of you. IRS employees, especially field employees such as revenue officers and revenue agents, are trained to ask tough questions to see if your story is consistent with other known facts.

Another example is that someone else had control of your tax records - an accountant or bankruptcy trustee or some other third party - so that is why you could not file on time. That is an acceptable reason, as long as you can show you attempted to get or got those records returned. The IRS will look at how long it took for you to file, after you finally got the records back. Again there can be other circumstances that occurred at the same time, such as you were in divorce proceedings, depressed, had lost your job, or other factors.

Perhaps you did not file a return or make tax payments in the time required, or you claimed credits, exemptions and deductions on your tax return and now you don't have the receipts to prove those deductions to the IRS. Maybe you never had them. At this point, it does not matter.

What matters is what you were thinking at the time that you made the decision to not file or pay or do whatever else the IRS is applying the penalty for. This is what the IRS calls "your intent". What did you intend to do at the time? Those are the facts of your case.

Now we ask that you remember what was happening in your life or your business that caused your IRS problems. This is not a blame game; it is seeking to tell your story truthfully because you may have what the IRS calls reasonable cause for the abating the penalties. In order for you to have penalties abated under the Reasonable Cause criteria, you must have "exercised ordinary business care and prudence" to take care of your tax obligations, but due to circumstances or events beyond your control, you were unable to meet the tax requirement that caused the penalty to be applied.

How to Write Your Penalty Appeal Letter

The letter should be addressed to whatever office sent you the most recent letter. You must include your name, address, Social Security number, and then you should state that you are protesting the penalties and interest on your case because you have either Reasonable Cause for Penalty Abatement or are requesting the abatement under First Time Penalty Abatement Waiver (FTAW). You have to ask for this to happen. The Inspector General for Tax Administration reported that in 2012, 1.65 million individual taxpayers qualified for FTAW but only 8.8% asked for it. This is because most taxpayers and even some tax representatives do not know about this valuable tool. If the IRS employee working your case refuses to take this penalty away, ask that your case be referred to the Office of Appeals.

Note: We have included two samples for you to use as a basis for a request for penalty abatement. Please see the Appendix of this book.

State what notice or letter that you are replying to. (Usually found in the upper right hand corner and starts out with "LT" or "CP", followed by numbers.)

State the questionable items, and, if known, explain which penalties you are requesting to be abated. If you do not know, then ask that all penalties assessed and accrued be abated.

Tell your story. Explain what circumstances were happening in your life. Remember that anything you say is completely confidential and will never be shared by the IRS with anyone. So if you are making accusations against a tax preparer or admitting to some substance abuse problems that you may have had at the time, write them down. This will be your chance to have the Appeals Office review your case and hopefully abate the penalties. You should also include the statement "Under penalty of perjury, I declare that this statement is to the best of my knowledge and belief true and complete." Then sign and date your letter, not electronically, but with ink on paper to meet the IRS requirements. Then send the letter using certified mail back to the address where your letter came from. In audit cases you can make a verbal appeal, but we do not suggest that you do that. Appeals are time sensitive - see Chapter 5 Service Center Processing to see exactly how many days you have to file a protest and request an appeal, based on the letter you have received.

The IRS will usually require that you are current with filing the current required tax returns. If you are applying for penalty relief for 2014 taxes in June of 2016, that means that you should have either already filed the 2015 income tax return or you have an extension to October 15, 2016 to file it.

Some penalty appeals can be made when you talk to the IRS, but it is always wise to also write down what you are appealing and send it to them. We have found that sometimes the IRS telephone agent will tell you that they are going to take away a penalty and then they do not. This leads you back to square one.

There are different types of penalty appeals. The first is where you ask your IRS contact to abate the penalties and you give your reasons in person, on the phone or in a letter. In collection, they use a system called Reasonable Cause Assistant (RCA). This is supposed to take the subjectivity out of penalty abatement. This system is not accurate, and is punitive with its determinations and wrong at least 70% of the time, in our experience. No matter what the IRS employee tells you, the RCA can be overruled (IRM 20.1.1.3.6.10.3 at www.irs.gov). It is only as good as the instructions in its programming. For instance, the IRS will abate penalties in cases of embezzlement. But the RCA system states that embezzlements must have been discovered in 6 months for this to be allowed. It is unfair, arbitrary and capricious. The RCA System usually rules against the taxpayer, no matter how good your reason or excuses for what happened. Most of the time they will deny your penalty appeal; you will receive a Notice of Disallowance which offers you penalty appeal rights.

What the IRS Looks for When It Reviews Your Protest Letter

IRS employees are not encouraged to abate penalties, even though they are authorized to do so in the IRM. They will always look for something that they think you did wrong and use as a reason to deny your request to abate the penalties. Additionally, you have to ask for penalty relief – it will not be just offered to you.

The Failure to Deposit penalty is applied at the rate of 2-15 % for businesses that fail to deposit payroll taxes. This penalty can be waived if the failure to deposit was due to reasonable cause and not due to willful neglect. Businesses that do not correctly make their tax deposits the first time they are required can have the penalty waived. IRC 6656 states that penalties can be abated if the failure to deposit was due to reasonable cause and not willful neglect.

Over the years IRS employees have discovered many cases of embezzlement that occurred in businesses and involved federal taxes. One case that was noteworthy involved a doctor who was very successful, bringing home $500,000 a year in income. He grew old and decided to sell his practice, so outside accountants came in and conducted a due diligence audit. They looked at his books and records going back seven years. They discovered that his office manager/bookkeeper had been embezzling for that whole time. He trusted her completely as they had known each other since high school and went to the same church.

Somewhere along the way, she became jealous of his lifestyle, and resented the fact that he only paid her $42,000 a year. At first she started slowly embezzling money to fund shopping and vacation trips. That should have been a signal, but the doctor never noticed. About 2 years in to the theft, an outside CPA conducted an audit and discovered that about $240,000 was missing. For some reason, instead of telling the doctor directly, he discussed it extensively over drinks with the office manager/bookkeeper and well, one thing led to another; they started having an affair, and stealing the money together.

How this relates to the taxes is that the doctor's employees had money taken out of their paychecks for income and Social Security taxes and the office manager never paid the money to the IRS. This happened in the last three years of the crime. That is how the balance grew so rapidly. Then the IRS came and told the doctor that he owed $1.7 million and about $700 thousand was just penalties.

The IRS audit and the due diligence audit happened about the same time. The doctor was very embarrassed and fired the office manager and tried to forget about it, and then the IRS showed up.

The IRS revenue officer reviewed what happened, plugged the facts into the RCA calculator and it rejected the claim for penalty abatement, because the embezzlement had gone over six months without discovery.

But the revenue officer did not feel right about that decision, so he chose to manually override it, because he said, "I don't think we should pluck a fat pigeon just because he can pay the $1.7 million."

The IRS decided that if the doctor would file criminal charges against the former office manager, they would abate $700 thousand in penalties, because he had conducted his business in a manner that was professional and exercised "ordinary business care and prudence in operating the company."

The fact that he had relied on professionals to do his accounting and audits helped. The office manager was sentenced to 4 years of probation after she claimed that she had a drinking and gambling problem and the CPA lost everything. She was mostly unemployable after that and never paid one dime in restitution.

Before going further into the return-related penalty discussion, it is important to mention penalties having to do with employment taxes.

To encourage prompt payment of withheld income and employment taxes, including Social Security taxes, Railroad Retirement taxes, or collected excise taxes, Congress passed a law that provides for the Trust Fund Recovery Penalty (TFRP.) These taxes are called trust fund taxes because the employer is supposed to hold the employee's money in trust until the employer is required to make a federal tax deposit in that amount. The TFRP may apply to you if these unpaid trust fund taxes cannot be immediately collected from the business. The business does not have to have stopped operating in order for the TFRP to be assessed. Further discussion of this penalty, and your rights to appeal, can be found in Chapter 8, regarding the Collection process.

When we talk about income taxes, we mean that you had income – actual money in your hand. The IRS wants the part of that money that you owe for taxes. Saying you never had the money does not count. That is not an excuse. You had the money; you just choose to do something else with it at the time. That is how the IRS views it.

The IRS Rarely Removes These Types of Penalties

The IRS never removes the bad check penalty.

Penalty abatement for abusive transactions, frivolous returns, accuracy-related penalty, civil and criminal fraud, negligence and other abusive conduct are usually very difficult to remove, but not impossible. This is because the IRS will be judging you on many different levels to determine if you are truly reformed from this behavior and attitudes. They will also look at your behavior if you are prominent in anti-government or anti-IRS groups, now or in the past. The IRS looks at what would the public perception would be if the penalty were abated. For instance, a CPA or tax preparer who has been filing returns and seeking fraudulent tax refunds for himself or his clients would not stand a chance of getting penalties abated. The same story applies to an activist who uses anti-IRS rhetoric.

The penalties that are eligible for penalty relief under the **First Time Penalty Abatement Waiver** include:

- Failure to file a tax return
- Failing to pay your taxes on time
- Failing to deposit taxes as required

Almost all other penalties can be abated under **Reasonable Cause** criteria.

Types of Penalty Relief:

- First Time Penalty Abatement
- Reasonable Cause
- Administrative Waiver (The IRS chooses to remove penalties)
- Statutory Exception (The law gives this right to remove penalties)

Reasonable Cause Arguments for Individuals and Businesses

Something happened that was beyond your control. This may include:

- You turned your records over to a tax professional, CPA, or to tax lawyers and they lost or destroyed them or refused to return them to you.
- You were affected by a fire, flood, theft, casualty, or other natural disaster. Or you were in a terrorist action or a war zone and were unable to meet your tax obligations.
- You acted in good faith to make sure that you were following the law and things happened that prevented you from doing so.
- You or a member of your family died, had a serious illness or you were unavoidably absent from your residence because you had to care for another person. Also, the date and the length of time you were absent is important.
- If you were out of the United States and unable to take care of your tax obligations.

- Despite your best efforts you were unable to obtain the records needed to file your return or support you in an audit.
- You relied on the advice of a tax professional, CPA or lawyer and it proved to be wrong. But you cannot blame another for failing to file your returns; it is always your responsibility.
- Ignorant of the law. This can be claimed due to your mental state, level of education, medical, emotional and mental problems that affected you.
- A claim of undue hardship could cause abatement of the failure to pay penalty due to **undue financial hardship.** Inability to pay claiming lack of funds does not apply. The taxpayer must have had enough funds on hand, but as result of unanticipated events was unable to pay the taxes. Perhaps you were robbed or you invested your tax money with Bernie Madoff. We have handled cases like this.
- Relied on advice from a tax professional. Was the advice given specifically and is there written evidence of that?

Penalties may also be abated due to **statutory exceptions**. This means that if the IRS gives you the wrong advice, then they will abate the penalty because of that, if you can prove it. If you talk to an IRS employee on the phone, always get their name and their employee identification number! Keep all correspondence received from the IRS.

Another way that penalties may be abated is called **administrative waiver**, where the IRS changes its position on some tax issue and in effect gives a group of taxpayers a onetime pass on a specific issue. The Internal Revenue Code allows typically compliant individual and business taxpayers to request abatement, or removal, of certain penalties that the IRS has assessed against them for the first time. In effect, the IRS rewards typically compliant taxpayers with one-time penalty amnesty which can save the taxpayer penalty dollars.

Businesses pay income, employment and excise taxes. They are held to a higher standard that the IRS uses to determine if they are making the effort to comply with the tax laws.

When you are in business, you must show that you "exercised ordinary business care and prudence." This means you operated your business with a profit motive, that you kept good books and records, and that you supervised every aspect of your business including monitoring what your employees were doing.

Examples of not being in control of your business are saying that you do not like to do the books or issue checks so you have a signature stamp made and then an employee authorizes checks and embezzles money from your company.

Being short of money because a customer filed bankruptcy or failed to pay their bill is not reasonable cause.

Could the company have anticipated what happened? Should they have reduced payroll or increased work load in order to make sure that taxes were being paid that they were able to pay? If so, the request for reasonable cause will likely be denied.

The IRS looks at the last three years of tax compliance; if you had that same penalty in the past, you are unlikely to get it abated now.

This is the standard used in the IRS - is this conduct what a reasonable person would do who owned a business? Would it be wise to take a two-month vacation to the south of France and leave people to run your business and then get you in tax trouble?

Audit/Exam Penalties

Tens of billions of dollars are assessed in penalties every year, penalties that are asserted by the Examination/Audit section of the IRS.

The most common penalties are the accuracy-related penalties, which account for 20-40% of the tax that the IRS is claiming that you underpaid.

Assessment of accuracy-related penalties by the IRS is up 800% for the period 2005-2010. Accuracy-related penalty (IRC 6662) types can be found in IRM 20.1.5.3.2 The IRS person you are working with, be it a revenue agent, revenue officer, tax compliance officer ("office auditor") or any other assistor, is required to explain penalties and, if you ask, should give you the reason for the penalty and explain it in "plain English". If you feel the IRS employee has not explained it adequately for your understanding, you should ask to speak to his/her supervisor.

The accuracy-related penalty is assessed if you overstate your deductions and expenses. There are many reasons for this penalty. This penalty is on top of the normal failure to file and pay penalties and interest is also charged on the penalty as well as the tax deficiency. The second penalty is the civil fraud penalty which is 75% of your new tax amount. Note that this is different from the criminal fraud penalty which comes with criminal cases.

Generally, taxpayers are not subject to the accuracy-related penalty if they establish that they had reasonable cause for the underpayment and acted in good faith. The most important factor is that the taxpayer made the effort to determine and present the correct tax return to the IRS. The burden of proof for establishing reasonable cause is on the taxpayer. In other words – you have to ask for it and prove why you deserve it.

The IRS looks at your compliance history, i.e. was this just a slip up in one or two years only? Did you maintain adequate books and records and take actions to ensure that the tax reported was correct? You must present your story about what happened and why it happened in order to have a greater chance of success with penalty abatement.

The Automated Under-Reporter System (AUR) is a computer program that matches information reported to the IRS by various sources required to report it. It matches that information to your return. It will automatically assess penalties if your tax return meets its selection criteria. Penalties are automatically assessed without any review by an IRS employee and are assessed without managerial approval of the penalty.

The IRS exam employees must have their managers' approval

to assess any penalties so the manager is your first line of appeal. The burden of proof to establish the penalty is on the IRS. Then the burden of proof shifts to you to establish why the penalty should not be assessed, such as reasonable cause. You can always pay the tax in full (including the penalty) and file a timely claim for refund which becomes a refund suit in U.S. District Court of Federal Claims. If your case looks like it is heading in that direction, then you need a tax attorney.

All accuracy-related penalties are charged to you if the IRS agent believes that you intentionally neglected to list the correct numbers or intentionally disregarded the tax laws.

Another common accuracy-related penalty, also assessed at 20% of the amount of your tax deficiency, is termed the substantial understatement penalty. This penalty is assessed only when the taxpayer has underreported the income on the return.

An understatement is considered substantial when it exceeds the greater of: 10 percent of the tax required to be shown on the return for a taxable year; or $5,000 ($10,000 for corporations, other than an S-Corporation or a personal holding companies, for taxable years beginning on or before October 22, 2004).

Your best defense in these cases is to appeal the penalties to the IRS agent, and then if you are unsuccessful, to their immediate manager. This will usually involve admitting to part or all of their proposed tax additions to you. It also makes the case easier for the IRS to process if you sign the Revenue Agent Report or Consent form to allow the agent to assess the additional tax. This puts them in a better mood, because they know that you will not go to the Office of Appeals or tax court to dispute the tax amount, which costs the government a whole bunch of money for them to have to prove their case again.

This is true if you have actually been caught hands down in not reporting income or you have no documentation to support your deduction and expense claims. If the IRS agent and their manager refuse to discuss or negotiate the penalties, then you can file a request to go to Appeals where there is a much higher probability that some or all of these penalties will be removed.

We have seen cases where the proposed new tax was $2 million and the fraud and accuracy penalties were $500,000 and a gifted tax attorney that we know persuaded the IRS to waive the penalties in full because the taxpayer consented to the new higher tax amount.

Does the IRS Ever Abate Interest?

The IRS will tell you that interest can never be abated, but that is not true. In fact, there are IRS employees who are known as "Interest Abatement Coordinators" who will make the final in-IRS decision if the IRS will abate interest. Appeals and U.S. Tax Court have this authority also.

Interest can be abated when:

- The IRS makes an error such as in processing or math error
- When the IRS is responsible for unreasonable delays in processing. (see IRM 20.2.7.4)
- When the tax is found to not legally be due
- Interest is also suspended when members of the military are in combat zones or under military deferment.
- Interest can be suspended or not assessed for taxpayers who are in a declared disaster area due to weather related disaster, terrorist or military action.
- When you are in bankruptcy, interest is suspended and sometimes is cancelled by the bankruptcy court.
- When the IRS fails to contact the taxpayer within 3 years of the filing of the tax return in question and then begins an audit.
- When an erroneous refund is issued due to no fault of the taxpayer and it is under $50,000.
- The IRS under IRC 6404 (a) and as explained in IRM 20.2.7.2, can abate interest that is:

- Excessive in amount
- Assessed after the statutory period of limitations has expired
- Erroneously or illegally assessed

With each of these arguments, the IRS will automatically fight you, but don't give up. If you believe that you have cause, you should always request that interest be abated also.

Interest abatement is never granted solely because of Reasonable Cause. It must fit the very strict and limited circumstances that you and your tax professional can find in the Internal Revenue Code.

A second line of defense is to contact the Taxpayer Advocate Service (www.irs.gov/Advocate) because trying to figure out what to do to defend yourself against IRS penalties and interest is very confusing. Some taxpayers have difficulty understanding their rights or obtaining a solution to a problem. This avenue is open to you when you have made or attempted to make two or more contacts; the IRS system or individual employees were not responsive; and the IRS was not able to resolve your case by the date promised.

See the Appendix of this book for sample letters to be used for applying for penalty abatement due to first time penalty abatement waiver and for abatement for reasonable cause and additional thoughts on how to prepare your letter.

Chapter 15
Identity Fraud, Refund Fraud and Other IRS-Related Frauds

Imagine finding a letter in your mailbox from the IRS telling you that you will not be receiving your tax refund for maybe a year, because someone else has already cashed your check.

Having your identity stolen is an assault on your name, your credit and your ability to conduct business. It violates innocent people every day, and often the IRS is who will notify you that someone is using your good name and tax data to steal refunds. We will share ways to make you more knowledgeable about the IRS Identity Fraud process to guide you in what you need to know to survive.

Tax-related identity fraud and refund fraud occur when someone uses your stolen Social Security number to file a tax return claiming a fraudulent tax refund. This happens because the IRS processes tax returns and sends out refunds before it has documents that it can use to match and verify the numbers reported on the tax returns.

In 2016, the IRS began processing income tax returns on January 19, but the Form W-2s that tell how much an employee made in wages and how much they had in withholdings are not required to be filed until January 31, 2016. The Form 1099s reporting income are not required to be issued to the receiver until January 31, 2016 but the IRS does not require a copy until February 28, 2016.

The IRS is giving the thieves at least 13 days to file fraudulent returns and receive refunds. But really it is far worse than that, because W-2s are required to be submitted electronically only if your employer has 250 or more employees. Otherwise, they are submitted on paper and the IRS has to enter the information by hand on the computer. It could take months or years for them to match. The IRS also has the mindset that refunds need to be issued within 45 days so that the government does not have to pay interest on the refunds. That may have made a difference when the IRS had to pay interest of 15%, but now the interest rate is only 3%. It is not an economic priority to do this anymore. In the quest for speed, the IRS pays refunds without the information needed to match to the correct recipient. They simply trust the word of whoever completes and mails or electronically files tax returns with the most speed.

The Revenue Reconciliation Act of 1998 (RRA 98) mandated that refunds would be issued more quickly. This ties in with a family needing their refund to pay off their Christmas bills or take vacations. It is good public relations to get the refunds out quickly. This is key to understanding the current refund/identity fraud problem. The IRS now has increased electronic filing and that made the demand increase for faster return processing and faster refunds, on average in 9.6 days. The computer does not ask questions or do a background search or match any of the information you put on the tax return. For instance - you have never filed before but now are claiming $10,000 in income and a refund of $5,000. The IRS will pay. Let's say you have not filed for the last two years but you now file for a refund of $314,000 and want it sent to an address in Hungary; you are likely to get your check. The IRS computer is unable to detect that multiple refunds were being sent to a single address and it makes no difference to the IRS computer if the check is heading to a place that does not use a zip code. We have heard of the IRS sending checks to one address in Hungary that received 603 refunds, other addresses in Hong Kong received 555 refunds, in Lithuania 655 refunds and a single address in Shanghai that received 343 refunds.

The IRS is using more filters than they have in the past, but is still unable to control the flow of money to the fraudsters. The IRS now is locking up the tax accounts of deceased individuals and that prevents others from using their name and Social Security number to commit identity theft refund fraud. According to a TIGTA report, the IRS locked up 26.3 million taxpayer accounts in the last 4 years.

Criminal types, thieves and swindlers are all aware of this loophole in the system and make sure to file their make-believe tax returns using other people's stolen identities and tax and financial data to file.

The IRS stated that its refund fraud program caught $24.2 billion in false refund claims, but admitted $5.2 billion was actually paid out in 2011. In 2012 $3.6 billion was paid out. In 2013, 3 million fraudulent refunds were filed and it is estimated that the number is even higher. The Treasury Inspector General projected that refund/identity fraud could cost $21 billion a year in 2016, despite the IRS efforts. This takes away taxpayer's confidence in the tax system. Most of the refunds are paid as direct deposits into bank accounts. Because of budget cuts, the IRS had to cut $200 million out of its information technology budget in 2015. Fraud detection software could be installed if only extra money was available for it.

The IRS claims that stopping identity theft and refund fraud is a top priority, but it probably won't feel like that if you are one of the people who has had their refund stolen. The IRS has assigned more than 10,000 IRS employees (12% of all employees) to work on identity theft-related issues. In addition, the IRS provides training to more than 35,000 employees who work with taxpayers to recognize identity theft indicators and help people victimized by identity theft. If you are a victim of identity theft, TIGTA reported that the IRS took an average of 278 days to resolve the identity fraud tax accounts. The IRS made errors in at least 17% of the cases which delayed refunds. This is a long time to have to wait to get your own money back. One solution to this is to adjust your tax withholdings so you receive a tax refund of $500 or less at the end of the tax year.

A recent poll by Bankrate.com reported that 62% of Americans are living paycheck to paycheck. Only 38% of those polled said that they would be able to cover a $500 repair bill or a $1,000 emergency room visit with funds from their bank account. Most would need to borrow or cut back elsewhere. The average IRS tax refund is the money that people "loan" the government.

The IRS does not crosscheck when a person files for a refund to see if they have any income or tax withholdings. It trusts that the taxpayer must be telling the truth. This is a strategy that does not work in today's business world. When was the last time you bought a car just on your good word and a handshake? It is as simple as looking at past income history and 1099's and W-2's that would be required to be filed electronically which would provide instant access. The IRS does not do this and that is the crime here. The IRS issues checks that no one in the business world would ever issue, based on "trust". The IRS issues refund checks to people who make false claims on tax returns.

That trust thing never works in business or government, because thieves will exploit it.

The IRS recently announced that it would stop processing suspicious tax returns that had indications of identity theft, but contained a real taxpayer's name and/or Social Security number and that they would send Letter 5071 C or Notice CP 01B requesting more information from the taxpayer of record. The IRS has now created a website where a person who is a victim of identity theft can go and verify who they are. It is: idverify.irs.gov.

If the taxpayer is able to verify their information and their refund claim, then the IRS should issue the refund within six weeks. If the IRS is still unable to verify the person filing the return or does not receive a response, they will treat the case as an identity theft case.

One of the ways to prevent future identity theft is that the IRS issues Identity Protection Personal Identification Numbers (IP PINS)

This six-digit number is issued annually to past victims of identity theft and is used along with their Social Security number to process their tax returns.

The IRS states that it is aware that identity theft is a frustrating, complex process for victims. It states that this type of case is extremely difficult to resolve, frequently touching on multiple issues and multiple tax years. Cases can be complicated even further because of identity thieves who contact the IRS and pretend to be the taxpayer. While identity thieves steal information from sources outside the tax system, the IRS is often the first to inform a victim that identity theft has occurred. The IRS claims that it is working hard to resolve identity theft cases as quickly as possible. In most cases we have seen delays of 6-12 months for the IRS to work the case and issue a refund to the correct taxpayer.

The fraudsters usually have your confidential data, like your Social Security number, address, date of birth, income, employer name and address, and bank information. They may also possibly have the same information on your spouse and children and other dependents. Where does the information come from? There are many companies, and payroll processing firms, that have access to a great deal of information: names, Social Security numbers, addresses and dates of birth. There is a growing black market for this information.

Large amounts of data have already escaped IRS attention. Many IRS employees have unlimited access to the Master File Computer. Despite numerous checks and balances in the system, some IRS employees have taken advantage of this opportunity to download millions of taxpayer accounts. These have a double value. They can be sold on the black market, or that individual can be a thief themselves. The IRS and its computers cannot question whether the refund you claim is good or not, because they always pay even though they have not received or processed the W-2 forms.

Identity theft is making some people very rich and few are caught, let alone convicted. It is white collar crime taken to the next level. The refunds - sometimes hundreds of them - go to a single address if they request a paper check, but more often than not, they go to pre-paid debit cards which are untraceable and a good source of cash and items. They also favor using direct deposit bank accounts. You can retire and have your Social Security check sent to most countries except North Korea and Cuba and the same goes for your fraudulent income tax refund. Tens of thousands of refunds are wired into either a foreign bank account or into domestic accounts and then transferred online to foreign banks. The IRS does not have any access or control over this once the refund is issued.

This happens because of another old IRS idea that every case can be worked in the "Service Center Processing Pipeline." That means that the cases are not worked by people, but mostly by the computer. The antique computer decides to send the checks out. That is what it was programmed to do 55 years ago. It only takes a new computer or extensive reprogramming to make this change. A clerk could look at tax refund claims that look suspicious. If you owe the IRS, you automatically lose your refund. But the computer sometimes sends you a refund on one year even though you have a balance due on another year. The IRS is consistent at being inconsistent and its chaotic refund system proves that.

The majority of the leaks of confidential tax information are occurring in the unsecured data transmission or leaks by employees in the IRS and Social Security Administration. There are dozens of IRS and Social Security employees who have been convicted of stealing tax data and using it to file false tax returns and receive tax refunds. There is too much identity fraud of old and disabled people to suggest otherwise. These people do not have active credit purchases, new mortgage loans or other financial transactions that would put their name, address and Social Security numbers out into the business world. Many of these people are not required to file tax returns because their income is too low. The information can also come from anyone you have credit with: doctors' offices, payroll companies, payroll clerks and scammers who have invaded your computer and stolen your tax and financial data.

Sometimes the IRS is afraid to be in charge. It holds the money, it has the power to require businesses to file all W-2 forms electronically, and it can program the computer to figure out when suspicious activity is happening. They do not have to wait until after it has happened and then try to correct it. The IRS is putting out small brush fires and failing to see that the whole forest is on fire. The IRS needs to "Just Say No," to this rapid refund program, even if that is unpopular with the public. But Congress mandated that refunds be issued rapidly, so that is the problem.

The first that the "victim taxpayer" hears about a problem is usually when they file their tax return and receive a letter back that there is a problem with their tax return and that their expected refund check is not going to be issued. That is when they enter the long, confusing path towards the Identity Fraud Unit hidden deep within IRS. That unit is: The IRS Identity Protection Specialized Unit and is available at 1-800-908-4490. Use Google or Bing to search this term: Form 14039.

What to Do if You Suspect Identity Fraud

Use Google or Bing to search for Publication 5027— Identity Theft Information for Taxpayers; it will tell you everything you need to know about identity fraud. There are basic warning signs of identity fraud explained there.

Be alert to possible tax-related identity theft if you are contacted by the IRS about:

- More than one tax return was filed for you,
- You owe additional tax, have a refund offset or have had collection actions taken against you for a year you did not file a tax return, or
- IRS records indicate you received wages or other income from an employer for whom you did not work.

Here is What to Do if You are a Victim of Identity Fraud

If you are a victim of identity theft, the Federal Trade Commission recommends these steps:

- File a complaint with the FTC at identitytheft.gov.
- Contact one of the three major credit bureaus to place a 'fraud alert' on your credit records:
  www.Equifax.com 1-888-766-0008
  www.Experian.com 1-888-397-3742
  www.TransUnion.com 1-800-680-7289
- Close any financial or credit accounts opened by identity thieves

If your SSN is compromised and you know or suspect you are a victim of tax-related identity theft, the IRS recommends these additional steps:

- Respond immediately to any IRS notice; call the number provided or, if instructed, go to IDVerify.irs.gov.
- Complete IRS Form 14039, Identity Theft Affidavit, if your e-filed return is rejected because of a duplicate filing under your SSN or you are instructed to do so. Use a fillable form at www.irs.gov, then print it and attach the form to your paper return and mail according to instructions.
- Continue to pay your taxes and file your tax return, even if you must do so by paper.
- If you previously contacted the IRS and did not have a resolution, contact the IRS for specialized assistance at 1-800-908-4490. The IRS has teams of employees available to assist.

More information is available at: www.irs.gov/individuals/identity-protection

It's important to know what type of personal information was stolen. If you've been a victim of a data breach, keep in touch with the company to learn what it is doing to protect you and follow the "Steps for Victims of Identity Theft."

How you can reduce your risk:

- Don't routinely carry your Social Security card or any document with your Social Security number on it.
- Don't give a business your Social Security number just because they ask – only when absolutely necessary.
- Protect your personal financial information at home and on your computer.
- Check your credit report annually.
- Check your Social Security Administration earnings statement annually.
- Protect your personal computers by using firewalls, anti-spam/virus software, update security patches and change passwords for Internet accounts.
- Don't give personal information over the phone, through the mail or the Internet unless you have either initiated the contact or are sure you know who is asking.

NOTE: The IRS does not initiate contact with taxpayers by email to request personal or financial information. This includes any type of electronic communication, such as text messages and social media channels.

What Happens Next

The IRS is supposed to provide an Identity Protection Personal Identification Number (IPIN) to each victim of refund/identity fraud. This would help them to get their refund faster in the future. The law requires it, but TIGTA found that 11% of taxpayers did not get this number and suffered because of it.

Some 759,446 taxpayers got an IPIN - but no instructions on what to do with it. The IPIN is like a second Social Security number.

Other Refund Frauds

The second part of this chapter deals with people who file false tax returns and collect big money from the IRS every year. It is a white collar crime that harms millions of taxpayers.

The Treasury Inspector General for Tax Administration (TIGTA) reports that nearly a quarter of the $63 billion worth of Earned Income Credits distributed in 2012 were improper payments. That's about $14.5 billion in payments to people who did not qualify for them.

In fact, there are areas of the country that are known for tax fraud, Miami being the best known. Anyone with a computer and some personal information of people can go into the identity fraud business and steal taxpayer's identities and refunds. It is not hard to do. You can buy stolen names, addresses, dates of birth and Social Security numbers on the internet as well as stolen credit reports. You can do anything you want with that information.

Abuse from taxpayers or in this case non-taxpayers included dozens of different fraudulent schemes:

- Earned Income Tax Credit fraud cost the IRS $17 billion a year in 2015
- Refund fraud/identity fraud is expected to cost the IRS $21 billion in 2016.
- Higher Education Tax Credit fraud costs $3.2 billion a year.
- Child Tax Credit fraud costs $5.9 billion a year.
- Alimony/child support fraud costs – in 2010 according to TIGTA, $2.3 billion was deducted from income by taxpayers paying alimony, but 47% of the people receiving the alimony don't report it at all.
- Additional Child Tax Credit fraud cost $7.2 billion a year

There is fraud associated with almost every line on the tax forms.

Two other major issues that show that the tax laws are not being applied fairly and equally are that by its own admission the IRS claims that **only 84% of all people with taxable income file and pay their**

taxes in a system that is based on voluntary compliance. All of the IRS Audit and Collection Activity only raise compliance by 2% to 86%. The audit and collection activity does yield $50 billion in increased revenue a year, but has little impact on the whole tax liable population.

The IRS acknowledges that at least 14% and some think as high as 20% of all income earners in the United States never file or pay income taxes. The IRS claims to not have the time, manpower or resources to go after them. It is much easier for the IRS to go after the W-2 wage earners and keep them in line, because that is where the income tax withholding and the Social Security and Medicare Tax Withholding come from.

Other scams are taxpayers who have learned that they do not need to file income tax returns and can still claim full credit for Social Security if they are W-2 wage earners, or if they are self-employed, they can file income taxes and claim the maximum Social Security benefit, but never pay the money in for the taxes. This can get involved, because they will have outstanding balances with the IRS, but usually they structure their financial affairs so they don't own anything anyway.

Business Identity Fraud

An emerging problem is with business identity fraud. This can occur because each 1099 or W-2 form contains a business's Employer Identification number (EIN) and address. This can be used to file for large tax refunds on business returns and is especially hard to find out about within the IRS system. Defunct businesses also have these EINs and they can be used without anyone knowing. In the past, every single county recorder's office in the United States had copies of the Notice of Federal Tax liens that contained names, addresses and Social Security numbers and Employer Identification numbers. About 12 years ago they reimaged the copies to block out the numbers. Originals of these documents still exist in most counties either on paper, computer images, microfiche or microfilm. These are all sources for Social Security numbers and Employer Identification numbers.

Individual Identity Fraud

The strange circumstances of each case are not considered. For instance – perhaps you have filed for years and make $24,000 a year. Suddenly you file and show income of $250,000 and request a $45,000 refund. Bam - you get the check. Estimates differ; as few as 40% of these refunds are issued up to a higher percentage for lower dollar refunds. Eighty percent of tax-related identity theft occurs through electronically filed tax returns. In 2014, the IRS processed 199 million individual income tax returns and 80% of them received refunds that averaged $3,000. Some received refunds in as little as 7 days. Let's think about that for a second. Approximately 159 million taxpayers in effect loaned the United States Government $374 billion, interest free, for up to a year. That is what happens. It is a huge scandal that taxpayers have grown comfortable with this system. Some use it as an automatic savings account - they are so happy to have the return of their own money - like it is an inheritance from some long lost uncle. You are losing potential income by not structuring your withholding to keep the minimum amount needed to satisfy your tax obligations. Any payroll manager or tax professional can assist you in filing a correct W-4 or you can compute it yourself using most tax software available.

Identity Fraud/Ghosting

This is when you or someone else uses your identity for fraudulent purposes. There are many cases like this before the IRS. Criminals steal the identities of people who are elderly, deceased, and mentally or physically disabled. It has become more frequent for them to use the identities of babies, children and teenagers who are deceased and create identities for them as well. In the past they could get information from a Notice of Federal Tax Lien. They would take advantage of the known lack of coordination between the IRS, Social Security and other federal agencies. Some people bribe employees who do payrolls for this information. They would manipulate the credit and banking systems to produce false entities that would then file for the IRS funds. That is why it is called ghosting.

Many people think white collar crime is one without a victim, as though it's no big deal. As you can see – identity fraud affects all of us, because of the strain upon the system to use resources to track and stop these criminals. These resources at the IRS and other federal agencies could be better utilized to assist taxpayers and help law-abiding citizens meet their obligations. If you suspect identity fraud against you or others, you should report the information to the IRS at 1-800-908-4490.

Chapter 16
Tax Planning For Your Life – From Birth to Death

This chapter will show you how tax laws can affect you from birth to death. It's also about all the life events that happen to you and your family in the process of life. There are so many tax laws and publications, forms and procedures that this chapter alone could be 1,000 pages. Instead of that we will refer you to a search term that can be used to bring you directly to the IRS search term that you need. The IRS website is very confusing and complex and does not use a Google search type of feature. So it is better to use Google or Bing with the appropriate search term to get you the information that you need to know right now. The best term to use for searching is underlined in each section below.

Because there are so many various laws and each person's life and tax situation is different, we suggest that if you read the Publication and cannot find an answer, then you can use the IRS Interactive Tax Assistant (ITA). Then if you have a lot of time and patience you can try to call the IRS at 1-800-829-1040. To find a local IRS office, use the search term IRS Contact Your Local Office and it will tell you what they do at that office and list their location and hours.

The Volunteer Income Tax Assistance (VITA) program offers free tax help to people who generally make $54,000 or less, persons with disabilities, the elderly and limited English-speaking taxpayers who need assistance in preparing their own tax returns. IRS-certified volunteers provide free basic income tax return preparation with electronic filing to qualified individuals.

In addition to VITA, the Tax Counseling for the Elderly (TCE) program offers free tax help for all taxpayers, particularly those who are 60 years of age and older, specializing in questions about pensions and retirement-related issues unique to seniors. The IRS-certified volunteers who provide tax counseling are often retired individuals associated with non-profit organizations that receive grants from the IRS. To locate the nearest VITA or TCE site, call 1-800-906-9887 or look for the VITA Locator Tool at irs.gov.

You can also consult a tax professional who will give you a more definitive answer. Many of the publications have been updated and made easier to read. They are still government publications and that can be like reading a legal document- lengthy, confusing and full of exceptions.

Use this search term IRS Tax Impact of Life Events. This page is organized by each type of life event and provides resources that explain the tax impacts of each event.

From Birth through Childhood

CREDITS

Earned Income Tax Credit Materials

The EITC is a tax credit for certain people who work and have an earned income under certain thresholds. A tax credit usually means more money in the pocket of those who qualify. Income and family size determine the amount of the EITC.

Health Coverage Tax Credit (HCTC)

The Health Coverage Tax Credit (HCTC) is a program that can help pay for nearly two-thirds of eligible individuals' health plan premiums. This website can help you figure out whether you are eligible for the HCTC and help you through the registration process. Please follow all instructions carefully so you and your family can receive the full benefit of this program.

Child Tax Credit

This credit is for people who have a qualifying child. It can be claimed in addition to the credit for child and dependent care expenses (see below). For more information on the Child Tax Credit, see Publication 972, Child Tax Credit.

Child and Dependent Care Credit

This is for expenses paid for the care of children under age 13, or for a disabled spouse or dependent, to enable the taxpayer to work. If you paid someone to care for a child or a dependent so you could work, you may be able to reduce your federal income tax by claiming the credit for child and dependent care expenses on your tax return.

There is a limit to the amount of qualifying expenses. The credit is a percentage of those qualifying expenses. For more information, see Publication 503, Child and Dependent Care Expenses.

Education Credits

There are two credits available, the American Opportunity Credit and the Lifetime Learning Credit, for people who pay higher education costs. The American Opportunity Credit is for the payment of the first four years of tuition and related expenses for an eligible student for whom the taxpayer claims an exemption on the tax return. The Lifetime Learning Credit is available for all post-secondary education for an unlimited number of years. A taxpayer cannot claim both credits for the same student in one year. For more information, see Publication 970, Tax Benefits for Education.

Child Adoption Issues

Use Google or Bing to search this term: EITC Home Page--It's easier than ever to find out if you qualify for EITC

If you worked but earned less than $53,267 during 2015, you may qualify for EITC. The Earned Income Tax Credit, sometimes called EIC, is a tax credit to help you keep more of what you earned. It is actually a work incentive program, where the Government pays you money just to go to work. You must file a return and claim the credit to receive it. Find out more about EITC and links to helpful tools and resources.

Adoption Credit at a Glance

The adoption tax credit is for qualified expenses paid to adopt an eligible child. The credit may be allowed for the adoption of a child with special needs, even if you do not have any qualified expenses.

Following are search terms to use to find additional information on the subjects listed:

- What is an Adoption Taxpayer Identification Number?
- Publication 972, Child Tax Credit
- Publication 970, Tax Benefits for Education
- Publication 929, Tax Rules for Children and Dependents
- Schedule EIC - Earned Income Tax Credit Can Lower Your Federal Tax Liabilities
- Form 8863, Education Credits (Hope and Lifetime Learning Credits)
- Publication 501, Exemptions, Standard Deductions, and Filing Status
- Form 8615, Tax for Children Under Age 14 Who Have Investment Income of More Than $1,600

Marriage

- Innocent Spouse
- Publication 555, Community Property
- Publication 971, Innocent Spouse Relief

- Marriage or Divorce - Check your Social Security Number

Divorce or Separations

- Pub 504, Divorced or Separated Individuals
- Publication 555, Community Property

Health Care Law

- Publication 5093, Health Care Online Resources
- Publication 5120, Facts about the Premium Tax Credit
- Publication 5120SP, Facts about the Premium Tax Credit
- Publication 5152, Report Changes to the Marketplace as They Happen
- Publication 5121, Facts about the Premium Tax Credit
- Publication 5156, Facts about the Individual Shared Responsibility
- Publication 5121SP, Facts about the Premium Tax Credit

Starting a New Career or Dealing With a Job Loss

- Withholding
- Unemployment
- Publication 531, Reporting Tip Income
- Independent Contractor or Employee?
- Publication 4128, Tax Impact of Job Loss
- Publication 969, Medical Savings Accounts
- Publication 529, Miscellaneous Deductions
- Publication 525, Taxable and Nontaxable Income
- Publication 505, Tax Withholding and Estimated Tax
- Form W-4, Employee's Withholding Allowance Certificate
- Publication 463, Travel, Entertainment, Gift, and Car Expenses
- Publication 587, Business Use of Your Home (Including Use of Home by Daycare Providers)
- Publication 4732, U.S. Taxpayers Living Abroad
- Publication 590 Individual Retirement Arrangements

PUBLICATIONS FOR OLDER AMERICANS

Planning for Retirement?

- Retirement Savings Contributions Credit (Savers Credit)
- Choosing a Retirement Plan: 403(b) Tax-Sheltered Annuity Plan
- Social Security and Equivalent Railroad Retirement Benefits
- Publication 554, Tax Guide for Seniors
- Publication 575, Pension and Annuity Income
- Publication 590A, Contributions to Individual Retirement Arrangements (IRAs)
- Publication 590B, Distributions from Individual Retirement Arrangements (IRAs)
- Publication 721, Tax Guide to U.S. Civil Service Retirement Benefits
- Publication 915, Social Security and Equivalent Railroad Retirement Benefits
- Mutual Fund Distributions
- Publication 4334, Simple IRA Publication
- Publication 17, Your Federal Income Tax
- Publication 523, Selling Your Home
- Form 8822, Change of Address
- Form 1040 (Schedule R), Credit for the Elderly or the Disabled

IRS Required Minimum Distributions for Retirement Plans

You generally have to start taking withdrawals from your IRA or retirement plan account when you reach age 70½. Roth IRAs do not require withdrawals until after the death of the owner.

Retirement Plan Contribution Limits

There are limits to how much employers and employees can contribute to a plan (or IRA) each year. The limits differ depending on the type of plan.

Withholding

- Pensions and Annuity Withholding
- Tax Withholding
- Form W-4P, Withholding Certificate for Pension or Annuity Payments
- Form 1040ES, Estimated Tax for Individuals
- Publication 3864, Brochure - Tax Facts for Seniors with a Change in Marital Status

Disasters and Casualties

- Tax Relief in Disaster Situations
- Publication 551, Basis of Assets
- Publication 547, Casualties, Disasters, and Thefts

Tax Scams/Consumer Alerts

The IRS urges taxpayers not to fall victim to tax scams. If it sounds too good to be true, it probably is.

Persons with Disabilities

- Disability and the Earned Income Tax Credit
- Publication 3966, Taxpayers with Disabilities
- Publication 502, Medical and Dental Expenses
- Publication 524, Credit for the Elderly or Disabled
- Publication 907, Tax Highlights for Persons with Disabilities
- Publication 3966, Taxpayers with Disabilities
- Publication 4334, Simple IRA Publication
- Publication 939, General Rules for Pensions and Annuities

First-Time Home Owner

- Publication 936, Home Mortgage Interest Deduction
- Publication 530, Tax Information for First-Time Homeowners

Moving?

- Form 3903, Moving Expenses
- Form 8822, Change of Address
- Publication 521, Moving Expenses Instructions Booklet
- Publication 523, Selling Your Home
- Publication 17, Your Federal Income Tax
- Publication 530, Tax Information for First-Time Homeowners

Bankruptcy

- Publication 908, Bankruptcy Tax Guide

Decedents (Deceased Taxpayer)

- Form 56, Notice Concerning Fiduciary Relationship
- Publication 559, Survivors, Executors and Administrators
- Form 1310, Statement of Person Claiming Refund Due a Deceased Taxpayer
- Form 4810, Request for Prompt Assessment under Internal Revenue Code Section 6501(d)

Local instructions on what to do- size of the estate- exemptions and what papers you need if you are going to do it yourself. This can be found by contacting your state taxing authority.

Get Transcript

You can get a transcript by mail to view your tax account transactions or line-by-line tax return information for a specific tax year. The method you used to file your return and whether you have a refund or balance due, affects your current year transcript availability. Note: If you need a copy of your return, you must use Form 4506, Request for Copy of Return.

You will need to go to irs.gov and enter "Get Transcript by Mail" in the search box. You will need your Social Security number (SSN) or your Individual Tax Identification Number (ITIN), date of birth, and address from your latest tax return.

The IRS will never send an email requesting that you obtain or access your transcripts. If you receive such an email, please forward it to the IRS fraud group at phishing@irs.gov.

There are five types of Transcripts. These can be used when you apply for a mortgage, student loans, state and local taxes, SBA loans, and FEMA/Disaster loans.

The types of transcripts available are:

- Tax Return Transcript – This is a line by line record of your tax return.
- Wage and Income - Best to order when you are trying to file your returns and are unsure what income was reported as being paid to you. These are not accurate and available until 13 months after the end of the tax year. For example, the 2015 tax information is not available until January, 2017. This is used for delinquent tax returns.
- Account Transcript – Best transcript if you have an audit or collection issue. It will tell you what your original tax was plus any additions to date.
- Record of Account – This shows that you have filed tax returns.

Tax Information for Students

Get Transcript

You can get a transcript to view your tax account transactions or line-by-line tax return information for a specific tax year.

Filing Your Taxes

Everything you need to file your individual federal income tax return.

Tax Benefit for Education Information Center

Many tax breaks are available to help with the cost of higher education.

Student Aid

This U.S. Department of Education Federal Student Aid website provides information about preparing for education, choosing a school, applying for admission, financial aid and more.

Interactive Tax Assistant (ITA)

The ITA tool is a tax law resource that takes you through a series of questions and provides you with responses to tax law questions.

This is similar to the way the popular program Turbo Tax guides you along to get an answer to your tax questions. This is supposed to replace the IRS Taxpayer Service assistance which no longer gives tax law or tax preparation advice.

Following are other topics by category and suggested search terms for use with Google or Bing. As you look through the topics, ask yourself or your tax professional the associated questions.

Affordable Care Act

- Am I eligible to claim the Premium Tax Credit?
- Am I eligible for a coverage exemption or required to make an Individual Shared Responsibility Payment?

General Filing Questions – use Google or Bing to search:

- Do I need to file a tax return?
- What is the due date of my federal tax return and am I eligible to request an extension?
- Who can I claim as a dependent?
- How much can I deduct for each exemption I claim?
- What is my filing status?
- What is the simplest form to use to file my taxes?
- How do I file a deceased person's tax return?
- Can I claim my personal and/or spousal exemption?

Deductions

- How much is my standard deduction?
- Can I deduct my charitable contributions?
- Can I deduct my mortgage-related expenses?

- Can I claim my expenses as miscellaneous itemized deductions on Schedule A (Form 1040)?
- Do I need to claim my gambling winnings and can I deduct my gambling losses?
- Can I deduct my medical and dental expenses?
- Can I deduct my moving expenses?
- Can I claim a deduction for student loan interest?

Credits

- Am I eligible for the Child Tax Credit?
- Am I eligible to claim an Education Credit?
- Do I qualify for the Credit for the Elderly or Disabled?

Income

- Is my pension or annuity payment taxable?
- Are my Social Security or Railroad Retirement Tier I benefits taxable?
- Do I have cancellation of debt income on my personal residence?
- Is my residential rental income taxable and/or are my expenses deductible?

Tax Information for Members of the Military

Get transcript

You can get a transcript to view your tax account transactions or line-by-line tax return information for a specific tax year. See above in this chapter for types of transcripts available.

Special tax considerations for veterans

Special tax considerations for disabled veterans occasionally result in a need for amended returns.

Filing your taxes

Everything you need to file your individual federal income tax return.

Publication 3, Armed Forces' Tax Guide

This publication covers the special tax situations of active members of the U.S. Armed Forces.

Special EITC rules

Special rules apply for calculating Earned Income Tax Credit or EITC for members of the military, ministers or members of the clergy.

FAQs regarding filing amended returns for disabled veterans

This covers frequently asked questions regarding special tax considerations for disabled veterans that may require filing amended returns.

Tax information for members of the U.S. Armed Forces

Members of the U.S. Armed Forces, especially those serving in combat zones, face some special tax situations and are entitled to some special tax benefits.

The Health Care Law: What's New for Individuals and Families

Most taxpayers will simply need to check a box on their tax return to indicate they had health coverage for all of 2015. This includes coverage from an employer, Health Insurance Marketplace coverage, and government-sponsored programs like most types of Medicare, Medicaid, CHIP, most types of TRICARE coverage, and comprehensive health care programs offered by the Department of Veterans Affairs.

Employers with employees in a combat zone

FAQs for employers whose workers deploy to a combat zone

Retirement plans FAQs regarding USERRA and SSCRA

Insights into the re-employment of veterans and the restoration of retirement plan benefits, as affected by the Uniformed Services and Reemployment Rights Act (USERRA) and the Veterans and Sailors Civil Relief Act (SSCRA).

Miscellaneous provisions — combat zone service

Deceased persons – probate, filing estate and individual returns, paying taxes due

This page provides information to help you resolve the final tax issues of a deceased person and their estate. As the surviving spouse, executor, estate administrator or other legal representative of a deceased person and their estate, you will have many responsibilities.

Deceased persons - Getting Information from the IRS

Find out how to receive tax information of a decedent or their estate.

Understanding the general duties as an estate administrator

Learn about the general responsibilities of the legal representative for the decedent and his or her estate.

Getting the IRS to file a proof of claim in a probate proceeding

Find out which IRS office to contact for assistance – search Contacting IRS.

Filing the final return(s) of a deceased person

Learn about filing requirements, getting transcripts and payment arrangements.

Filing the estate/trust income tax return (Form 1041)

The fiduciary of a domestic decedent's estate, trust, or bankruptcy estate files this form to report:

- The income, deductions, gains, losses, etc. of the estate or trust,
- The income that is either accumulated or held for future distribution or distributed currently to the beneficiaries,
- Any income tax liability of the estate or trust, and
- Employment taxes on wages paid to household employees.

Selling real property that is part of the decedent's estate

This page provides instructions on how to obtain a release of lien on the decedent's property.

Protecting the deceased's identity from ID theft

Here you will find tips to reduce the risk of having a deceased person's identity stolen.

Filing estate and/or gift tax returns (Forms 706 or 709)

Provides links to various topics on Estate and Gift tax issues.

Getting an International Estate Transfer Certificate

When tax due resulting from the filing of Form 706-NA is paid, the estate administrator may request a Transfer Certificate so that the decedent's property may be transferred without liability. Transfer Certificates are releases of the federal estate tax lien on a decedent's property.

Publication 559, Survivors, Executors, and Administrators

This publication is designed to help those in charge (personal representatives) of the property (estate) of an individual who has died (decedent). It shows them how to complete and file federal income tax returns and explains their responsibility to pay any taxes due on behalf of the decedent.

Chapter 17
Church and Charity Work- What You Need to Know Before You Volunteer

In this chapter we will talk about how to help others or causes that you are attracted to through the use of a not-for-profit organization. These are called 501(c)(3) entities. Many people do their own private works of charity, but being involved with a tax-exempt organized charity gives you a tax benefit for doing so. Your cash contributions become tax deductions. We will present what you can expect when you are on a board of directors and what liability you may have personally and how to protect yourself. Then we will touch on how you may also be able to protect the organization from problems common to non-profits.

How to Form a Charitable/Not for Profit Group

APPLYING FOR 501(C)(3) TAX-EXEMPT STATUS

Federal tax law provides tax benefits to nonprofit organizations recognized as exempt from federal income tax under section 501(c)(3) of the Internal Revenue Code (IRC). It requires that most organizations apply to the Internal Revenue Service (IRS) for that status. Use Google or Bing to search for IRS Publication 4220, which presents general guidelines for organizations that seek tax-exempt status under section 501(c)(3) of the IRC. Content includes references to the statute, Treasury regulations, other IRS publications that explain the requirements for tax-exempt status, and IRS forms with instructions. Publication 4220 is neither comprehensive nor intended to address every situation. As an alternative to applying for exemption, an organization may obtain many of the benefits of 501(c)(3) status by affiliating with an existing charity that acts as its agent.

It is important to note that the existing charity must be given full control and authority over the program. To learn more about the rules and procedures that pertain to organizations applying for exemption from federal income tax under section 501(c)(3) of the IRC, see Publication 557, Tax-Exempt Status for Your Organization. For assistance on 501(c)(3) status, you may also want to consult a tax adviser, attorney, or CPA.

WHY APPLY FOR 501(C)(3) STATUS?

The benefits of having 501(c)(3) status include exemption from federal income tax and eligibility to receive tax-deductible charitable contributions. To qualify for these benefits, most organizations must file an application with, and be recognized by, the IRS as described in Publication 4220. Another benefit is that some organizations may be exempt from certain employment taxes.

Individual and corporate donors are more likely to support organizations with 501(c)(3) status because their donations can be tax deductible. Recognition of exemption under section 501(c)(3) of the Internal Revenue Code assures foundations and other grant-making institutions that they are issuing grants or sponsorships to permitted beneficiaries.

An IRS determination of 501(c)(3) status is recognized and accepted for other purposes. For example, state and local officials may grant exemption from income, sales or property taxes. In addition, the U.S. Postal Service offers reduced postal rates to certain organizations.

WHO IS ELIGIBLE FOR 501(C)(3) STATUS?

There are three key components for an organization to be exempt from federal income tax under section 501(c)(3) of the IRC. A not-for-profit (i.e., nonprofit) organization must be organized and operated exclusively for one or more exempt purposes.

Organized – A 501(c)(3) organization must be organized as a corporation, trust, or unincorporated association. An organization's organizing documents (articles of incorporation, trust documents, articles of association) must: limit its purposes to those described in section 501(c)(3) of the IRC; not expressly permit activities that do not further its exempt purpose(s), i.e., unrelated activities; and, permanently dedicate its assets to exempt purposes.

Operated – Because a substantial portion of an organization's activities must further its exempt purpose(s), certain other activities are prohibited or restricted including, but not limited to, the following activities. A 501(c)(3) organization: must absolutely refrain from participating in the political campaigns of candidates for local, state, or federal office; must restrict its lobbying activities to an insubstantial part of its total activities; must ensure that its earnings do not inure to the benefit of any private shareholder or individual; must not operate for the benefit of private interests such as those of its founder, the founder's family, its shareholders or persons controlled by such interests; must not operate for the primary purpose of conducting a trade or business that is not related to its exempt purpose, such as a school's operation of a factory; and must not have purposes or activities that are illegal or violate fundamental public policy.

Exempt Purpose – To be tax exempt, an organization must have one or more exempt purposes, stated in its organizing document. Section 501(c)(3) of the IRC lists the following exempt purposes:

charitable, educational, religious, scientific, literary, fostering national or international sports competition, preventing cruelty to children or animals, and testing for public safety.

501(C)(3) ORGANIZATIONS

The most common types of 501(c)(3) organizations are charitable, educational, and religious.

CHARITABLE

Charitable organizations conduct activities that promote: relief of the poor, the distressed, or the underprivileged; advancement of religion; advancement of education or science; erection or maintenance of public buildings, monuments, or works; lessening the burdens of government; lessening neighborhood tensions; eliminating prejudice and discrimination; defending human and civil rights secured by law; or combating community deterioration and juvenile delinquency.

EDUCATIONAL

Educational organizations include: schools such as a primary or secondary school, college, or a professional or trade school; organizations that conduct public discussion groups, forums, panels, lectures, or similar programs; organizations that present a course of instruction by means of correspondence or through the use of television or radio; museums, zoos, planetariums, symphony orchestras, nonprofit day-care centers; and youth sports organizations.

RELIGIOUS

The term church includes synagogues, temples, mosques, and similar types of organizations. Although the IRC excludes these organizations from the requirement to file an application for exemption, many churches voluntarily file applications for exemption. Such recognition by the IRS assures church leaders, members, and contributors that the church is tax exempt under section 501(c)(3) of the IRC and qualifies for related tax benefits. Other religious organizations that do not carry out the functions of a church, such as mission organizations, speakers' organizations, nondenominational ministries, ecumenical organizations, or faith-based social agencies, may qualify for exemption. These organizations must apply for exemption from the IRS. See Publication 1828, Tax Guide for Churches and Religious Organizations, for more details.

All of these organizations are required by law to have a board of directors who tell the charity what it can do and how it will do it. The laws of the state where it is incorporated or otherwise organized require that the charity has Articles of Incorporation that describes what the charity can and might do. For instance, a charity formed to help the homeless cannot use the money collected to own and run a dog shelter instead. The charity cannot pay the volunteers or members of its board of directors for all the work that they do. That is why they are called volunteers, after all. Nonprofits have Articles of Incorporation that govern everything that they can do. It is a good idea to solicit help from an attorney or CPA to prepare the documents as well as get them a place on your board of directors, because a little knowledge about nonprofits and tax laws goes a long way. The third most important person is your insurance agent who will issue a liability policy that will protect you from lawsuits that you might face personally because of your actions on the board of directors.

WHAT RESPONSIBILITIES ACCOMPANY 501(C)(3) STATUS?

While conferring benefits on 501(c)(3) organizations, federal tax law also imposes responsibilities on organizations receiving that status.

RECORDKEEPING

Section 501(c)(3) organizations are required to keep books and records detailing all activities, both financial and nonfinancial. Financial information, particularly information on its sources of support (contributions, grants, sponsorships, and other sources of revenue) is crucial to determining an organization's private foundation status. See Publications 4221-PC and 4221-PF, Publication 557, and the instructions to Forms 990, 990-EZ, and 990-PF for more information.

FILING REQUIREMENTS

Annual Information Returns – Organizations recognized as tax exempt under section 501(c)(3) of the IRC may be required to file an annual information return- Form 990, Form 990-EZ, 990-N (see below) or Form 990-PF along with certain schedules that may be required for the organization. Certain categories of organizations are exempt from filing Form 990 or Form 990-EZ, including churches.

See the instructions with each of these forms for more information. See the listed publications and instructions in the "Recordkeeping" section above for more information and guidance.

Annual Electronic Notice – To meet their annual filing requirement, organizations with gross receipts normally $50,000 or less may choose to submit an annual electronic notice using Form 990-N, Electronic Notice (e-Postcard) for Tax-Exempt Organizations Not Required to File Form 990 or 990-EZ. The e-Postcard can only be filed electronically; there is no paper version. For more information about the e-Postcard, go to www.irs.gov/Charities-&-Non-Profits.

Any organization that fails to file a required annual return or notice for three consecutive years will automatically lose its tax-exempt status, by act of law, as of the due date of the return for the third consecutive year.

Right of Public Inspection – All Section 501 (c)(3) organizations must make their applications and annual returns (Form 990, Form 990-EZ and Form 990-PF) available to the public for three years starting with the filing date of the return. We have found that a private organization called The Foundation Center makes this information easy to access. See FoundationCenter.org

Unrelated Business Income Tax – In addition to filing Form 990, 990-EZ, or 990-PF, an exempt organization must file Form 990-T if it has $1,000 or more of gross income from an unrelated trade or business during the year. The organization must make quarterly payments of estimated tax on unrelated business income if it expects its tax liability for the year to be $500 or more. The organization may use Form 990-W to help calculate the amount of estimated payments required. In general, the tax is imposed on income from a regularly carried-on trade or business that does not further the organization's exempt purposes (other than by providing funds). See Publication 598, Tax on Unrelated Business Income of Exempt Organizations, and the Form 990-T instructions for more information.

ORGANIZATIONS NOT REQUIRED TO FILE FORM 1023

Some organizations are not required to file Form 1023 or 1023-EZ. These include:

Churches, interchurch organizations of local units of a church, conventions or associations of churches, integrated auxiliaries of a church, such as a men's or women's organization, religious school, mission society, or youth group.

Any organization (other than a private foundation) normally having annual gross receipts of not more than $5,000 (see Gross receipts test, later).

These organizations are exempt automatically if they meet the requirements of section 501(c)(3).

Filing Form 1023 to establish exemption - If the organization wants to establish its exemption with the IRS and receive a ruling or determination letter recognizing its exempt status, it should file Form 1023 or 1023-EZ (if eligible). By establishing its exemption, potential contributors are assured by the IRS that contributions will be deductible. A subordinate organization (other than a private foundation) covered by a group exemption letter does not have to submit a Form 1023 for itself.

Private Foundations - See Private Foundations and Public Charities, later in this chapter, for more information about the additional notice required from an organization in order for it not to be presumed to be a private foundation and for the additional information required from a private foundation claiming to be an operating foundation.

Gross Receipts Test – for purposes of the gross receipts test, an organization normally does not have more than $5,000 annually in gross receipts if:

1. During its first tax year the organization received gross receipts of $7,500 or less,
2. During its first 2 years the organization had a total of $12,000 or less in gross receipts, and
3. In the case of an organization that has been in existence for at least 3 years, the total gross receipts received by the organization during the immediately preceding 2 years, plus the current year, are $15,000 or less.

WHAT YOU ARE RESPONSIBLE FOR AS A MEMBER OF THE BOARD OF DIRECTORS

You might have been a member of an organization or have done volunteer work for them. One day you receive a call from someone on the board of directors asking you if you would be interested in helping to direct the affairs of the nonprofit. You have no idea what that means, but you like the sound of your name being associated with being on a board of directors and you really like the cause that they are fund raising for; you really believe in its values and goals. Additionally, you may have some fun doing what you do to help others.

Welcome to the world of the board of directors. It is very simple at first. You show up at the first board meeting and everyone is happy you have joined and shakes your hand. You smile, they smile and then they tell you what they expect from you. It could be a minimum donation every year, or so many hours per month of your time, or you may be assigned to be the president, vice president, secretary or treasurer. You will also be assigned to committees like the fundraising committee or the finance committee. You might be assigned to travel to national conventions of your parent group. Time, money and your ability to make decisions will affect what the charity does and how it does it, and other than a free lunch or reimbursement of expenses, you are not being paid. So hopefully you are getting a warm feeling in your heart for doing good deeds.

Let's start by figuring out what you might be doing for the organization. If it has a manager and employees, then the board will become the boss/employer of those people. The board will authorize collecting and receiving donations so that these employees can be paid. If the board does not have enough money to do this, you will have to lay off or fire employees. The whole board will vote on it of course, but you are now part of the board.

You are protected from personal liability in most of the actions of the board, but you should insist that the organization pay for at least a $1 million umbrella liability insurance policy. Depending what your organization does, you may need a much larger policy as well. The corporation, which is how most charities are organized, provides you with the protection of the corporate shield. There are things you can do, however, that could cause you to be personally liable for your actions as a member of the board:

- If you personally sign any payroll checks and do not pay the payroll taxes into the IRS or state authority, you could be liable for the Trust Fund Recovery Penalty. It used to be that just being on a board could make you personally liable, but that changed in 1998. So unless you do some direct action, like authorizing that only the net payroll be funded without providing for tax payments, you can escape liability.

- If you sign for a bank loan or business loan personally and the organization defaults, you can be held personally liable for the debt.
- If you co-mingle nonprofit and personal funds or embezzle money, you are personally liable for that.
- If you as a member of the board authorize anything that is not in the charter of the organization or is illegal or fraudulent, you can be held personally liable.

Being a part of the charitable organization is all well and good and makes people feel good about themselves and the cause to which they are contributing. Now the real work has to be done: the many hours planning what the board of directors wants to do with the money, making a list of the priorities and goals of the organization. There is never enough money for all that the volunteers want to do. So if you are on the board, you need to make tough decisions on where to spend what was donated.

If you have a social services program, such as one that houses runaway children and you have a 24-hour residential facility, you need to pay the rent, the utilities, and the cost for the managers and employees, the food, transportation costs and medical costs. You probably need social workers and counselors to minister to the children and also probably a coordinator to figure out how much the federal and state government and other charities are willing to pay for some of the services that you provide. Of course, if any of these are paid employees, you will need to budget the various employment taxes.

So far so good, right? But what if there is an accusation of child abuse? If that accusation is reported to the government agency that is funding your organization, they usually immediately cut off your funding pending an investigation. So what do you do? You have workers there 24 hours a day. You try to make it up by getting new donations, but that is hard because people will shy away from the charity if they believe that the allegations are true.

In one case that we saw, the manager of a not-for-profit and a board member were both required to sign each check issued at the bank. The manager was told by the board of directors to continue paying the employees, but not to pay in the income and Social Security taxes for them. This is called funding the net payroll only. For every $100,000 in payroll, he should have been withholding $30,000 and sending the money into the government. He did what he was told and the board member also agreed. The board assured him that although hefty tax balances were piling up, they would protect him and cover it when the money came in again.

The child abuse investigation against the not-for-profit took one and a half years and the organization was cleared of any wrong doing. At that point the charity owed $400,000 in back taxes; it had taken money from its daily outreach programs to fund the 24/7 operations and finally were so far behind, that they were bankrupt. So the organization closed its doors and this poor manager and the board member who had so believed that the money would be paid were personally assessed $280,000 in Trust Fund Recovery Penalty assessments. No one else on the board of directors was found to be personally liable for these taxes. Both the manager and the board member also received a Notice of Federal Tax Lien that destroyed his credit for the next ten years. The Trust Fund Recovery Penalty is not dischargeable in bankruptcy.

Trust Fund Recovery Penalty Assessments - The Trust Fund Recovery Penalty, applicable to withheld income and employment (Social Security and Railroad Retirement) taxes or collected excise taxes, will be used to facilitate the collection of tax and enhance voluntary compliance. If a business has failed to collect or pay over income and employment taxes, or has failed to pay over collected excise taxes, the Trust Fund Recovery Penalty may be asserted against those determined to have been responsible and willful in failing to pay over the tax. Responsibility and willfulness must both be established. The withheld income and employment taxes or collected excise taxes will be collected only once, whether from the business, or from one or more of its responsible persons.

DETERMINATION OF RESPONSIBLE PERSONS

Responsibility is a matter of status, duty, and authority. Those performing ministerial acts without exercising independent judgment will not be deemed responsible.

In general, non-owner employees of the business entity, who act solely under the dominion and control of others, and who are not in a position to make independent decisions on behalf of the business entity, will not be assessed the trust fund recovery penalty. The penalty shall not be imposed on unpaid, volunteer members of any board of trustees or directors of an organization referred to in section 501 of the Internal Revenue Code to the extent such members are solely serving in an honorary capacity, do not participate in the day-to-day or financial operations of the organization, and/or do not have knowledge of the failure on which such penalty is imposed.

In this case, the whole board was also considered for the assessment but the IRS decided to go after only the manager and the one board member who signed checks. The case is significant because when they knowingly voted to approve a payroll budget that did not also pay the taxes, they exposed themselves to personal tax liability. In this case, the board members had few personal assets and that is why the IRS chose not to assess the penalty against them.

BENEFITS YOU CAN RECEIVE FROM YOUR ORGANIZATION

Your nonprofit can educate its volunteers that some of the expenses that they incur are tax deductions to them. These are small dollar amounts and can be for out of pocket expenses, mileage, and travel expenses.

For example, board members might deduct unreimbursed phone, postage, and copying charges associated with preparing for meetings.

THE EFFECT OF CHARTER DOCUMENTS

Any specific requirements for Articles of Incorporation and other corporate charter documents will be found in the nonprofit corporation statute of the state of incorporation. Generally, these requirements are pretty limited and place most of the responsibility for defining what the corporation will do, and how it will do it, on the people who draft each organization's documents. Not surprisingly, nonprofit corporation statutes usually prohibit the distribution of profits to owners, stockholders, or anyone else. (Payments for services rendered, and for anything used in the work, are of course allowed.) "Profit" is the surplus an organization has at the end of an accounting period. There is no prohibition on nonprofit corporations having profits. What can't happen is paying any part of such profits to owners or anyone else.

Every nonprofit's Articles of Incorporation will have to state the purposes for which the corporation is formed. It's common for the Articles to list some specific purposes and then to add a phrase like "and for any lawful purpose." This part of the drafting needs to be done with care—the advice of a knowledgeable attorney is usually very helpful—to be sure the corporation will qualify as exempt from federal corporate income taxes under the Internal Revenue Code. There's more about this topic below in the federal tax exemption section.

Any organization that wants to qualify for federal tax exemption will also need to take care in drafting the section of its Articles that addresses the question of what happens when or if it ceases operations. The basic point is that any assets that remain (money, furniture, buildings, etc.) when the organization is no longer operating for its "exempt purposes" must be distributed to another tax-exempt organization with similar purposes. The IRS will not recognize an organization that doesn't undertake to follow that rule, and any other disposition of assets at the time of dissolution is calling out for trouble with state or federal authorities.

Charitable nonprofits are divided into two broad categories by the Internal Revenue Code. "Private Foundations" is the category for organizations (primarily grant makers) that are supported by investment earnings or a small group of large donors (often a family or a corporation). The others are known as "Public Charities" - groups that are supported by program service income, grants and contracts from governments or foundations, and larger numbers of individual donors. Private foundations pay an excise tax on their investment earnings and are subject to stricter rules about their operations than public charities.

WHO IS LIABLE WHEN YOU OR A VOLUNTEER GETS HURT WHILE WORKING FOR THE CHARITY?

Our experience is that that the largest bodily injury exposure often comes from accidents or incidents caused by volunteers.

When they hear "volunteer liability", many people think about liability to volunteers, and not always about liability caused by volunteers for the organization.

Because of this misconception, some volunteer organizations do not purchase adequate insurance. Some buy "volunteer accident" insurance policies only and feel well protected from liability. But this kind of insurance addresses only one kind of liability associated with the utilization of volunteers — that of injury to the volunteer. Injury caused by a volunteer is generally not covered by such a policy.

Volunteer accident policies provide a certain limit of coverage, usually for medical expenses. They respond when a volunteer is injured in an accident while engaged in activities for the benefit of the organization.

HOW DO YOU PROTECT YOURSELF?

When you are on a board of directors, you need to make sure that you are financially and legally protected. You need liability insurance protection. Board members have been named as defendants in lawsuits due to some neglect or actions that they took or failed to take as a board member.

As a board member you are the trustee for the business side of the charity. You have a fiduciary duty to the organization. Many board members do not understand this legal liability and how important it is to both them and the organization.

You should have liability insurance for the organization, for each board member and possibly for yourself. In the end, you should be covered so you never have to pay out of your pocket for tax professionals or attorneys to protect you in the event of lawsuits or government actions,

"State and federal laws provide some protection with volunteer-immunity laws when a person is acting in good faith. But insurance also can safeguard board members and the organization from federal civil-rights and antidiscrimination suits, which aren't typically covered by those immunity laws," according to Illona Bray, J.D.

Churches and charitable organizations can do amazing work and actually make you feel good, because you are part of that work. But you need to protect yourself, in case something goes wrong. If you need more information talk to a tax professional for more information. Some CPAs specialize in working with not-for-profit organizations.

—∾—

Chapter 18
What Do You Really Pay in Taxes?

"I am proud to be paying taxes in the United States. The only thing is I could be just as proud, for half the money." Arthur Godfrey, Entertainer

The object of this book is to figure out how you can take advantage of IRS tax laws and procedures, loopholes and other methods that will save you money on your taxes.

This can get very confusing. You probably already think that you pay a lot in taxes. You do, but some of it is hidden. Tax systems are designed to be confusing. Otherwise people would truly understand what was going on and revolt.

If you are an employee, as of 2015, you are paying 6.2% for Social Security plus 1.45% for Medicare - and your employer pays the same. This totals 15.3%. This tax only applies to the first $117,000 you earn. A person earning $50 million a year pays the same amount as you. Senator Bernie Sanders claims that "if we lifted this cap on income above $250,000, we could extend the solvency of Social Security for another 47 years." Plus, unemployment insurance is paid for you through your employer. We estimate it to be 1% in most cases.

If you are self-employed you have to pay 12.4% for Social Security and 2.9% for Medicare. That equals 15.3%.

You may also have income tax withholding. In this estimate we will say 20% is being withheld for the IRS and 3% to your state of residence.

Depending on where you live you also have state income tax (average 3%) and township, county, city income tax, plus taxes for local school districts. In some places there is also a real estate transfer tax that you pay just for buying a house. State income taxes are all over the board and vary widely. They range from no state income tax in Alaska, Florida, Nevada, South Dakota, Texas, Washington and Wyoming to the highest tax rates of California 12.3%, Hawaii 11%, and Massachusetts 12%.

So just for going to work, for every $1000 you earn the government takes approximately 7.65% for Social Security/Medicare Tax plus your income tax withholding of 20% and your State Income tax withholding of 3%. So for starters you are paying almost 31% in taxes.

You are left with $690.00; less if you contribute to an IRA or pension plan. If you are self-employed, you are only left with $657.00.

OK, so you got out of your office with what is left of your check. Then you get into your car, which was already taxed with a sales tax when you bought it. Then you have licenses, stickers and other fees from the government (they can be 6-10 %.) You look at your tires; they seem worn out. There is a special excise tax just for tire sales. Then you put gas in the car and yes, gas is taxed at the federal, state and sometimes local levels. Federal excise taxes are 18.4 cents per gallon for gas and diesel. The State of Arizona adds 18.4 cents per gallon and the California state fuel tax is 39.5 cents per gallon. There is also the LUST Tax which is 1 cent per gallon. Sounds exciting right? This is paid on leaking underground storage tanks. (This applies to old gas stations that have closed and left their rotting tanks in the ground.)

You get in the car and turn on the air conditioning and you have already paid a tax on the Freon gas that is used to make the system work. If you stop at the store on the way home there are taxes on your food and non-food items, sometimes at different rates. You are taxed on your cigarette and cigar purchases; this is a separate excise tax over the sales tax. You also pay a federal liquor tax on your spirits, wine and beer. There may also be a tax from state and local liquor agencies. Actually, the truck that brought all that food and liquor and supplies to the store had to pay the federal highway use tax, just to get what you need to the store.

If you stop and buy a gun, watercraft, bullets, a bow and arrow or a fishing rod you pay a special excise tax. When you go home your real estate taxes might be 3% or more of the value of your home. If you rent, these taxes are included in your rent. Sometimes your landlord will also have to pay taxes for the right to rent to you, which is also included in your rent.

These taxes are built into the price that you pay for the goods and services you want. If you buy an RV for traveling you pay a recreational vehicle tax. There used to be luxury taxes on furs, diamonds, jewelry and other luxury items.

Sales taxes are not charged in five states - Alaska, Delaware, Montana, New Hampshire and Oregon. They are the highest in California where the state sales tax is 7.5% but when county and local taxing districts add on their taxes they can approach 12%. Sales taxes, especially on food, are regressive. A poor person and a rich person both buying a loaf of bread pay at far different levels, because the rich person has more money to spend and the poor person is paying a tax, but has far fewer dollars to spend. In this example, regressive means unfair. In some places, food and prescriptions are not taxed at all or are taxed at a lower rate.

All of your utilities are taxed, often from federal, state and local levels.

While you drive and talk on the phone you are also paying federal excise taxes, federal universal service taxes, and well as state and local telephone taxes. In some places you pay taxes on internet and cable access. Airplane tickets have a federal tax of 7.5% of every ticket plus $4.

Federal and state governments have other taxes that you pay

indirectly, like corporate income tax - this is usually passed along to the consumer as a higher cost to the item.

On top of all this you pay other taxes when you are required to get a building permit, a driver's license, a vehicle license plate, tolls and fees for toll roads, bridges and ferries.

The spread of taxation and the complexity of it are overwhelming and terrifying. People are trained by society to just try to earn more money to get the things that they want.

Some financial experts estimate that you may only have 40-50% of your paycheck after you have paid all these taxes.

When you add in the fact that your money is worth less every year due to inflation, it is no wonder that citizens at all levels are financially challenged. Since 1975, according to the Bureau of Labor Statistics and the Consumer Price Index, one study says the inflation rate has been 352% or about 3.85% a year. The federal minimum wage was $2.10 in 1975 so using this calculation it should be $9.49 in 2015 rather than the current $7.25. The minimum wage is almost 24% lower than it should be, so people that are working are hurt by this thief, inflation. Inflation is like a quiet tax, because it erodes the buying power of taxpayers.

Seventy percent of the income earners in the United States make less than $60,000 per year, which is why most Americans (53%) do not pay federal income taxes. This is because of their income levels, and because they qualify for credits, exemptions and deductions that reduce their taxable income.

According to IRS data in 2011:

- The top 1% of earners paid 35% of all income taxes
- The top 10% paid 56% of all income taxes
- The top 25% paid 86% of all income taxes.

Now when we say the top, we might think of very wealthy people but only a small percentage are super wealthy.

Thirty-six percent in the top of the upper 25% of earners have adjusted gross incomes of $120,136 to $388,905.

The top 1% has adjusted gross incomes of $388,905 or more, and while that certainly makes them comfortable, it does not make them super rich.

Only 1% of the top one percent made more than $1 million.

About half of the top 1% percent had incomes of $368,000 to $443,000. That income does not go far in Manhattan, Chicago or San Francisco, but it is very comfortable for most people living elsewhere. While income is taxed more at higher levels, the taxes that these taxpayers pay are usually lower because of various tax breaks for the wealthy, and the fact that stock dividends are taxed at only 15% when the taxpayer's tax rate is 25% on other income. People with wealth are more likely to own stocks, and this is a huge benefit to those with dividend income.

The multi-billionaire Warren Buffett has claimed on more than one occasion that his secretary pays more in income taxes than he does. This is true because she has wages that are taxed at the rate of 10% to 39.5%. Mr. Buffett is more likely to have income from dividends, interest and capital gains. Capital gains were only taxed at 15% for years. Now capital gains have increased to 20% but it is still less than many people pay for wage and self-employment income.

Sixty percent of the people who are in the top 25% of income earners only make from $70,492 to $120,136.

The income tax falls heavily on the middle and upper income levels.

Whatever we pay in taxes, it seems like too much for most people, so we hope that this chapter helps to keep you focused on creating tax strategies to lower your tax burden, even such things as simple as opening an IRA or having a side business.

Chapter 19
Are Income Taxes Really Legal?

A client asked us, "My friend told me I don't have to file or pay taxes because the 16th Amendment, which created the income tax laws, was not properly ratified. Plus, I heard that the Supreme Court overruled the income tax and said it was unconstitutional. Is this true?"

We responded that the United States Congress made the Internal Revenue Code (IRC) which is a collection of tax laws that are administered by the Internal Revenue Service. The current IRC was ratified by Congress in 1916, 1926, 1939, 1954, and 1986. It is also codified as Title 26 of the United States Code. No one could possibly know everything in the IRC. It is 73,854 pages long and growing. It is complex and confusing and that is exactly the way that Congress likes it.

We responded to our client that part of his friend's story is correct; the Supreme Court said the Income Tax of 1894 was found to be unconstitutional and it was struck down in 1895.

The legality of the current Internal Revenue Code has been upheld in U.S. Courts and the Supreme Court, time after time.

Many clients and friends have told us that they "know a guy" who just stopped paying income taxes. Sometimes they learn about this information at club meetings, union meetings, churches or from family or friends. There are many stories being circulated about how to quit your connection with the Internal Revenue Service. All might be considered helpful in figuring out what you should do, but none are legal. If you try this, you can lose everything you own.

In our years of experience in the IRS we have known some former taxpayers who have dropped out of the tax system. There are penalties and consequences for their choices which we will explain later in the chapter.

Still there are many people who listen to and believe the arguments that tax protester promoters make as to why you should leave the tax system. So it may not be you who is thinking of "dropping out of the IRS System" but you may know some people who are considering that option.

The top arguments used by "tax protesters" against income taxes are:

- The most frequently heard argument is that the 16th Amendment which established the right for the federal government to institute an income tax was not properly ratified.
- The second argument is that the Supreme Court has ruled that the income tax was illegal and overturned the law. Completely correct! But that was the Income Tax Law of 1895 which was overturned, not the 1916 version of the Internal Revenue Code.
- The Constitution says that filing a tax return violates a person's 5th amendment right to not incriminate themselves.
- The 13th amendment to the Constitution prohibits involuntary servitude and slavery. Some people think that compulsory taxation is a form of slavery.
- Article 1, Section 10 of the Constitution gives the federal government the power to create and regulate money, which excludes Federal Reserve Notes (your dollars) because they are not backed by silver or gold. So your dollars are not really taxable according to them.
- Filing a tax return is "voluntary". In fact, the IRS uses this term frequently. If you fail to "volunteer" then the IRS will prepare income tax and business tax returns for you. These returns will always overstate your real tax liability.

- Some people declare themselves to be "sovereign citizens" of their own country. This sovereign citizen movement is very closely watched by the IRS and other federal law enforcement agencies.
- Some people say that any money you earn on federal land is taxable, but not anywhere else in the United States. So if you were selling cold drinks on the steps of the U.S. Capital it would be taxable income for you. But if you were across the street on private land your sales would be non-taxable. Some of these people think that the only "real United States" is in the District of Columbia (Washington D.C.) and federal territories like Puerto Rico and Guam and military bases.

There is an excellent summary of these tax protester arguments found on Wikipedia under "Tax Protester Sixteenth Amendment Articles."

One woman in Chicago filed 13 false tax returns for herself, her family and her friends who then received $8 million in fraudulent refunds after they declared themselves "sovereign citizens". The IRS paid out the money, before it figured out that this was a tax refund scam. Some of the so-called "sovereign citizens" ended up in prison.

Violate Tax Laws at Your Own Risk!

The IRS spends a disproportional amount of time and resources working on tax protester/frivolous return/tax avoidance filer cases. By giving so much time, resources and energy to these cases they are actually empowering these tax resistors and their causes. We do believe that cases where the protesters are actively recruiting other taxpayers to stop filing and paying taxes should still be followed.

The National Taxpayer Advocate, Nina Olson in her annual statement said that under "Internal Revenue Code 6702 which deals with frivolous returns, that the law was not supposed to aimed at taxpayers who had acted erroneously and had done so in good faith." She said "that the IRS is applying the frivolous return penalties so broadly to some taxpayers that it encompasses unintentional tax errors and occasionally even undermines constitutional protections that taxpayers have."

Consequences of Not Filing or Paying Taxes

There are people who do not want to pay taxes at all. One such group of people advocates bringing down the government through passive or violent methods. This group was once classified by the IRS as "Illegal Tax Protesters". Tax protestor was a term that the IRS used to describe a person or organization that advocated non-filing and/or non-payment of federal tax returns and balances due. Technically the IRS was required to stop using that term after 1998, but you can believe that it still vigorously tracks such illegal activity. Now the IRS refers to taxpayer's anti-tax arguments as frivolous or by quoting tax law that refers to such argument(s) as "tax protester arguments or rhetoric." Another relatively new term used is "tax deniers."

There are people who are either protesting the use of the tax money, saying they do not wish to pay for war or atomic weapons, or they are people who are challenging the legality of the tax laws. Protesting is not against the law. Regardless of why they are protesting, these people are still being tracked by the IRS. You can protest but still pay, or can stop filing and paying. The latter is against the law and will get you into trouble eventually. Now, the IRS may classify violent people as PDT - Potentially Dangerous Taxpayers - or others as Frivolous Return Filers, or non-filers. This is kind of like being found guilty of something but without any legal hearing. No 1st Amendment rights or due process rights are in force here; however, you should become familiar with the IRS Taxpayer Bill of Rights found on www.irs.gov.

Some people will make claims that they do not want to pay taxes and then see if they can get away with it. Others are violent and promote violence against the U.S. government or IRS agents/officers. They post signs around their properties that their home is not in the United States of America and that they are sovereign citizens in their own sovereign countries and that IRS and other U.S. government agents will be shot, if they trespass.

A prime example is a story of what happened to two Revenue Officers in a southern state known for harboring violent tax protesters. The ROs were sent to do a seizure of property for nonpayment of taxes. The taxpayer had been afforded many opportunities to pay, but had refused. When the ROs arrived at the site where the property was located, they were met by the taxpayer and friends, all well-armed. The protesters threw gasoline on one of the RO's personal vehicle and attempted to throw a lit match into the bed of that pick-up truck. The ROs left quickly and the case was turned over to Criminal Investigation and TIGTA. Those taxpayers were classified as Potentially Dangerous and were arrested, tried in criminal court and sentenced to a federal prison.

The former IRS Historian Shelly L. Davis stated that the IRS kept lists of citizens "for no other reason than their political activities might have offended someone at the IRS." She charged that "anyone who offers even legitimate criticism of the tax collector is labeled as a tax protester."

Financial Penalties of Not Filing and Paying Taxes

The accuracy related penalty can be 20%, (Internal Revenue Code 6662), civil fraud penalty 75% (IRC 6663), and erroneous claim for refund penalty 20% (IRC 6676). Late filing of a return penalty regarded as being frivolous can be another 75% in penalties (IRC 6651 (f)). The IRS has a list of what it describes as frivolous tax positions at www.irs.gov. If you claim that the income tax is illegal or you don't have to pay, and you refuse to pay, you will be assessed the penalty.

When a person files a return that claims what the IRS calls frivolous arguments, the IRS will send out a Letter 3176C which gives the person 30 days to change their mind about whatever it was they were claiming on the tax return. If they do not "take it back," then the IRS will assess a $5,000 to $20,000 penalty for each tax year where the taxpayer submits frivolous returns. This is on top of any tax, penalty or interest that the person might already owe.

This is a bad place to be, since getting the penalties taken away is very difficult. In fact, even to ask that they take the penalties away will cost $250 to $500 just to ask the IRS to consider abating the penalty. This is only for Form 14402 Internal Revenue Code (IRC) Section 6702 (d) Frivolous Tax Submissions Penalty Reduction. It does everything short of making you swear allegiance to the United States again. If you have been penalized and also owe income tax balances the IRS won't even consider your request for penalty abatement, until you become current with filing and paying all of your taxes.

Tax Protester Promoters

We have also met several well-known people who organized thousands of people by telling them they did not need to file or pay taxes. The IRS called them "Tax Protesters Promoters." They officially advertised they had never filed or paid federal income taxes. People believed them. The ones who did not file or pay went to jail. Really now, don't you think the other tax avoidance promoters really did file and pay their taxes? Makes you wonder. The IRS could never say yes or no publicly without the alleged tax protester's consent. And since your tax records are always confidential, that would never happen. Those people make a lot of money traveling around fleecing people who get into trouble with the IRS years later.

Voluntary Compliance

We want to be very clear how the IRS feels about people who do not follow their directive to voluntarily comply with filing and paying tax returns. The system is "voluntary" until you do not volunteer to do it and then it becomes mandatory and you will be forced to comply with the tax laws. Policy Statement 5-1 (IRM 1.2.14.1.1) states that "Enforcement is a necessary component of a voluntary assessment system", and that a tax system based on voluntary assessment would not be viable without enforcement programs to ensure compliance. The IRS is responsible for compelling non-compliant taxpayers to file their returns and pay their taxes. Enforcement actions should be taken promptly against those who have not shown a good faith effort to comply with the tax laws.

These actions include enforcement necessary to move the taxpayer toward compliance.

We have seen taxpayers who have attempted to withdraw from the tax system and although they survive, they have no secure income, they cannot own anything, and they live in fear that the IRS will seize whatever they have whenever they find it. Their greed develops into a sort of madness of selfish isolation.

We can acknowledge that taxes are high and the only way to get them lower is through referendums, Constitutional Amendments and Acts of Congress. An unfair tax system alienates citizens from their own government.

The Consequences of Dropping Out of the Tax System

If you try to go it alone and declare yourself no longer part of the United States, you would need to learn to live without a Social Security card, bank accounts or savings in your own name. You would not be able to hold a wage-paying job, and whatever your work it would need to be temporary and transitory. You could not rent or own a car, truck, apartment or house in your own name. You would live in constant fear that the IRS or other taxing agencies would come and seize everything that you own. You would not be able to have a health insurance or life insurance policy. If you became unemployed as a wage earner, you would not be able to receive unemployment benefits or Social Security Disability Income. You would no longer be qualified for or able to claim a Social Security check even if you are old and feeble.

You might be able to beat the IRS, and we have seen a few cases where former taxpayers have done this. You will only be able to get by with a lot of help from your friends and family who will have to give you space in their homes and take care of you if you are unable to work.

The safest place for you to be is to file and pay your taxes in a timely manner. Make full use of all legitimate tax breaks that you qualify for, because the costs of being a sovereign citizen, patriot or tax protester are great.

The results of using those methods can be litigation, loss of income and property and even jail. As convincing as all those arguments are, they are not true and valid.

The IRS should stop trying to draw a line in the sand and prove a point with people who refuse to pay their taxes due to moral, constitutional, anti-war or other reasons to protest. We have seen the IRS spend so much money on tax protester programs where it brought no increased filing or paying compliance. So much money is being spent there that could be going to other places where their efforts would result in increased filing and paying compliance.

Chapter 20
IRS Survival Strategies

—∞—

The following is a list of the most often asked IRS questions and answers to guide you in your contacts with the IRS.

Question: I don't know how to respond to the IRS. What do I do?
Answer: Read what they have sent you. There is important information regarding your rights buried in that pile of papers that you received in the mail. Study the system and figure out what you have to do first. Then give them exactly the information they request. Determine what they are trying to use that information for and then learn your rights; be prepared to file an appeal at every opportunity. If you are talking to an employee, then write down their employee number and also request their eFax phone number or you may never be able to locate them again.

Question: I have been calling the IRS for days and they never pick up, or leave me on hold for over 2 hours before they answer. What should I do?
Answer: The IRS is so short staffed that it admits that at least 60% of all calls will not be answered during peak periods. A written letter of inquiry or response should be sent certified mail to the address found on the last letter that you received.

Question: I am poor with keeping receipts and records. Now I got a notice that the IRS is going to audit me. What do I do?
Answer: Do not despair! There is a rule named the Cohan Rule, after the composer of the song "I'm a Yankee Doodle Dandy," by George M. Cohan. It is a ruling by Judge Learned Hand that establishes that if you are busy earning a living and not keeping track of your expenses you can still be entitled to estimate your expenses and receive credit for them on your tax return, as long as they can establish some basis for the deduction. In Mr. Cohan's case he was also an entertainer who traveled and did shows all across the United States, so he could back-track and explain that he had train fare and food while on the road and hotel room expenses.

The IRS would prefer to use Section 274 of the Internal Revenue Code, but with a good CPA or Tax Attorney, you might find relief using, at least in part, the Cohan Rule.

Question: Can I go to jail for not paying my taxes?
Answer: Yes, but the odds are against it. Eighty-two percent of all people convicted go to prison. That number is less than 4,000 a year on average. If you are being audited or owe the IRS, your life will seem like a living hell for a while, but jail will not be involved. If you have income and do not file tax returns, then yes you can be investigated by the Criminal Investigation (CI) special agents and their goal is for you to be found guilty in court and go to jail. Fraud or misrepresentations made to the government will also get IRS attention. However, because of significantly lower staffing numbers in CI, many fraud cases with amounts under $100,000 are not even accepted for criminal investigation.

Question: I have an approved installment agreement to pay my back taxes, but they still keep charging me a failure to pay penalty. Why?
Answer: Because that is what Congress put in the law. You pay this penalty even when you are making payments. The failure to pay

penalty is applied even when a person is in an installment agreement. It can be applied at the rate of 5% per month up to a maximum of 25%. Congress can change this but has not. Also a delinquent taxpayer faces penalties for failure to file in an amount as high as 25%, penalties for failure to pay in an amount as much as 25%, plus an estimated tax payment penalty of approximately 1%, with the potential for other penalties for accuracy errors, or fraud and interest. Penalties can be as much as 150% of the original tax balance. A $1,000 can quickly grow to $1,500.

Question: I have an installment agreement and I had extra money so I sent three monthly payments all at the same time. Now I got a letter that they are defaulting my agreement. Why?
Answer: You can send three separate checks towards your installment agreement and hope they post them correctly, but mostly they won't. Just send one check every month. There is a built in skip on every installment agreement. If you miss one payment it will not automatically default the agreement. The IRS does not advertise this. Many people miss a payment and then worry and start calling or writing the IRS, which is not prepared to respond.

Question: I am a small businessman, I report my credit card sales, but not my cash income. The IRS can never catch me - right?
Answer: The IRS identifies all businesses that have assets less than $10 million as small businesses. It does not depend on the amount; you are structuring your business to evade taxes. That is illegal. They can catch you in a dozen ways. In one case, prostitutes were targeted for nonpayment. It was a massage parlor. So the IRS went to the laundry that supplied its sheets and towels and used that number to back into the number of clients that they provided with services and the average that they would have paid. Or there was the case of the blacksmith/metal fabrication workshop. He had never filed tax returns and claimed to have no income. The IRS went to his steel supplier and

reconstructed his income that way. It may have been too high - but he was forced to either accept that the IRS prepared number or file his own returns with the proof of what he put on the returns. So yes you can get caught. IRS revenue agents are well trained in those types of indirect methods of reconstructing cash basis business income. There are even handbooks for various industries with average income and expenses expected for that industry. When the IRS has the will there is always a way.

The informal motto of The IRS Criminal Investigation is "Greed follows prosperity and we follow greed." They will look for the most egregious cases of non-tax compliance and prosecute them. The IRS claims a 92% conviction rate. Tax criminals usually receive 18-25 month sentences in a Federal Prison. The chances of you getting caught are about the same as you winning the lottery. If you are unlucky or extremely greedy and this happens to you, the mental, emotional, and health-related costs of a criminal investigation will depress, deplete and destroy you.

Question: My tax return is going to be different from what other people file, because I donate a lot of money to charity. What should I do?
Answer: When you file your return, make sure you keep all of your donation records and the copy of the receiver's letter proving it and the check you used to make the donation. You should attach photocopies of all your proof to the return and that will prevent an audit. There are many audit triggers and this includes high donations to charity - especially if they exceed 50% of Adjusted Gross Income.

Question: I want to avoid an audit. What will trigger an audit?
Answer: There are many things that will trigger an audit. Most of them are only known by a few in the IRS. This is determined by what areas the IRS wants to investigate in that tax year. Sometimes it will go after certain types of business, like realtors or beauty shops/barbers.

Or it will question certain types of expenses like losses or business expenses.

The Nation Research Project (NRP) audit is an audit on everything in your life, and returns are randomly selected for this project. They will want to see your marriage certificate, Social Security cards, spouse and children's cards and birth certificates, etc. Some audits are based on your lifestyle. You must be able to show that you make enough money and that you report it to show how you pay for your lifestyle.

Question: I have a corporation and corporations hardly ever get audited. My CPA told me the odds are good it will not get audited. Is this true?

Answer: Every year about 33,000 corporate income tax returns are audited by Revenue Agents who come to your business and sit there looking at your records for days or weeks. They always are there to come up with a tax balance. Don't put anything on the return that you cannot prove or does not have some basis in the law. Large businesses get even closer attention, because anything that corporation does will have a major and far reaching impact that could have large and immediate tax consequences. NRP projects are also being done on corporate and partnership returns. As stated above, these are the "luck of the draw", so never assume you are safe.

Question: I heard that all my income is taxable. I sold my comic book collection, my car and had a garage sale. Is this all taxable income? How would the IRS ever find out?

Answer: The Internal Revenue Code states that all "gross income from whatever sources legal or illegal is taxable." You have some basis in the collections and the car that you can subtract from the sales prices (what you paid for the comic books or car and the contents of the garage). The IRS can find out if you make a lot of money because most people are afraid to keep cash and put money in the bank or buy something for cash - beyond their known income level. Cash leaves an audit trail. This can occur with sales on Amazon and EBay or selling antiques, or expensive automobiles that have increased in value. People who watch shows like CSI think that the IRS and the Treasury Department already know everything about everyone, and if they don't, they can easily find it out. It is true that with a summons, the IRS can get all of your information; it is not instant and it is not easy. They can get access to every detail about your life. The IRS may request every transaction, every financial document, phone records, credit card records, passport records, once an audit is started or when there is a tax balance due.

Question: I have a $6.5 million estate and am trying to avoid the estate tax by using "pay on death" and joint tenant's accounts at the bank and on my properties.
Answer: Good idea, but it is illegal. You are trying to evade taxation. If the IRS finds out, they will construct an Estate Tax Return for you and assess taxes and go to all those people you left your estate to and collect from them directly. There are many legal ways to reduce estate taxes. Consult a tax attorney.

Question: Can I get an installment agreement if I owe the IRS?
Answer: Yes, if you owe under $10,000 or can pay it down to that amount, you qualify for an automatic agreement. You also easily qualify for an installment agreement if you owe $50,000 or less. Under this agreement it can be without a Notice of Federal Tax Lien being filed.

Question: I like to receive my refund every year. It is usually about $3,000. It is like a forced savings account. Is this a good idea?
Answer: Let's see: you are making an interest free loan to the Government every year and you are happy? The Government holds your money for 12-16 months and you are paying interest on any credit card balances that you have. Think about it; this forced IRS savings plan is probably costing you 10-25% in credit card interest every year.

You should adjust your withholding and then pay off any credit cards balances, then set up an automatic savings plan.

Question: I was told the IRS tracks when people buy vacation homes, expensive cars, homes, artwork and other collectibles. Is that true?
Answer: No myth - it is correct that they can. However, they do not systematically track these purchases. Large cash transactions leave a trail for the IRS to follow. It is likely to come up if you are under audit or your tax preparer is under audit.

Question: I heard that you can get cash awards from turning in your neighbors, friends, family and employer for tax crimes. Is that true?
Answer: Yes, it is true that you can collect 15-30% of the amount the government eventually collects because of the information that you provided. The largest payout was to a convicted criminal who was also an informant. He also spent 2 ½ years in jail. He received $104 million, which worked out to be $4,600 for every hour he spent in prison. The IRS hotline number is 1-800-829-0433 for information. You will need to file Form 211 to actually report the alleged tax violation. They no longer accept information over the telephone. All reports can be done anonymously, but then you will not be able to claim the informant's award.

Question: I filed my return and forgot to include income. I am afraid to amend the return because someone told me that would trigger an audit. Is this correct?
Answer: Wrong. Amended returns are routinely processed. It is rare for them to be assigned to a field auditor.

Question: I was really scared by the IRS Agent when he was at my door; he said horrible things. Is this what will happen when I try to deal with them in the future or should I hire a tax professional?
Answer: Each IRS employee is different. You will find many of the

stories and orders that you were told to do by the Agent or Officer were not actually what they were supposed to legally say to you. You will notice how differently they speak if you hire a tax professional. If you feel that you have been harassed you can contact TIGTA and report that employee: 1-800-366-4484.

Question: Someone told me that he has a business and writes off all of his expenses so he ends every tax year with no taxable income. Is that possible?
Answer: It is for a while. The IRS expects that you should make a profit in 3 out of the first 5 years of a business, or the IRS may disallow all expenses and reclassify your business as your hobby. There are exceptions to every type of business. In fact, the Internal Revenue Code does not use the term "hobby." The business may have a loss that can be supported beyond the first three years. The IRS looks at a person's total income and lifestyle to determine if it is a business that is motivated to make a profit.

Question: When I was finally able to pay my many-years-old IRS tax balance, I was given a payoff amount by the government agent and then 4 months later the IRS came back and said I owe something called accrued failure to pay penalty and interest for another $12,154. How can this be - what can I do about it?
Answer: Nothing can be done, unless you can convince that agent and his manager that the government made false representations and made an error that damaged you. That is rare. The reason that this happened is because the old IRS computer can only assess failure to pay penalty if there is a credit balance on the account. So when you made a large payment, a credit was on the account that triggered the computer to calculate the failure to pay penalty, which can grow to 25% of what your tax was to be calculated. The worst part of this is that it may have been years since this penalty was last calculated. You can ask for the penalty to be abated but this is rare; plus, the IRS will

generally not abate interest in a case like this either. In the meantime, that old computer cannot charge interest on the penalty that is accruing but has not been assessed. This hurts both the taxpayer and the Government and costs millions of dollars every year. This is not fair or equitable to those taxpayers who pay earlier. The Treasury Inspector General estimates that this costs the Government $171 million a year in lost interest.

Question: My friend said she had identity fraud happen to her where someone used her name and address and Social Security number to get a large refund. She said it took over a year for her to get her actual refund and for the IRS to resolve it and she felt like the IRS was treating her like a criminal. She is a retired old lady - she only gets Social Security - how can this happen?
Answer: It happens because the IRS is overwhelmed and unprepared to identify and battle identity fraud. TIGTA has issued its own reports that find that customers with identity and refund fraud do not receive quality customer service. Currently, the IRS is training more employees to resolve identity theft as the number of cases has increased dramatically over the years.

Question: The IRS sent a letter telling me they were holding my current year's refund (which I need to pay medical expenses) because I have not filed in the last five years. I was taking care of my dying mother and had no income. What should I do?
Answer: Write or call them immediately to explain the circumstances. It is better to write and send the details as to why you did not file. Send it certified mail with a return receipt requested. After six months they have to issue the refund with 3% interest. Request a copy from the IRS of any income reported under your name and Social Security number for the past five years. If you do not get a fast resolution, you should file a Form 911 telling that this is causing you hardship. You will talk to the Taxpayer Advocate which is a watchdog part of the IRS.

The Taxpayer Advocate will only accept your case if you have made numerous contacts with the IRS and have been unable to resolve your case. They can be very effective when they help a taxpayer. Or you can seek help from the manager of the person that you speak to on your phone call. Or you can write to your Senator, Member of Congress or the President seeking help.

Question: I am afraid the IRS will come and seize my house or car or business. What can I do?
Answer: The IRS can seize your house, but probably won't. Happily, the number of seizures is down from 12,000 a year to an average of 764 a year, in the last 5 years. The IRS did 25% less seizures in 2013 than in 2012 and we project this number will continue to decline due to loss of experienced employees who know how to use the seizure tool effectively.

Question: What triggers an audit?
Answer: Just filing a tax return enters you in the "IRS Tax Lottery". Every single item on a return can be questioned. Using the DIF (Discriminant Index Function) (the score used to determine which cases should be audited. The IRS will scrutinize large, unusual or questionable items. (LUQ). They will compare your return to millions of other people or businesses like you. They will make sure that your income is sufficient to support your exemptions claimed and your lifestyle.

Question: If I sell my house, can I keep all the profits and pay no income tax?
Answer: Yes and no. Consult a tax professional. You will have to live in your house for a certain amount of time and only a certain amount of money is exempt. The IRS does not have an effective online computer follow-up that allows them to monitor when and how much you sold your last home for and how much you made or lost on the sale. This

is what you must provide in an audit. If you have a cash sale, there is usually no record monitored by the IRS to track that, unless the cash transaction is large and is processed through a bank or title company.

Question: I received an IRS letter that said I should have tip income. Why?
Answer: What did you write on your tax return under occupation? Waiter? Bartender? Taxi driver? Beautician? Barber? Hair designer? Porter? Doorman? The IRS keeps it pretty simple. They respond to what you tell them. If you are in a job where tips are the norm, they will ask why you do not have any tips. If you receive a W-2 it will indicate if you should be reporting tips. That is how the IRS knows to look for tip income.

Question: How do I get out of the tax system once and for all?
Answer: You can die and in most cases that will get your Social Security number permanently closed on both the IRS and the Social Security computers. That computer program is known as the "Death Master File." Some people have tried to bribe employees to do that. Some IRS and Social Security employees have been arrested for taking money for doing just that.

Otherwise, you can try to live with the IRS after you. No Social Security, no disability, no unemployment, and no benefits of our society, like food stamps, welfare or medical assistance. Today you need a Social Security number for almost everything, even to open a bank account or to have credit. So it is almost impossible to disappear these days. That is why many people have figured out how to use corporations and LLCs and holding companies to water down income and pay no income taxes.

Question: A friend told me that tax avoidance is illegal. Is that true?
Answer: Tax avoidance is both legal and encouraged by the IRS. Tax evasion is illegal.

Question: I am old and disabled. I want to file my taxes but am unable to pay for it. I just want to walk-in to the IRS and have them answer my questions and help me do my returns. How do I do this?
Answer: As of January, 2014, IRS walk-in offices/taxpayer assistance sites stopped providing answers to tax law questions, no longer gives tax law advice, and they will not help old, sick or handicapped people file their tax returns. There are programs outside the IRS such as Tax Counseling for the Elderly (TCE) administered by AARP. Look in the local phone book for VITA (Volunteer Income Tax Assistance) or check with your local library.

If you try to call the IRS with a question, good luck! Due to budget cuts they answered roughly 40% of incoming calls in 2015. Some weeks they only answered 10% of incoming calls. Even tax professionals can be on hold for 2 hours. We have heard of one story where a taxpayer called in the late afternoon and the IRS employee picked up the phone and said her shift ended in ten minutes and that she could not help them, so she hung up!

If you write them a letter you may just receive a letter telling you that they are behind and need 45-60 days to respond to you and then you may not ever hear from them again. There are some free software programs where you can prepare your own tax return. The IRS website will post "free file" links that can be used for free tax preparation, but only online. Unfortunately, many people do not own or have access to a computer or even know how to use a computer.

Question: I want to do one of those Offer in Compromises that they talk about so much on the radio and television. What are the odds of me getting such a deal?
Answer: There were 11.5 million delinquent taxpayers in 2013; of these only 74,000 offers were filed and only 31,000 (42%) offers in compromises were accepted. That is only .002% of all delinquent tax cases. The IRS does accept some offers because the taxpayer is old, sick or has access to money that the Government would not be able to

reach. You have a better chance at getting an installment agreement, or having your collection or audit account deferred for a few years. If you have a financial hardship, ask that your case be declared "currently not collectible". Your odds might be better if you buy a lottery ticket and then win enough money to just pay the IRS and be done with it. The ads on TV showing that everyone is settling their tax debts with the IRS for pennies on the dollar are wrong. Do not think that you can negotiate with the IRS by threatening bankruptcy or because you want a better deal. Offers are determined by your numbers, not your speech.

Question: I don't make enough to get audited. True?
Answer: If your income is less than $25,000, there is a less than .1% chance that you will be audited. If your income is under $25,000 you probably have more important things to worry about like paying your rent, car payment and buying food.

If your income is under $200,000, there is only a 1% (or less!) chance that you will be audited. Incomes above $200,000 have an audit chance of 3%. This has made some people reckless with the information that they put on tax returns. In 2015 the IRS did 1.2 million individual audits, 350,000 less than five years ago. This is down 22%. These are the fewest audits since the 1980s. In part this is because additional information filing requirements allow the IRS to match more data reported to them with the data you put on your tax return. Audits are a way to bring fear into the equation. The audit is where you have to bring in your actual books and receipts and prove what you claimed on the tax return. Unlike the IRS of the old days, when the auditors had more discretionary power, now there is very little reasonableness during an audit. You either have the records or you lose that deduction. During an audit, you will be asked dozens of questions that are designed to make you disclose income or gifts that you may have forgotten to list on the tax return. In that forum, you are presumed guilty until you can prove yourself innocent.

There were 100,000 fewer audits in 2014. There was be no collection on 190,000 cases in collection in 2015, due to a reduced number of employees. This means 3 billion dollars will not even attempt to be collected in 2015. In fact, three Automated Collection Sites (ACS) were closed and the employees were reassigned to work on identity fraud cases instead. These do not yield any tax money to the government. The odds are against being selected for an audit, if the taxpayer puts down reasonable expenses in relation to their income. The IRS tracks this and builds accounting models via the NRP program. So they know the percentage that people would normally have for housing/ mortgage interest, real estate taxes, medical expenses and charitable contributions.

The IRS has business models by industry and by market. The IRS knows that a dentist, for instance, would have certain expenses in a statistical range. They look for deviations from the norm. It works pretty well at locating audit targets.

Question: I move often, and I file every year, so the IRS always knows where I am. So I don't think I need to file a change of address (Form 8822) - Is that correct?

Answer: Wrong. Part of the IRS may know where you are. The auditor or tax collector may not. He may send letters raising your taxes to the address you listed on the return. Your mail forwarding order will have expired and they will audit you, make big tax assessments and then start collection against you. This includes the Notice of Federal Tax Lien, one of the greatest tools of IRS Collection, all without your knowledge. In our credit based society, this can destroy your financial life for the next ten years. All because the auditor does not try to find out your new address - which might already be somewhere else on the IRS computer. You must file Form 8822, the IRS Change of Address Form.

Question: If I just ignore these letters from the IRS will they stop some day?
Answer: Sorry! The IRS never forgets you. One day they will come to your door. Seize the day and if you can't handle talking to the IRS, hire a tax professional to help you out.

Question: If I have an installment agreement, then will the IRS stop charging me the Failure to Pay Penalty?
Answer: No! You pay this penalty up to 25% for as long as you have a tax balance due, installment agreement or not.

Question: My friend told me I don't have to file or pay taxes because the 16th Amendment, which created the Income Tax laws, was not properly ratified. Plus I heard that the Supreme Court overruled the income tax and said it was unconstitutional. Is this true?
Answer: This is misinformation. All federal courts have upheld the income tax law that was passed in 1916. It is correct that the Supreme Court said that an older, different income tax law passed in 1894 was unconstitutional and it was struck down in 1895. Following this advice will get you in big trouble and the IRS will assess huge penalties against you.

Question: The Internal Revenue Service advertises that the tax system is based on voluntary compliance. Can I refuse to "volunteer?"
Answer: Bad choice! The IRS likes you to think that you have some choice about whether you should file and pay taxes. When you don't, watch how fast they force you into compliance.

Question: Cash income like gambling winnings, tips, and other cash income is non-taxable. The IRS can't prove it anyway. Am I right?
Answer: Wrong! The IRS can look at your lifestyle and see what you have paid for rent, mortgage, car payments, education costs, insurance utilities, etc. and add it all up and then make up tax returns for you and

you will owe money. Plus, casinos are required to file 1099-G for any amounts over $600. Other tools are in place to trace large cash transactions. Eventually, you will get caught if you live a lifestyle beyond the income expressed on your tax return.

Question: Will I get a bigger refund if I go to a CPA or tax preparer?
Answer: If you have a complex return you can go to ten tax professionals and get 10 different tax returns results. Some unscrupulous preparers will prepare fraudulent returns that will guarantee you large refunds. Later they get caught and you get audited. If something sounds too good to be true, it usually is. Many IRS employees and ex-employees use Turbo Tax - but there are many programs that are pretty easy to use if you choose to do the returns yourself.

Question: Can the IRS revenue officers, revenue agents or tax compliance officers arrest me and put me in jail?
Answer: No! They do not have that power. They can make your life a living hell and you may wish you were in a quiet jail cell. IRS criminal special agents can make arrests and so can TIGTA special agents. Revenue officers, revenue agents and tax compliance officers can refer you to IRS Criminal Investigation for investigation for tax evasion, tax fraud or perjury. This can then lead to your arrest for tax crimes.

Question: If I wait to file until October 15 (on extension) is it true that I will not get audited, because the IRS runs the lists comparing income reported with income reporting systems in June?
Answer: Wrong! All returns get a DIF Score (Discriminate Index Function) and that score will always be reviewed and if it is high enough you will get audited (if the IRS has enough people to work the audit).

Question: What does the DIF score look for when it is comparing my numbers to other taxpayers?

Answer: We have seen home office, travel and entertainment, casualty losses and charitable contributions deductions most often. We have also seen Foreign Bank and Financial Account Form (FBAR) as a cause for an audit. The funny part of this is that each return is reviewed by a DIF examiner who may have their own standards - so it is a very subjective process.

Question: A friend told me that the IRS also uses special projects to audit groups of people. They choose different businesses and individuals each year. Is that true?
Answer: Very true. In a recent year, the IRS went after S-corporations, real estate partnerships, construction companies and individuals earning over $1 million. They also like to audit people who list numbers in their tax returns that do not match up to other data that has been reported to the IRS.

Question: If I don't have any assets in my name, the IRS cannot do anything to me, right?
Answer: Partially correct; instead you can live a life where you work for cash and are paid every day and own nothing; you have no bank account, car or ownership in anything. The IRS can come after your friends, family and significant others and for example ask why they have assets when they do not have any means of support - no way to pay the mortgages or other expenses. One attorney who was a big gambler and playboy had a huge house and put it in his girlfriend's name and went out drinking, gambling and carousing every night but not with her. When the IRS knocked on the door, the girlfriend answered. She talked at length, she shared some information about how she owned the house according to public records and that she could do whatever she wanted with it. One day a month later she had kicked him out of the $600,000 house that was in her name and paid for in cash and had taken back his expensive BMW also in her name and also paid for in cash.

Question: If I am fair and honest with the IRS, will the IRS be fair and honest and reasonable with me?
Answer: Keep dreaming! Many people have wished for this to happen, failed to get representation on complex tax matters (because they thought they could do it themselves and save money) and have lost millions of dollars, experienced hardships and lost valuable rights that they did not even know they had. Protect yourself first, get the best advice you can afford about your tax situation.

Question: Can I ever get the IRS off my back? I filed on time and owe back taxes from 5 years ago. They keep sending me threatening letters.
Answer: Taxes that were filed on time and are more than three years since the due date and filing of the return may be dischargeable in bankruptcy court. See a bankruptcy lawyer.

Question: Will the Taxpayer Bill of Rights make the IRS protect me?
Answer: No! The IRS is run by people and some people are nice and some are not. Wake up! You may get some protections from it, but you have to exercise all your rights. Most IRS rights expire in time.

Question: The IRS can't take my wages or bank account or my retirement account or my house without going into court and allowing me to have my day in court, right?
Answer: Very wrong! The IRS can take most everything you own, just based on the testimony of the IRS revenue officer or criminal special agent in a secret session they hold with a federal Judge. You have some rights after the seizure. If you don't have a good tax professional even those rights will evaporate with time.

Question: If I disagree with the IRS - can I fight them in court?
Answer: Yes and no. To even get into U. S. Tax Court will cost you as much as $20,000 for the attorney and filing fees. Many people would be helped if they used the IRS Appeals system first if they have a

disagreement. It is very rare for an individual to be able to go to tax court and win against the IRS.

Question: I always thought the IRS was there to help me.
Answer: Wrong! The IRS is here to audit tax returns, look for tax cheats, unreported income, collect money and close cases! It is designed to assess and collect new tax balances. It talks about doing the right thing, but its first mission is to audit and collect money.

Question: I heard I don't need to keep my receipts or tax records because of the tax law changing. Is that true?
Answer: Wrong! That is very limited and applies to tax court. If you are audited or suspected of tax fraud you will need your records. The IRS can assess new taxes against you generally for 3 years, but if you have omitted over 25% of your income it can assess up to 6 years. There is no statute of limitations on fraud. I have seen cases going back 25 years. So in a criminal case it is common for the last ten years to be looked at. If record storage is a problem, you should scan them into your computer and then also save them on a cloud. Be aware that many cash register receipts have ink that fades and will disappear in a year or so. Having adequate tax records means that you have both the bill and the proof that you paid that bill. That is how you can defend your deductions in an audit.

Question: I don't want to file tax returns or pay taxes because I don't like big government; I don't want to pay for armies and wars; I don't want to pay for nuclear weapons, and I don't want to pay for food stamps and welfare. Can't the government just leave me alone?
Answer: Remember high school civics class. You vote and elect people to represent you and they determine how much to tax you and how the money will be spent. If the IRS knows you have income and you do not file taxes it will make up perfectly legal returns allowing you no deductions under the Substitute for Return (SFR) program. No one

in the IRS cares what you think about the tax system or public affairs.

Question: I have a business and don't want to file the employment tax returns. What can happen?
Answer: The IRS will estimate how much they think you owe - add 20% - and then file returns for you. The good part of both of this is if you pay the tax balances plus penalty and interest, you are accepting the tax returns as filed and so is the IRS. So they can't come after you later to make changes. This will hurt your employees if they need Social Security disability or unemployment checks when they file their tax returns.

Question: Do I have rights before the IRS?
Answer: You only have rights if you know about them and use them. Read Publication 1 - Your Taxpayer Rights. Most people don't. Either they don't read all the letters explaining the rights or they don't understand them or they don't file timely responses and appeals.

Question: It is time to file my tax return and I am short $10,000. I am just going to wait until I get the money and then I will file and send the money I owe. Will this work?
Answer: No. File on time or the IRS will assess a Failure to File Penalty of 5% a month for 5 months up to 25%. If you file five months late you will owe another 5 % per month up to 25%.

Question: If I have an installment agreement with the IRS - I don't have to pay any penalties. Right?
Answer: Wrong. You will be charged either 5% a month for failure to pay penalty - even while you are making payments or if they choose .5% a month for up to 50 months, the IRS will decide.

Question: I heard that if I structure my business with many partners in a large partnership, it makes it too hard for the IRS to audit the business. Is this true?
Answer: Yes, an effective Audit Avoidance Plan is to form a Large Partnership. In fact, when the person does not want the IRS to monitor their tax affairs then, it is good to be organized as a partnership. Large partnerships (assets over $100 million) have an audit rate of only .8% according to the Government Accountability Office. Because a partnership does not pay any tax itself, it passes whatever loss or profit down to its partners. So the IRS has to audit not just the partnership, but also the individual partners at least on that issue. This results in huge audit cases and most of the time the IRS is not prepared for that. Audit rate for corporations with assets over $10 million fell by 20% between 2013 and 2014. There were 300,000 less of these audits in 2015.

Question: Is it true that the IRS can't make me do anything -even respond to their summons and subpoenas?
Answer: You are incorrect and wrong. The IRS will document that you are ignoring your tax obligations and you will be in contempt of the Internal Revenue Service and they will refer you to the Department of Justice which will bring you before a federal judge who will give you a chance to testify or produce records and then if you refuse - the Judge will throw you in jail for being in contempt of court. Usually the U.S. Marshal will actually arrest you. Many people are currently in jail for this offence.

Question: If I get audited will I owe more in taxes?
Answer: Not always. In fact, about almost 2 in 10 people who get audited get refunds or no change is made to their taxes.

Question: My friend told me that if I get my refund check, then the IRS believes what I put on my return and then they forget about me.

Answer: The IRS is under great pressure to pay out tax refunds within 45 days of filing or within 45 days of the due date of the return, whichever is later. So the IRS usually pays your refund first and asks questions later - sometimes two years later.

—〰—

Chapter 21
How to Find a Qualified Tax Professional and Avoid Preparer Fraud

—◦◦◦—

This is a difficult chapter to write, because even we, as retired IRS employees and now enrolled agents, find it difficult to determine from the outside who is good and who is qualified to help you in your tax case. Most return preparers are professional, honest and provide excellent services to their clients, but some engage in fraud and other illegal activities. Return preparer fraud involves the preparation and filing of false income tax returns by preparers who claim inflated personal or business expenses, false deductions, unallowable credits or excessive exemptions on returns prepared for their clients, according to the IRS.

Preparers may, for example, manipulate income figures to fraudulently obtain tax credits, such as the Earned Income Tax Credit. In some situations, the client, or taxpayer, may not even know of the false expenses, deductions, exemptions and/or credits shown on his or her tax return. Some preparers will tell their clients that they are entitled to credits such as the Slave Reparations Tax Credit because they are African American, or market to Hispanic clients and allow them to erroneously claim dependents living far away in foreign countries or file tax returns for illegal immigrants.

When the IRS detects a fraudulent return, it is the taxpayer – not the return preparer - that has to pay the additional taxes, penalties and interest and may be subject to other penalties as well.

The IRS advises that when you choose a tax preparer or tax professional you need to be very careful – as careful as you would be in choosing a doctor or lawyer.

Helpful Hints When Choosing a Return Preparer

- Avoid tax preparers that are in temporary locations. They pop up for tax season and then close shop after tax season. If they can't afford to have a decent office that is open year round and provides tax work and also bookkeeping, just walk on by.
- If a tax preparer wants to meet you at Starbucks or in the parking lot and works out of the trunk of his car, or at your kitchen table, avoid him or her.
- If the tax preparer does not have a PTIN (Preparer Tax Identification Number), a number required by the IRS for all people who prepare and file tax returns, then avoid them.
- The IRS issued a report that identified 19,496 tax preparers with PTINs who were noncompliant with filing and paying their tax obligations. These preparers had $367 million in tax due as of January 26, 2015. In addition, 3,055 preparers failed to file tax returns for one or more years and eight tax return preparers failed to file required returns for five years.
- If the tax preparer refuses to sign the tax return or put their business name or PTIN on your tax return, then you should not sign it either.
- Be cautious of tax preparers who claim that they can get you larger tax refunds than other tax preparers.
- Avoid preparers who base their fee on a percentage of the refund. Use a reputable tax preparer who signs the return and gives you a copy.

- Consider if the tax preparer will be around after the tax season to answer questions, handle a tax audit for you, or explain what happened if you do not receive a tax refund.
- If you are doing direct deposit of your refund it should be deposited directly into your bank account, not the tax preparer's. Debit cards should come to your home address, not the tax preparer's address.
- Find out if the preparer is affiliated with a professional organization that provides its members with continuing education and resources and holds them to a code of conduct and ethics.
- Never sign a blank return or sign the E-Filing authorization (Form 8879) until you have reviewed the return and gotten a copy of it.

Should You Prepare Your Own Tax Return?

This is a good question. The IRS states that 70% of Americans can do their taxes for free since their income is $62,000 or less. Go to **irs.gov/freefile** to get connected. The IRS contracts with various private companies that offer free tax software for the federal income taxes. They offer state returns; some are free and some will cost you. This can be a challenge for many people who are unable to understand the tax terminology. Many uneducated, illiterate, poor, non-English speakers and elderly persons may have trouble following the instructions on how to prepare tax returns.

If your income is over $62,000 the **irs.gov/freefile** also offers free, fillable, electronic versions of the federal income tax returns and schedules. You must know how to do your taxes yourself. It does prevent math errors, but offers only basic tax preparation. State tax preparation is not available. This software does not guide you along or ask pertinent questions about your individual tax situation.

This is no problem if you live in one of the states that have no personal income tax like Alaska, Florida, Nevada, South Dakota, Texas, Washington, or Wyoming. New Hampshire and Tennessee that do not tax wage income, just interest and dividend income. So this free software may be useful to residents of those states.

The easiest solution would be for the IRS to calculate and prepare tax returns, and it has the technology to do so. Then they would send a postcard tax return to each taxpayer and they could approve it by checking a box on a postcard or they could prepare their own tax return and submit it. In the past this has been pushed by the IRS, but the H&R Block Corporation and others who make billions of dollars in the tax preparation industry have successfully lobbied Congress to bury this idea.

The IRS, in its local walk-in offices, used to provide answers to tax questions and situations that taxpayers could not figure out for themselves. It stopped doing this and also stopped preparing tax returns for the elderly, the poor and the disabled in January, 2014.

The new policy of the IRS is to refer taxpayers to the IRS website, where they are sent to private organizations. It as though the IRS does not want to see or hear from the taxpayers it is sending letters to. Now the IRS refers taxpayers to private organizations, some of whom receive money from the IRS to help taxpayers. One program is called the **Volunteer Income Tax Assistance (VITA)** program, which offers free tax help to people who generally make $54,000 or less, persons with disabilities, the elderly, and limited English-speaking taxpayers who need assistance in preparing their own tax returns. IRS-certified volunteers provide free basic income tax return preparation with electronic filing to qualified individuals.

Low Income Taxpayer Clinics (LITCs) represent low income individuals in disputes with the Internal Revenue Service, including audits, appeals, collection matters, and federal tax litigation. LITCs can also help taxpayers respond to IRS notices and correct account problems. Some LITCs provide education about taxpayer rights and responsibilities for low income taxpayers and taxpayers who speak English as a second language (ESL).

LITC services are free or low cost for eligible taxpayers. LITCs are independent from the IRS but receive up to $100,000 in grants to fund their organizations. See IRS Low Income Taxpayer Clinic List on irs.gov.

The **IRS Tax Counseling for the Elderly (TCE)** program offers free tax help for all taxpayers, particularly those who are 60 years of age or older, specializing in questions about pensions and retirement-related issues unique to seniors. The IRS-certified volunteers who provide tax counseling are often retired individuals associated with non-profit organizations that receive grants from the IRS.

The AARP (the American Association of Retired Persons) operates the majority of TCE sites and you can call 1-888-227-7669 to find a location near you.

Several authors of this book have trained VITA and TCE volunteers over the years and many people have been helped by these groups. If you have a tax situation where you feel in over your head, you should see a tax professional. Otherwise the money you lose will be your own. Find out more information on irs.gov under "Free Tax Return Preparation for Qualifying Taxpayers."

The simplest tax return is if you are a single person with W-2 income, and no children or dependents. The Form 1040 EZ takes about 3 minutes to prepare. Anything else that you add to the mix will complicate your tax return. As we saw in the Chapter on Tax Planning for Your Life, many life events can affect your tax situation.

Big Name Tax Preparers

Going with big name tax preparers like H&R Block, Liberty Tax, etc. is the answer for some people. They have many levels of employees who can be very knowledgeable, but their services cost a lot of money. Last year H& R Block, the largest independent tax preparation company with 11,000 offices, had revenues of $3 billion from people just like you. Jackson Hewitt is a company that has 5,800 local offices as well as online software. Some of its stores are located in K-Marts, Walmart's and mall locations.

They offer loans on your tax refund- these are called refund anticipation loans and come with high fees and interest charges. As an alternative, we recommend that you adjust your income tax withholding so that you get more back in each paycheck and a smaller refund at the end of the year. Ask your employer to file a Form W-4, Employees Withholding Allowance Certificate to increase your paycheck.

Do It Yourself Tax Returns

Then there is the option of using software that guides you and asks you questions to help you complete your tax return. It seems like they ask you a million questions, but these programs are pretty accurate in our collective experience.

Some of the authors of this book have used Intuit's Turbo Tax for many years and so have many other IRS employees that we know, for our own tax returns and for friends' and families' returns. It used to be that most employees took it as sign of pride that they could still do their returns on paper; all but one of the authors no longer can do that, due to the complexity of the tax laws.

The largest self-help/guided computer software programs are:

- Intuit Turbo Tax
- H & R Block Online
- Tax Act
- Tax Slayer
- E Smart Tax
- Jackson Hewitt Online

For some people, even thinking about doing their own tax return makes them uneasy. Every return is different and can quickly become complex. The term "simple returns" is a misnomer, because what is simple for one person is mind boggling for another. Just the word "tax" gets some people tense.

Tax Preparer Fraud

The IRS does prosecute those it catches engaging in preparer return fraud. Over a three-year period, 218 cases were investigated and 127 of the tax preparers investigated went to jail for an average of 21 months.

There are 1,200,000 known tax preparers and tax professionals in the United States, so it is likely that many more are not being identified or prosecuted.

Some tax preparers, both large and small, have been able to steal huge amounts from the IRS through their fraudulent refund returns.

One preparer in Washington D.C. received $500,000 in refunds after he increased itemized deductions and credits for hundreds of his clients. He served 3 years in prison.

Another preparer who together with his daughters owned several income tax preparation businesses stole $15 million by filing false tax returns. The returns that they prepared caused the IRS to lose $45 million in taxes, because of the false data on the tax returns. They each received six years in prison.

There are tax attorneys and CPAs that are known to us that also owe the IRS tax income and employment tax balances. One owed over $1 million and actually did tax resolution work and used his Notice of Federal Tax Lien as advertising, saying that if he could get away with not paying the taxes, then he could help his clients to do that also.

A Chicago tax preparer was very generous in spending the government's money. She filed 3,200 tax returns, which gave tax refunds of $8 million to her clients. She said she just wanted to help the residents of her Southside Chicago neighborhood. She only received the return preparation fees, not any of the money. She must be thinking about that now as she sits in her prison cell for her 63-month sentence.

There are many people in business who prepare tax returns, and some are registered and licensed by the IRS to practice, but their work is not endorsed or approved by the IRS. There are some who are good, honest and very professional and there are some who you will visit who actually ask you how big a tax refund you want that year and then they will prepare false returns to make that happen for you. The problem is that when you sign your tax return or any related financial statements, you are legally and financially responsible for everything that is listed on that tax return.

We will divide this section into those people who prepare tax returns and those who will represent you in IRS audit and collection cases.

Unenrolled Preparers

Some preparers are called unenrolled preparers. They cannot talk to the IRS about your return, they have little or no education in tax law and are not regulated or monitored by anyone, especially not the IRS. Usually they set up a lucrative practice in a store front and then stay one or two tax seasons and have been known to do outrageous things with tax returns that include fraudulent returns and even forging a client's signature and stealing their refunds. Then they close the business when the IRS starts to match up all the information on the returns with information that it has from other sources. This usually takes one or two years before the IRS does this matching. An example of an unpaid preparer might be a family member or friend.

Tax professionals who represent you before the IRS are called Tax Resolution Professionals. They may or may not also do tax preparation. They are all required to be registered by the IRS.

When Do You Need a Tax Attorney?

Attorneys are licensed by state courts, the District of Columbia or their state bar association. Generally, tax attorneys have earned a degree in law and have passed a bar exam. Attorneys are required to take continuing professional education (CPE) and must maintain professional character standards. Attorneys may also be CPAs, and some specialize in tax planning, preparation and practice before the U.S. District Court and the U.S. Tax Court. The best place to locate individuals who are both qualified as Attorneys and Certified Public Accountants is on the website for the American Association of Attorney-Certified Public Accountants (AAA-CPA. See http://www.attorney-cpa.com).

Some attorneys specialize in tax law. You may need a **tax attorney** if:

- Your case is very technical, involves large dollar amounts, or requires filing suit against the IRS
- You plan to go before the U.S. Tax Court for a more favorable tax ruling
- You are under investigation by the IRS Criminal Investigation Division. You will need a criminal attorney who is also a tax attorney.
- You have filed false tax returns, failed to file tax returns or have been indicted, this is very serious and you will need a criminal tax attorney whose expertise is in this field.
- You have filed returns and listed false refunds, credits, deductions or exemptions, you will need an attorney because you can tell them your whole story and it is all confidential – because of the attorney-client privilege. Never lie to your attorney or hold back any information or you can both suffer when it is found out by the IRS.
- Your case involves more than just you and your small business. This would be the case in large businesses or partnerships.

Some tax attorneys are also CPAs. The larger the numbers in your audit case and the more people that are affected by it, the more you need this type of individual to help you. However, large dollar amounts in a collection case do not mean that you necessarily need a tax attorney.

Certified Public Accountants (CPAs) are licensed by state boards of accountancy, the District of Columbia and U.S. Territories. Certified public accountants have passed the Uniform CPA Examination. They have completed a study in accounting at a college or university and also met experience and good character requirements established by their respective boards of accountancy. In addition, they must comply with ethical requirements and complete specified levels of continuing education in order to maintain an active CPA practice. CPAs may offer a range of services from bookkeeping, to tax planning, tax preparation and financial planning. The American Institute of Certified Public Accountants (AICPA) is the world's largest member association representing the accounting profession. (http://AICPA.org)

CPAs bring an unmatched level of knowledge, experience and education to the tax planning and preparation process.

Many CPAs specialize in certain types of businesses such as partnerships, or corporate tax work. Most do a mix of business and personal tax clients.

CPAs may be very qualified to represent you in an audit or appeals situation, but have no idea how to help you in a collection or criminal case. A CPA can save you a lot of money because they can make a tax plan for you that will save you tax money and provide for retirement planning long into the future. A CPA is a great choice for an audit case.

The best CPA will interview you about your financial situation, family situation, life goals and will listen to you and respond to your questions. They will also be available for year-end tax planning from October to December.

Enrolled Agents

An enrolled agent is a person who has earned the privilege of representing taxpayers before the Internal Revenue Service. Enrolled agents are subject to a suitability check and must pass a three-part Special Enrollment Examination, which is a comprehensive exam that requires them to demonstrate proficiency in federal tax planning, individual and business tax return preparation, and representation. They must complete 72 hours of continuing education every three years.

Enrolled agents, like attorneys and certified public accountants (CPAs), are generally unrestricted as to which taxpayers they can represent, what types of tax matters they can handle, and in which IRS offices they can represent clients.

Some enrolled agents are retired or former IRS employees with at least 5 years' experience who automatically qualify for enrolled agent status because of their experience.

An enrolled agent can be your best advocate in the case of correspondence audits or office audits if they were tax auditors or revenue agents for field audits, in their IRS lives.

Retired revenue officers are great advocates for collection and appeals and offer in compromise cases. They will need to be your advocate and they have a fiduciary responsibility to take care of you in a competent professional manner. They know the tax law and IRS procedures and how the IRS will review or decide your case.

Attorney-Client Privilege

The most important difference in these tax professionals is that with the attorney you have the attorney-client privilege. That means that anything you tell the attorney, he/she can never repeat that information to another person, even if he/she is under a summons or subpoena. Your private financial business stays just between the two of you. A

CPA or enrolled agent has limited confidentiality protection. They of course must not go about sharing your business; they must keep all of your communications private and confidential. If they are summoned or subpoenaed they have to tell everything that you told them.

Some clients hire a tax attorney and then the tax attorney hires the CPA and/or the enrolled agent as needed to work your case and then the attorney-client privilege covers the attorney, the CPA and the enrolled agent.

Tax Professionals

- There is no current effective way to determine if your tax preparer or tax professional is trustworthy or competent. The IRS does maintain a Directory of Federal Tax Return Preparers with Credentials and Select Qualifications. Search on the irs.gov site for this. This just tells you that they have a Preparer Tax Identification Number (PTIN); it does not rate their competence.
- The IRS could publish statistics that it controls over these tax professionals regarding their error rate and any disciplinary action or complaints recorded by professional organizations, bar associations or licensing authorities or the IRS.

Let's start with the tax professionals that abuse the taxpaying public with false and unethical ads promising that they will get offers in compromise and tax settlements for pennies on the dollar. What they promise is illegal.

The IRS is afraid to control or regulate or censure these practitioners, even though many in the IRS are strongly in favor of it. The IRS is afraid that it would give the appearance that they were trying to deny taxpayers their rights to representation.

The reason that these firms do so well and are able to generate so much income to buy television and radio ads, is because they are selling hope - a glimmer of hope. They want you to think that by hiring them, you will be able to get the IRS off your back for good - that you will be able to settle your tax debt with the IRS for pennies on the dollar. It is a nice dream, but in most cases they are unable to deliver on their promises.

We advocate avoiding the big box tax resolution firms, the ones you see advertising all the time on radio and television. They make many promises and charge up to ten times what a local tax professional would charge.

We recommend finding someone who is local to your area or in a larger city near where you live so you can drive over and meet in person with them, maybe get a free consultation, leave your records. That way you can meet them, see their office, meet their assistant or secretary and get a feel for how they treat you. This is important. If they don't treat you special and take the time to ask you important questions at the initial interview, then don't hire them.

We have all worked with tax professionals who were aging, not connected with reality or recent IRS tax law and procedures. You should use Google or Bing to search them on the internet. There you will see ratings by past clients, the Better Business Bureau, Yelp.com, AngiesList.com, the American Institute of Certified Public Accountants, the National Association of Enrolled Agents and the IRS Office of Enrollment for enrolled agents.

Tax professionals should explain up front exactly what they will do and approximately what it will cost for them to do it. They should tell you that to represent you in an audit will take approximately so many hours, and disclose their rate per hour. If going to the Office of Appeals on your case is an option, they should give you a separate quote for how much that is expected to cost. We have seen some tax professionals who charge clients for travel to cities where the appeal is to be held. We have seen where they fly from Phoenix to Las Vegas or Los Angeles, charge their clients to fly there, and stay for 1-2 days. This is wrong and unnecessary. The same thing can be accomplished over email, with letters. The appeals officer does not want to see them in person - just evaluate their arguments and make a decision.

Some tax professionals will give you a flat rate quote and then if you want to go to higher levels like appeals or tax court, they will offer you a different price quote.

Most tax professionals will use an engagement letter that tells what they will do and then you review and sign it. Usually they expect at least 1/3 of the retainer up front and the rest with interest over the next 3-6 months. They will stop servicing you when your retainer runs out, no matter what the IRS is doing to you. We have seen them stop audit meetings because their time was up. Some will expect full payment of the full fee up front, because especially in collection cases, they think – this person did not pay the IRS, why would they make paying their tax advisor a priority?

This is why we advise that you hire someone you have met and had a good feeling about. Your tax case is very important to your life and financial well-being. To some you are just another case.

Also remember that attorneys and CPAs have to be licensed in each state where they operate. Enrolled agents are licensed to practice in every U.S. state.

You also need to remember that if your tax representative is going to handle your IRS work, and you have balances owed also to your state, then you will need to sign a separate power of attorney form for that state.

The best thing about signing your power of attorney over to a tax professional is that the IRS cannot call you or contact you. The IRS has to contact your representative. The only time that you would be required to speak to the IRS is if you receive a summons to appear and provide books and testimony. Even then you can have your representative by your side. You need to know that the collection efforts of most states are very aggressive and you have fewer rights than with the IRS. In fact, many of the states use private collection firms to collect their debts. It is usually best to make an agreement with the state and then go to the IRS and show that you are paying the state and they will usually allow the whole payment to the state as long as it looks reasonable to them.

When you interview the tax preparer, you need to ask questions about your situation and listen to what they say. Some tax professionals are very aggressive and will put many deductions on your return. These could create a high probability of being selected by the IRS for an audit - an audit that would probably end with you owing more taxes.

Tax preparation and tax resolution are things you should not attempt to save money on, because a tax professional can save you thousands of dollars when they apply their knowledge and wisdom to your tax case.

Finally, some people recommend that you ask your friends for their referrals. This can be good or bad; if the preparer is very aggressive, they might be able to get you big refunds now that are illegal and you will owe the IRS big money later.

Who Can Represent You Before the IRS

Tax preparers who are not enrolled agents, CPAs or attorneys are called "unenrolled preparers". They still have to have a PTIN, but are not licensed by the IRS. They may only represent clients whose returns they prepared and signed, and only before revenue agents, customer service representatives, and similar IRS employees, including the Taxpayer Advocate Service. They cannot represent clients whose returns they did not prepare and they cannot represent clients regarding appeals or collection issues even if they did prepare the returns in question.

Have a Complaint about a Tax Preparer/Tax Professional?

If you have been financially impacted by a tax preparer or tax professional's misconduct, malpractice or improper tax preparation practices, you have several avenues open to you.

The first is: The IRS Director of Practice office in the Internal Revenue Service. (fax number 202-317-6338)

The second is whatever board licenses the tax preparer/professional.

The third is your local police, district attorney or state's attorney. If you have experienced a financial fraud, embezzlement or refund fraud, call the police.

Chapter 22
What to Do About the IRS Situation

The IRS is an agency broken by years of budget cuts, an antique computer system, inexperienced employees who lack adequate training, an aged workforce (half of its employees are nearly as old as the computer system), and a failed approach to its mission. The IRS budget has been cut over $1.2 billion since 2010 and new laws from Congress placed more responsibilities on the IRS and are quickly destroying the existing tax administration system. The IRS cannot continue to do more with less. The IRS is at its lowest staffing level since 2008.

Cutting the IRS budget costs more money than the budget cuts save. IRS Commissioner Koskinen said that "From 2005 to 2010, IRS compliance averaged $14.7 billion in collections annually. Over the next five years, collections averaged $10.5 billion a year, leaving an estimated $20 billion uncollected."

While it is true that IRS management is responsible for gross mismanagement of resources, inefficiency, waste and confusion of their mission and purpose, it is not something that is likely to be corrected by throwing more money at the IRS. The atmosphere of low morale, poor working conditions and lack of tools to do their jobs has weakened the IRS employees. This situation has been created and condoned by the IRS management. This organizational philosophy is that all taxpayers are trying to get away with something and that the

IRS employees need to "draw a line in the sand," and push the taxpayers down into the dirt.

This way of thinking is wrong and actually costs the government money in lost tax collections and should be a thing of the past. We, the majority of taxpaying citizens, pay for the IRS to exist and we, the American taxpayers, deserve better than this.

The National Taxpayer Advocate Nina Olson stated that while the IRS needs more resources to support its compliance and enforcement actions, the IRS also needs to see taxpayers as human beings through such means as face-to-face appeals hearings. Besides efficiency in collections, it should promote practices that respect taxpayers' rights and enhance voluntary compliance broadly and for the long term.

However, the Service's trend, she said, has been to reduce direct taxpayer contacts. A low level of service is the result of reductions in the number of employees available to both service walk-in taxpayers as well as taxpayers who are trying to call the IRS and receive no answer, despite calling over and over. If taxpayers try but are unable to contact IRS to make payment arrangements, the IRS through its Automated Collection System may next send out a levy notice or file a lien. Ms. Olson asked "Now, how does that make you feel as a taxpayer? The environment today will, no question about it, erode trust in the IRS, if it hasn't already been eroded, and will erode voluntary compliance."

The result of the waste and inefficiency of the IRS is that fewer taxpayers are filing or paying their taxes and there are fewer audits of those who do file tax returns.

The IRS, at present, is a dying agency that has lost control of administering a fair, equitable and balanced tax system.

In the long term, this will be good for the American people, because the IRS was out of control for decades. It went beyond its role of tax administrator to an agency that enjoyed the power that it had because most taxpayers lived in fear of any contact from the IRS. This created enormous power that was abused by IRS management and some employees. This is an opportunity for a new IRS to rise up from the ashes of its former self; to be reborn with a fresh crop of employees who are young and trainable and motivated to treat taxpayers with respect, while at the same time increasing compliance and tax collections.

The IBM Corporation created a unique, powerful and state-of-the-art computer system that still is used by the IRS today, over fifty years later. Now a new state-of-the-art system is what the IRS needs, together with forward thinkers from private business who can raise the platform of tax administration for the next 50 years.

A neutral outside private company should evaluate existing tax laws and tax administration requirements, the existing IRS systems, and then come up with a plan that can address what the IRS of the future will be. The IRS needs computers, training, employees and systems that will need to be in synch with other large financial services businesses.

Politicians who advocate a flat tax or a national sales tax do not know what they are talking about. Those are regressive taxes that harm the middle and working classes. Their words are spoken in ignorance. So are mandates from Congress that private collection agencies be awarded IRS work. Tax collection is a fundamental responsibility of the government. Past attempts to contract it out to private businesses resulted in worse abuse than what the IRS had done.

The use of private tax collection agencies is now mandatory, per a long-term highway funding bill signed into law in December, 2015. The law includes provisions that require the use of private tax collectors to collect federal taxes and uses critically needed customer user fees to pay for unrelated projects. It also allows for a delinquent taxpayer to have their passports revoked if they owe more than $50,000 in back taxes.

The IRS of the future needs fresh, new employees who want to provide "true" customer service and collections and fair audits as their goal and then move quickly into the future. The IRS comes up with new plans all the time, but they always flounder and die. That is because these plans are placed on employees instead of seeking grass roots solutions to tax problems that come from the IRS employees.

The United States economy is at a place where much more revenue will be needed just to pay the interest on the national debt and fund the Social Security checks of the baby boomer generation and beyond.

Killing the Beast that the IRS system has become would start with less interference from Congress and more input from tax attorneys, CPAs, enrolled agents and members of the general public who can guide the system forward, with a minimum of political interaction.

It will take an uprising of all taxpayers to make this happen. When the spotlight is focused on the IRS and its failure to seek out those who never file or pay taxes and who allow businesses to skirt tax laws and hide money offshore - forever free of U.S. taxation - then we are at a place where true public confidence in the tax system could be restored.

When the tax laws are fair and balanced, all will benefit - income earners at all levels - not just the top 10% of influential and wealthy income earners. Or is “income earners” even a correct term? Does someone who is making $40,000 a year work any harder than a person who is a hedge fund manager who earns between $40 million and $2 billion a year? Wealth inequality is contained and rewarded in the Internal Revenue Code; it is legal and acceptable for the rich to get richer. Just because this happens does not make it right.

When the taxpayers of the United States band together and demand that all income earners pay similar tax rates, based not just on income, but on income that exceeds the basic costs to survive, then the laws will eventually change.

Today 47% of people do not pay income taxes at all because their income is too low. All income and wage earners still pay Social Security taxes of 7.65% as a wage earner and 15.3% if self-employed, even if it causes them financial hardship. Maybe we should have a law that says that no one earning under $50,000 pays any income taxes at all. This could then be adjusted upwards to include any dependents and adjusted for the higher cost of living by some geographic areas.

The complex and confusing Internal Revenue Code is a problem created by Congress, not the majority of the people who voted them into office. Recent polls show that 78% of people disapprove of Congress. So when will the people who pay for this country rise up and start to demand a fair and balanced tax system? It starts with you, as a registered voter. You are responsible for holding your elected representatives accountable for their actions (and inactions) and you shouldn't send them back to office if they don't deliver.

A broken tax system corrupted by greed hurts all of us. For far too long the IRS has used internal management that has come up through the ranks and lacked the education, experience, knowledge and credentials to effectively administer the tax system. IRS management is myopic, fearful and paranoid of outside assistance.

The IRS is capable of doing excellent tax administration if it is allowed to do what it is supposed to do. The IRS deserves credit for being able to operate at all, given its antiquated computer system, its aging employee population, the increasingly complex tax laws and the budget cuts it has suffered for the last five years. Looking at how the IRS is still operating is remarkable – it is like watching a tired, old, three-legged dog go for a run.

In the IRS we had all been taught that old maxim of government: "Good enough for government work." That is just not good enough anymore, because some people never pay taxes and that is hurting all of us who do pay taxes. We need a more equal and fair tax system.

Changing the IRS will come out of need and it will not come easily. Old ideas die hard. Lack of money to pay the expenses that the government owes will help.

The future IRS must be an audit and collection business that is operated with the idea of fairly and efficiently serving all the taxpayers of the United States.

"You cannot use the old IRS managers and old IRS employees who were abusers under the old system and allow them to train the IRS employees of the future to be bad too. The school for dinosaurs needs to close!" Lauri Goff.

The Congressional Budget Office projected that from 2013 to 2024 federal government spending would increase from $3.5 trillion to $6.0 trillion, an increase of $2.5 trillion. The money will not come from the existing revenues and tax collections of the federal government. So we must look outside of current revenue sources and seek to make all transactions and income subject to a fair and equal tax system. Small changes in current tax law will produce tens of billions of dollars more in excise and income taxes. Transactions that affect business in the United States will cause trillions of dollars to appear as new income to the federal government.

The military budget uses up 55% of the revenue of the United States. Add another 9% to pay the interest on the national debt which is currently almost 19 trillion dollars. The United States owes $41 trillion dollars to Social Security and Medicare. There is much work to be done to not only improve the tax administration system in the United States, but also to make it fair for future generations.

We hope that you have enjoyed this book and that it will save you time and money in your dealings with the IRS. We cannot stress enough the rewards of good tax planning and how much that will save you in the future.

Appendix

Sample - Penalty Abatement Letter Due to First Time Penalty Abatement Waiver

Sample - Penalty Abatement Letter Due to Reasonable Cause

Form 12203

Form 433-A, Collection Information Statement for Wage Earners and Self-Employed Individuals

Form 433-A (OIC) Collection Information Statement for Wage Earners and Self-Employed Individuals – Offer in Compromise Version.

Form 433-B, Collection Information Statement for Businesses

Form 433-B (OIC) Collection Information Statement for Businesses

Form 433-F Collection Information Statement for Service Center and ACS

Form 9465 Installment Agreement Request

Appendix

Penalty Abatement Letters: Two letters have been provided - one for first time penalty abatement waiver request and the second for reasonable cause penalty abatement. You can use these letters as a template for your own letter. Information in brackets [...] is for your guidance and is where you should tailor the letter.

First Time Penalty Abatement Waiver Letter

Date:

To: Internal Revenue Service

From: [Your name and your spouse's name]

[Your address, and both of your Social Security Numbers]

Regarding: [On upper right corner of the latest IRS letter that you receive- it will begin with CP or LT and then a number and tell the date of the letter]

I request First Time Penalty Abatement Waiver for my individual income tax return based on my compliance history for Form 1040 for the year ended [12/31/201x]. I had an issue that prevented me from filing and/or paying my taxes on time. I request abatement of failure to file and failure to pay and failure to deposit penalties as applicable under Internal Revenue Manual Section 20.1.1.3.6.1.1A.

In the three years before this subject tax year, I filed and paid my taxes in a timely manner, I did not have any penalties of a significant amount that were not resolved. Any estimated tax penalty does not apply to this situation.

I request that my case be manually reviewed as the Reasonable Cause Assistant is unreliable. If this request is denied I also am presenting a letter which asks for penalty abatements for all years under the reasonable cause section of IRM 20.1.1.3.2.2.2. (See attached if applicable)

Please process this application for penalty abatement promptly. I am seeking to resolve the tax and interest portion of the tax assessment separately. Thank you for your consideration of this matter. My telephone number is [XXX-XXX-XXXX] if you require any more information. If you reject my penalty abatement request, please send this case to the Office of Appeals.

Sincerely,

[Name and business name, if applicable]

[On business tax returns, you can also request abatement of the above penalties plus the failure to deposit penalty as well.]

Reasonable Cause Penalty Abatement Letter Request

Date:

To: Internal Revenue Service

From: [Your name and your spouse's name]

[Your address, and both of your Social Security Numbers]

Regarding: [On upper right corner of the latest IRS letter that you receive- it will begin with CP or LT and then a number and tell the date of the letter]

I request that all penalties and interest (if applicable) be abated from my [income tax or employment or other type of tax] returns for the years ended [12/31/201x or which quarters] because I have reasonable cause for the abatement of the penalties. I request this because of the following reasons.

I exercised ordinary business care and prudence in determining my tax obligation, I acted in good faith and did not willfully neglect my duty to comply with the tax laws, because of the following reason or reasons: [Delete any reason not applicable!]

- Due to a natural disaster, floods, hurricanes, earthquakes, tornados
- Due to military or terrorist action that affected me
- Due to my personal illness
- Due to illness of family or persons close to me
- Due to destruction of my records
- Due to negligence from my tax professional
- Due to hospitalizations, required because of accidents, injuries or death of family or people close to me
- Due to loss of records or records not being obtainable by me
- Due to loss of my job or spouses job
- Due to death of family or close friend
- Due to business closing or bankruptcy or other financial disaster

- Due to divorce
- Due to alcohol abuse
- Due to drug abuse (prescription or other)
- Due to mental issues including depression, bi-polar etc
- Due to physical abuse, sexual abuse, mental and emotional abuse
- Due to sexual addiction
- Due to gambling addiction
- Due to these conditions affecting me or the rest of my family and close friends.
- Due to fire
- Due to a theft or burglary of records needed to prepare my return
- Due to being out of the country for business
- Due to being deployed with the military

I request that my case be manually reviewed as the Reasonable Cause Assistant is unreliable. If this request is denied I also am presenting a letter which asks for penalty abatements for all years under the reasonable cause section of IRM 20.1.1.3.2.2.2. (See attached if applicable)

Please process this application for penalty abatement promptly. I am seeking to resolve the tax and interest portion of the tax assessment separately. Thank you for your consideration of this matter. My telephone number is [XXX-XXX-XXXX] if you require any more information. If you reject my penalty abatement request, please send this case to the Office of Appeals.

Sincerely,

[Name and Business name, if applicable]

Form **12203** (February 2016)	Department of the Treasury - Internal Revenue Service **Request for Appeals Review**

Complete the information in the spaces below, including your signature and the date.

Taxpayer name(s)		Taxpayer Identification Number(s)
Mailing address		Tax form number
City		Tax period(s) ended
State	ZIP Code	
Your telephone number(s)		Best time to call

Identify the item(s) *(for example: filing status, exemptions, interest or dividends)* you disagree with in the proposed change or assessment report you received with the enclosed letter. Tell us why you disagree. You can add more pages if this is not enough space.

Disagreed item	Reason why you disagree

Disagreed item	Reason why you disagree

Disagreed item	Reason why you disagree

Disagreed item	Reason why you disagree

Name of Taxpayer	Signature	Date
Name of Taxpayer	Signature	Date

Name and signature of authorized representative **(If a representative is signing this form, please attach a copy of your completed Form 2848,Power of Attorney and Declaration of Representative.)**

Name	Signature	Date
Your telephone number	Best time to call	

Catalog Number 27136N www.irs.gov Form **12203** (Rev. 2-2016)

Purpose of this form: You can use this form to request a review in Appeals when you receive Internal Revenue Service (IRS) proposed adjustments or other changes of $25,000 or less to a tax year questioned in the IRS letter you received with this form.

When you take no action and your case involves income taxes, we will send you a formal Notice of Deficiency and bill for the amount you owe. The Notice of Deficiency allows you to go to the Tax Court and tells you the procedure to follow.

When you don't agree with the IRS proposed adjustments or changes and you have submitted all supporting information, explanations, or documents, you may:

(1) discuss the IRS findings with the person identified *(or their supervisor)* in the heading on the IRS letter that provided you this information; and if you can't reach agreement,

(2) appeal your case by requesting an Appeals Review.

If you want to request an Appeals Review, complete this form and return it in the envelope provided to the address in the heading of the IRS letter.

Appeals is independent of the IRS office proposing the action you disagree with. Appeals conferences are conducted in an informal manner. Most differences are settled in these conferences without expensive and time consuming court trials. Appeals will independently consider the reason(s) you disagree, except for moral, religious, political, constitutional, conscientious objection, or similar grounds.

You can represent yourself in Appeals. If you want to be represented by another person, the person you choose must be an attorney, a certified public accountant, or an enrolled agent authorized to practice before the IRS. If you plan to have your representative talk to us without you, we need a signed copy of a completed power of attorney *(Form 2848,* Power of Attorney and Declaration of Representative*)*.

If you don't reach an agreement in Appeals, the Appeals office will send you a Notice of Deficiency. After you receive the Notice of Deficiency, you may take your case to the United States Tax Court before paying the amount due as shown on the Notice of Deficiency. If you want to proceed in the United States Court of Federal Claims or your United States District Court, see Publication 5, Your Appeal Rights and How to Prepare a Protest if You Disagree, for more information.

You can get more information about your appeal rights by visiting the IRS Internet Web Site at http://www.irs.gov or the Appeals Web Site at http://www.irs.gov/appeals. You also can order blank tax forms, schedules, instructions and publications by calling toll-free 1-800-829-3676. Once you've placed your order, allow two weeks for delivery. For IRS Tax Fax Services, call (703) 487-4160 *(not a toll-free number)*.

PRIVACY ACT STATEMENT

Under the Privacy Act of 1974, we must tell you that our legal right to ask for information is Internal Revenue Code Sections 6001, 6011, 6012(a) and their regulations. They say that you must furnish us with records or statements for any tax for which you are liable, including the withholding of taxes by your employer. We ask for information to carry out the Internal Revenue laws of the United States, and you are required to give us this information. We may give the
information to the Department of Justice for civil and criminal litigation, other federal agencies, states, cities, and the District of Columbia for use in administering their tax laws. If you don't provide this information, or provide fraudulent information, the law provides that you may be charged penalties and, in certain cases, you
may be subject to criminal prosecution. We may also have to disallow the exemptions, exclusions, credits, deductions, or adjustments shown on the tax return. This could make your tax higher or delay any refund. Interest may also be charged.

Form **433-A**

(Rev. December 2012)

Department of the Treasury
Internal Revenue Service

Collection Information Statement for Wage Earners and Self-Employed Individuals

Wage Earners Complete Sections 1, 2, 3, 4, and 5 including the signature line on page 4. *Answer all questions or write N/A if the question is not applicable.*

Self-Employed Individuals Complete Sections 1, 3, 4, 5, 6 and 7 and the signature line on page 4. *Answer all questions or write N/A if the question is not applicable.*

For Additional Information, refer to Publication 1854, "How To Prepare a Collection Information Statement."

Include attachments if additional space is needed to respond completely to any question.

Name on Internal Revenue Service (IRS) Account	Social Security Number *SSN* on IRS Account	Employer Identification Number *EIN*

Section 1: Personal Information

1a Full Name of Taxpayer and Spouse *(if applicable)*	**1c** Home Phone ( )	**1d** Cell Phone ( )
1b Address *(Street, City, State, ZIP code) (County of Residence)*	**1e** Business Phone ( )	**1f** Business Cell Phone ( )
	2b Name, Age, and Relationship of dependent(s)	
2a Marital Status: ☐ Married ☐ Unmarried *(Single, Divorced, Widowed)*		

	Social Security No. *(SSN)*	Date of Birth *(mmddyyyy)*	Driver's License Number and State
3a Taxpayer			
3b Spouse			

Section 2: Employment Information for Wage Earners

If you or your spouse have self-employment income instead of, or in addition to wage income, complete Business Information in Sections 6 and 7.

Taxpayer		Spouse	
4a Taxpayer's Employer Name		**5a** Spouse's Employer Name	
4b Address *(Street, City, State, and ZIP code)*		**5b** Address *(Street, City, State, and ZIP code)*	
4c Work Telephone Number ( )	**4d** Does employer allow contact at work ☐ Yes ☐ No	**5c** Work Telephone Number ( )	**5d** Does employer allow contact at work ☐ Yes ☐ No
4e How long with this employer *(years)* *(months)*	**4f** Occupation	**5e** How long with this employer *(years)* *(months)*	**5f** Occupation
4g Number of withholding allowances claimed on Form W-4	**4h** Pay Period: ☐ Weekly ☐ Bi-weekly ☐ Monthly ☐ Other	**5g** Number of withholding allowances claimed on Form W-4	**5h** Pay Period: ☐ Weekly ☐ Bi-weekly ☐ Monthly ☐ Other

Section 3: Other Financial Information *(Attach copies of applicable documentation)*

6 Are you a party to a lawsuit *(If yes, answer the following)* ☐ Yes ☐ No

☐ Plaintiff ☐ Defendant	Location of Filing	Represented by	Docket/Case No.
Amount of Suit $	Possible Completion Date *(mmddyyyy)*	Subject of Suit	

7 Have you ever filed bankruptcy *(If yes, answer the following)* ☐ Yes ☐ No

Date Filed *(mmddyyyy)*	Date Dismissed *(mmddyyyy)*	Date Discharged *(mmddyyyy)*	Petition No.	Location Filed

8 In the past 10 years, have you lived outside of the U.S for 6 months or longer *(If yes, answer the following)* ☐ Yes ☐ No

Dates lived abroad: from *(mmddyyyy)*	To *(mmddyyyy)*

9a Are you the beneficiary of a trust, estate, or life insurance policy *(If yes, answer the following)* ☐ Yes ☐ No

Place where recorded:		EIN:
Name of the trust, estate, or policy	Anticipated amount to be received $	When will the amount be received

9b Are you a trustee, fiduciary, or contributor of a trust ☐ Yes ☐ No

Name of the trust:	EIN:

0 Do you have a safe deposit box (business or personal) *(If yes, answer the following)* ☐ Yes ☐ No

Location *(Name, address and box number(s))*	Contents	Value $

1 In the past 10 years, have you transferred any assets for less than their full value *(If yes, answer the following)* ☐ Yes ☐ No

List Asset(s)	Value at Time of Transfer $	Date Transferred *(mmddyyyy)*	To Whom or Where was it Transferred

Section 4: Personal Asset Information for All Individuals

12 **CASH ON HAND** Include cash that is not in a bank **Total Cash on Hand** $

PERSONAL BANK ACCOUNTS Include all checking, online and mobile *(e.g., PayPal)* accounts, money market accounts, savings accounts, and stored value cards *(e.g., payroll cards, government benefit cards, etc.)*.

	Type of Account	Full Name & Address *(Street, City, State, ZIP code)* of Bank, Savings & Loan, Credit Union, or Financial Institution	Account Number	**Account Balance** As of ________ *mmddyyyy*
13a				$
13b				$
13c				$

13d **Total Cash** *(Add lines 13a through 13c, and amounts from any attachments)* $

INVESTMENTS Include stocks, bonds, mutual funds, stock options, certificates of deposit, and retirement assets such as IRAs, Keogh, and 401(k) plans. Include all corporations, partnerships, limited liability companies, or other business entities in which you are an officer, director, owner, member, or otherwise have a financial interest.

	Type of Investment or Financial Interest	Full Name & Address *(Street, City, State, ZIP code)* of Company	Current Value	Loan Balance *(if applicable)* As of ________ *mmddyyyy*	**Equity** Value minus Loan
14a		Phone	$	$	$
14b		Phone	$	$	$
14c		Phone	$	$	$

14d **Total Equity** *(Add lines 14a through 14c and amounts from any attachments)* $

	AVAILABLE CREDIT Include all lines of credit and bank issued credit cards. Full Name & Address *(Street, City, State, ZIP code)* of Credit Institution	Credit Limit	Amount Owed As of ________ *mmddyyyy*	**Available Credit** As of ________ *mmddyyyy*
15a	Acct. No	$	$	$
15b	Acct. No	$	$	$

15c **Total Available Credit** *(Add lines 15a, 15b and amounts from any attachments)* $

16a **LIFE INSURANCE** Do you own or have any interest in any life insurance policies with cash value *(Term Life insurance does not have a cash value)*

☐ **Yes** ☐ **No** If yes, complete blocks 16b through 16f for each policy.

16b	Name and Address of Insurance Company(ies):			
16c	Policy Number(s)			
16d	Owner of Policy			
16e	Current Cash Value	$	$	$
16f	Outstanding Loan Balance	$	$	$

16g **Total Available Cash** *(Subtract amounts on line 16f from line 16e and include amounts from any attachments)* $

REAL PROPERTY Include all real property owned or being purchased

	Purchase Date *(mmddyyyy)*	Current Fair Market Value (FMV)	Current Loan Balance	Amount of Monthly Payment	Date of Final Payment *(mmddyyyy)*	**Equity** FMV Minus Loan
17a Property Description		$	$	$		$
Location *(Street, City, State, ZIP code)* and County	Lender/Contract Holder Name, Address *(Street, City, State, ZIP code)*, and Phone Phone					
17b Property Description		$	$	$		$
Location *(Street, City, State, ZIP code)* and County	Lender/Contract Holder Name, Address *(Street, City, State, ZIP code)*, and Phone Phone					
17c Total Equity *(Add lines 17a, 17b and amounts from any attachments)*						$

PERSONAL VEHICLES LEASED AND PURCHASED Include boats, RVs, motorcycles, all-terrain and off-road vehicles, trailers, etc.

Description (Year, Mileage, Make/Model, Tag Number, Vehicle Identification Number)		Purchase/ Lease Date *(mmddyyyy)*	Current Fair Market Value (FMV)	Current Loan Balance	Amount of Monthly Payment	Date of Final Payment *(mmddyyyy)*	**Equity** FMV Minus Loan
18a Year	Make/Model		$	$	$		$
Mileage	License/Tag Number	Lender/Lessor Name, Address *(Street, City, State, ZIP code)*, and Phone Phone					
Vehicle Identification Number							
18b Year	Make/Model		$	$	$		$
Mileage	License/Tag Number	Lender/Lessor Name, Address *(Street, City, State, ZIP code)*, and Phone Phone					
Vehicle Identification Number							
18c Total Equity *(Add lines 18a, 18b and amounts from any attachments)*							$

PERSONAL ASSETS Include all furniture, personal effects, artwork, jewelry, collections *(coins, guns, etc.)*, antiques or other assets. Include intangible assets such as licenses, domain names, patents, copyrights, mining claims, etc.

	Purchase/ Lease Date *(mmddyyyy)*	Current Fair Market Value (FMV)	Current Loan Balance	Amount of Monthly Payment	Date of Final Payment *(mmddyyyy)*	**Equity** FMV Minus Loan
19a Property Description		$	$	$		$
Location *(Street, City, State, ZIP code)* and County	Lender/Lessor Name, Address *(Street, City, State, ZIP code)*, and Phone Phone					
19b Property Description		$	$	$		$
Location *(Street, City, State, ZIP code)* and County	Lender/Lessor Name, Address *(Street, City, State, ZIP code)*, and Phone Phone					
19c Total Equity *(Add lines 19a, 19b and amounts from any attachments)*						$

If you are self-employed, sections 6 and 7 must be completed before continuing.

Section 5: Monthly Income and Expenses

Monthly Income/Expense Statement *(For additional information, refer to Publication 1854.)*

Total Income		Total Living Expenses		IRS USE ONLY
Source	Gross Monthly	Expense Items [6]	Actual Monthly	Allowable Expenses
20 Wages (Taxpayer) [1]	$	35 Food, Clothing and Misc. [7]	$	
21 Wages (Spouse) [1]	$	36 Housing and Utilities [8]	$	
22 Interest - Dividends	$	37 Vehicle Ownership Costs [9]	$	
23 Net Business Income [2]	$	38 Vehicle Operating Costs [10]	$	
24 Net Rental Income [3]	$	39 Public Transportation [11]	$	
25 Distributions (K-1, IRA, etc.) [4]	$	40 Health Insurance	$	
26 Pension (Taxpayer)	$	41 Out of Pocket Health Care Costs [12]	$	
27 Pension (Spouse)	$	42 Court Ordered Payments	$	
28 Social Security (Taxpayer)	$	43 Child/Dependent Care	$	
29 Social Security (Spouse)	$	44 Life Insurance	$	
30 Child Support	$	45 Current year taxes (Income/FICA) [13]	$	
31 Alimony	$	46 Secured Debts (Attach list)	$	
Other Income (Specify below) [5]		47 Delinquent State or Local Taxes	$	
32	$	48 Other Expenses (Attach list)	$	
33	$	49 Total Living Expenses (add lines 35-48)	$	
34 Total Income (add lines 20-33)	$	50 Net difference (Line 34 minus 49)	$	

1 **Wages, salaries, pensions, and social security:** Enter gross monthly wages and/or salaries. Do not deduct tax withholding or allotments taken out of pay, such as insurance payments, credit union deductions, car payments, etc. To calculate the gross monthly wages and/or salaries:

If paid weekly - multiply weekly gross wages by 4.3. Example: $425.89 x 4.3 = $1,831.33

If paid biweekly (every 2 weeks) - multiply biweekly gross wages by 2.17. Example: $972.45 x 2.17 = $2,110.22

If paid semimonthly (twice each month) - multiply semimonthly gross wages by 2. Example: $856.23 x 2 = $1,712.46

2 **Net Income from Business:** Enter monthly net business income. This is the amount earned after ordinary and necessary monthly business expenses are paid. **This figure is the amount from page 6, line 89.** If the net business income is a loss, enter "0". Do not enter a negative number. If this amount is more or less than previous years, attach an explanation.

3 **Net Rental Income:** Enter monthly net rental income. This is the amount earned after ordinary and necessary monthly rental expenses are paid. Do not include deductions for depreciation or depletion. If the net rental income is a loss, enter "0." Do not enter a negative number.

4 **Distributions:** Enter the total distributions from partnerships and subchapter S corporations reported on Schedule K-1, and from limited liability companies reported on Form 1040, Schedule C, D or E. Enter total distributions from IRAs if not included under pension income.

5 **Other Income:** Include agricultural subsidies, unemployment compensation, gambling income, oil credits, rent subsidies, etc.

6 **Expenses not generally allowed:** We generally do not allow tuition for private schools, public or private college expenses, charitable contributions, voluntary retirement contributions or payments on unsecured debts. However, we may allow the expenses if proven that they are necessary for the health and welfare of the individual or family or the production of income. See Publication 1854 for exceptions.

7 **Food, Clothing and Miscellaneous:** Total of food, clothing, housekeeping supplies, and personal care products for one month. The miscellaneous allowance is for expenses incurred that are not included in any other allowable living expense items. Examples are credit card payments, bank fees and charges, reading material, and school supplies.

8 **Housing and Utilities:** For principal residence: Total of rent or mortgage payment. Add the average monthly expenses for the following: property taxes, homeowner's or renter's insurance, maintenance, dues, fees, and utilities. Utilities include gas, electricity, water, fuel, oil, other fuels, trash collection, telephone, cell phone, cable television and internet services.

9 **Vehicle Ownership Costs:** Total of monthly lease or purchase/loan payments.

10 **Vehicle Operating Costs:** Total of maintenance, repairs, insurance, fuel, registrations, licenses, inspections, parking, and tolls for one month.

11 **Public Transportation:** Total of monthly fares for mass transit *(e.g., bus, train, ferry, taxi, etc.)*

12 **Out of Pocket Health Care Costs:** Monthly total of medical services, prescription drugs and medical supplies *(e.g., eyeglasses, hearing aids, etc.)*

13 **Current Year Taxes:** Include state and Federal taxes withheld from salary or wages, or paid as estimated taxes.

Certification: *Under penalties of perjury, I declare that to the best of my knowledge and belief this statement of assets, liabilities, and other information is true, correct, and complete.*

Taxpayer's Signature	Spouse's signature	Date

After we review the completed Form 433-A, you may be asked to provide verification for the assets, encumbrances, income and expenses reported. Documentation may include previously filed income tax returns, pay statements, self-employment records, bank and investment statements, loan statements, bills or statements for recurring expenses, etc.

IRS USE ONLY *(Notes)*

Sections 6 and 7 must be completed only if you are SELF-EMPLOYED.

Section 6: Business Information

51 Is the business a sole proprietorship *(filing Schedule C)* ☐ **Yes**, Continue with Sections 6 and 7. ☐ **No**, Complete Form 433-B.
All other business entities, including limited liability companies, partnerships or corporations, must complete Form 433-B.

52 Business Name & Address *(if different than 1b)*

53 Employer Identification Number	54 Type of Business	55 Is the business a Federal Contractor ☐ Yes ☐ No
56 Business Website (web address)	57 Total Number of Employees	58 Average Gross Monthly Payroll
59 Frequency of Tax Deposits	60 Does the business engage in e-Commerce *(Internet sales)* If yes, complete *lines 61a and 61b* ☐ Yes ☐ No	

	PAYMENT PROCESSOR *(e.g., PayPal, Authorize.net, Google Checkout, etc.)* Name & Address *(Street, City, State, ZIP code)*	Payment Processor Account Number
61a		
61b		

CREDIT CARDS ACCEPTED BY THE BUSINESS

	Credit Card	Merchant Account Number	Issuing Bank Name & Address *(Street, City, State, ZIP code)*
62a			
62b			
62c			

63 **BUSINESS CASH ON HAND** Include cash that is not in a bank. **Total Cash on Hand** $

BUSINESS BANK ACCOUNTS Include checking accounts, online and mobile *(e.g., PayPal)* accounts, money market accounts, savings accounts, and stored value cards *(e.g., payroll cards, government benefit cards, etc.)*. Report Personal Accounts in Section 4.

	Type of Account	Full name & Address *(Street, City, State, ZIP code)* of Bank,Savings & Loan, Credit Union or Financial Institution.	Account Number	**Account Balance** As of ______ *mmddyyyy*
64a				$
64b				$
64c	**Total Cash in Banks** *(Add lines 64a, 64b and amounts from any attachments)*			$

ACCOUNTS/NOTES RECEIVABLE Include e-payment accounts receivable and factoring companies, and any bartering or online auction accounts. *(List all contracts separately, including contracts awarded, but not started.)* **Include Federal, state and local government grants and contracts.**

	Accounts/Notes Receivable & Address *(Street, City, State, ZIP code)*	Status *(e.g., age, factored, other)*	Date Due *(mmddyyyy)*	Invoice Number or Government Grant or Contract Number	**Amount Due**
65a					$
65b					$
65c					$
65d					$
65e					$
65f	**Total Outstanding Balance** *(Add lines 65a through 65e and amounts from any attachments)*				$

Form **433-A** (Rev. 12-2012)

BUSINESS ASSETS Include all tools, books, machinery, equipment, inventory or other assets used in trade or business. Include a list and show the value of all intangible assets such as licenses, patents, domain names, copyrights, trademarks, mining claims, etc.

	Purchase/ Lease Date *(mmddyyyy)*	Current Fair Market Value (FMV)	Current Loan Balance	Amount of Monthly Payment	Date of Final Payment *(mmddyyyy)*	**Equity** FMV Minus Loan
66a Property Description		$	$	$		$
Location *(Street, City, State, ZIP code)* and Country	Lender/Lessor/Landlord Name, Address *(Street, City, State, ZIP code)*, and Phone Phone					
66b Property Description		$	$	$		$
Location *(Street, City, State, ZIP code)* and Country	Lender/Lessor/Landlord Name, Address *(Street, City, State, ZIP code)*, and Phone Phone					
66c Total Equity *(Add lines 66a, 66b and amounts from any attachments)*						$

Section 7 should be completed only if you are SELF-EMPLOYED

Section 7: Sole Proprietorship Information *(lines 67 through 87 should reconcile with business Profit and Loss Statement)*

Accounting Method Used: ☐ Cash ☐ Accrual

Use the prior 3, 6, 9 or 12 month period to determine your typical business income and expenses.

Income and Expenses during the period *(mmddyyyy)* to *(mmddyyyy)*

Provide a breakdown below of your average monthly income and expenses, based on the period of time used above.

Total Monthly Business Income		**Total Monthly Business Expenses** (Use attachments as needed)	
Source	Gross Monthly	Expense Items	Actual Monthly
67 Gross Receipts	$	**77** Materials Purchased [1]	$
68 Gross Rental Income	$	**78** Inventory Purchased [2]	$
69 Interest	$	**79** Gross Wages & Salaries	$
70 Dividends	$	**80** Rent	$
71 Cash Receipts not included in lines 67-70	$	**81** Supplies [3]	$
Other Income (Specify below)		**82** Utilities/Telephone [4]	$
72	$	**83** Vehicle Gasoline/Oil	$
73	$	**84** Repairs & Maintenance	$
74	$	**85** Insurance	$
75	$	**86** Current Taxes [5]	$
76 Total Income (Add lines 67 through 75)	$	**87** Other Expenses, including installment payments (Specify)	$
		88 Total Expenses (Add lines 77 through 87)	$
		89 Net Business Income (Line 76 minus 88) [6]	$

Enter the monthly net income amount from line 89 on line 23, section 5. If line 89 is a loss, enter "0" on line 23, section 5. Self-employed taxpayers must return to page 4 to sign the certification.

1 Materials Purchased: Materials are items directly related to the production of a product or service.

2 Inventory Purchased: Goods bought for resale.

3 Supplies: Supplies are items used in the business that are consumed or used up within one year. This could be the cost of books, office supplies, professional equipment, etc.

4 Utilities/Telephone: Utilities include gas, electricity, water, oil, other fuels, trash collection, telephone, cell phone and business internet.

5 Current Taxes: Real estate, excise, franchise, occupational, personal property, sales and employer's portion of employment taxes.

6 Net Business Income: Net profit from Form 1040, Schedule C may be used if duplicated deductions are eliminated (e.g., expenses for business use of home already included in housing and utility expenses on page 4). Deductions for depreciation and depletion on Schedule C are not cash expenses and must be added back to the net income figure. In addition, interest cannot be deducted if it is already included in any other installment payments allowed.

IRS USE ONLY *(Notes)*

Form **433-A (OIC)** (Rev. February 2016)	Department of the Treasury — Internal Revenue Service **Collection Information Statement for Wage Earners and Self-Employed Individuals**

Use this form if you are

- An individual who owes income tax on a Form 1040, U.S. Individual Income Tax Return
- An individual with a personal liability for Excise Tax
- An individual responsible for a Trust Fund Recovery Penalty
- An individual who is self-employed or has self-employment income. You are considered to be self-employed if you are in business for yourself, or carry on a trade or business.
- An individual who is personally responsible for a partnership liability (only if the partnership is submitting an offer)
- An individual who operates as a disregarded single member Limited Liability Company (LLC) taxed as a sole proprietor
- An individual who is submitting an offer on behalf of a deceased person

Note: Include attachments if additional space is needed to respond completely to any question.

Section 1 Personal and Household Information

Last Name	First Name	Date of Birth *(mm/dd/yyyy)*	Social Security Number - -
Marital status ☐ Unmarried ☐ Married	Home Address *(Street, City, State, ZIP Code)*	Do you: ☐ Own your home ☐ Rent ☐ Other *(specify e.g., share rent, live with relative, etc.)*	
County of Residence	Primary Phone ( ) -	Mailing Address *(if different from above or Post Office Box number)*	
Secondary Phone ( ) -	Fax Number ( ) -		

Provide information about your spouse.

Spouse's Last Name	Spouse's First Name	Date of Birth *(mm/dd/yyyy)*	Social Security Number - -

Provide information for all other persons in the household or claimed as a dependent.

Name	Age	Relationship	Claimed as a dependent on your Form 1040?	Contributes to household income?
			☐ Yes ☐ No	☐ Yes ☐ No
			☐ Yes ☐ No	☐ Yes ☐ No
			☐ Yes ☐ No	☐ Yes ☐ No
			☐ Yes ☐ No	☐ Yes ☐ No

Section 2 Employment Information for Wage Earners

Complete this section if you or your spouse are wage earners and received a Form W-2. If you or your spouse have self-employment income (that is you file a Schedule C, E, F, etc.) instead of, or in addition to wage income, you must also complete Business Information in Sections 4, 5, and 6.

Your Employer's Name		Employer's Address *(street, city, state, zip code)*
Do you have an ownership interest in this business? ☐ Yes ☐ No	If yes, check the business interest that applies: ☐ Partner ☐ Officer ☐ Sole proprietor	
Your Occupation	How long with this employer (years) (months)	
Spouse's Employer's Name		Employer's Address *(street, city, state, zip code)*
Does your spouse have an ownership interest in this business? ☐ Yes ☐ No	If yes, check the business interest that applies: ☐ Partner ☐ Officer ☐ Sole proprietor	
Spouse's Occupation	How long with this employer (years) (months)	

Section 3 Personal Asset Information

Use the most current statement for each type of account, such as checking, savings, money market and online accounts, stored value cards *(such as, a payroll card from an employer)*, investment and retirement accounts *(IRAs, Keogh, 401(k) plans, stocks, bonds, mutual funds, certificates of deposit)*, life insurance policies that have a cash value, and safe deposit boxes. Asset value is subject to adjustment by IRS based on individual circumstances. Enter the total amount available for each of the following *(if additional space is needed include attachments)*.

Round to the nearest dollar. Do not enter a negative number. If any line item is a negative number, enter "0".

Cash and Investments (domestic and foreign)

☐ Cash ☐ Checking ☐ Savings ☐ Money Market/CD ☐ Online Account ☐ Stored Value Card		
Bank Name	Account Number	(1a) $
☐ Checking ☐ Savings ☐ Money Market/CD ☐ Online Account ☐ Stored Value Card		
Bank Name	Account Number	(1b) $
	Total of bank accounts from attachment	(1c) $
	Add lines (1a) through (1c) minus ($1,000) =	**(1) $**
Investment Account: ☐ Stocks ☐ Bonds ☐ Other		
Name of Financial Institution	Account Number	
Current Market Value $ ____ X .8 = $ ____	Minus Loan Balance – $ ____ =	(2a) $
Investment Account: ☐ Stocks ☐ Bonds ☐ Other		
Name of Financial Institution	Account Number	
Current Market Value $ ____ X .8 = $ ____	Minus Loan Balance – $ ____ =	(2b) $
Total investment accounts from attachment. [current market value X.8 minus loan balance(s)]		(2c) $
	Add lines (2a) through (2c) =	**(2) $**
Retirement Account: ☐ 401K ☐ IRA ☐ Other		
Name of Financial Institution	Account Number	
Current Market Value $ ____ X .8 = $ ____	Minus Loan Balance – $ ____ =	(3a) $
Retirement Account: ☐ 401K ☐ IRA ☐ Other		
Name of Financial Institution	Account Number	
Current Market Value $ ____ X .8 = $ ____	Minus Loan Balance – $ ____ =	(3b) $
Total of retirement accounts from attachment. [current market value X .8 minus loan balance(s)]		(3c) $
	Add lines (3a) through (3c) =	**(3) $**
Cash Value of Life Insurance Policies		
Name of Insurance Company	Policy Number	
Current Cash Value $ ____	Minus Loan Balance – $ ____ =	(4a) $
Total cash value of life insurance policies from attachment $ ____	Minus Loan Balance(s) – $ ____ =	(4b) $
	Add lines (4a) through (4b) =	**(4) $**

Section 3 *(Continued)* Personal Asset Information

Real Estate (Enter information about any house, condo, co-op, time share, etc. that you own or are buying)

Property Address *(Street Address, City, State, ZIP Code)*	Primary Residence ☐ Yes ☐ No	
	Date Purchased	
County and Country	Date of Final Payment	
How title is held *(joint tenancy, etc.)*	Description of Property	
Current Market Value $ ______ X .8 = $ ______	Minus Loan Balance *(Mortgages, etc.)* – $ ______ (Total Value of Real Estate) =	(5a) $
Property Address *(Street Address, City, State, ZIP Code)*	Primary Residence ☐ Yes ☐ No	
	Date Purchased	
County and Country	Date of Final Payment	
How title is held *(joint tenancy, etc.)*	Description of Property	
Current Market Value $ ______ X .8 = $ ______	Minus Loan Balance *(Mortgages, etc.)* – $ ______ (Total Value of Real Estate) =	(5b) $
Total value of property(s) from attachment [current market value X .8 minus any loan balance(s)]		(5c) $
	Add lines (5a) through (5c) =	**(5) $**

Vehicles *(Enter information about any cars, boats, motorcycles, etc. that you own or lease)*

Vehicle Make & Model	Year	Date Purchased	Mileage	
☐ Lease ☐ Loan	Name of Creditor	Date of Final Payment	Monthly Lease/Loan Amount $	
Current Market Value $ ______ X .8 = $ ______		Minus Loan Balance *(Mortgages, etc.)* – $ ______	Total value of vehicle *(if the vehicle is leased, enter 0 as the total value)* =	(6a) $
			Subtract $3,450 from line (6a) (If line (6a) minus line (6b) is a negative number, enter "0")	(6b) $
Vehicle Make & Model	Year	Date Purchased	Mileage	
☐ Lease ☐ Loan	Name of Creditor	Date of Final Payment	Monthly Lease/Loan Amount $	
Current Market Value $ ______ X .8 = $ ______		Minus Loan Balance *(Mortgages, etc.)* – $ ______	Total value of vehicle *(if the vehicle is leased, enter 0 as the total value)* =	(6c) $
			If you are filing a joint offer, subtract $3,450 from line (6c) (If line (6c) minus line (6d) is a negative number, enter "0")	(6d) $
Total value of vehicles listed from attachment [current market value X .8 minus any loan balance(s)]				(6e) $
			Total lines (6a) through (6e) =	**(6) $**

Section 3 *(Continued)* **Personal Asset Information**

Other valuable items *(artwork, collections, jewelry, items of value in safe deposit boxes, interest in a company or business that is not publicly traded, etc.)*
Note: Do not include clothing, furniture and other personal effects.

Description of asset:			
Current Market Value $	X .8 = $	Minus Loan Balance – $ =	(7a) $
Description of asset:			
Current Market Value $	X .8 = $	Minus Loan Balance – $ =	(7b) $
Total value of valuable items listed from attachment [current market value X .8 minus any loan balance(s)]			(7c) $
Add lines (7a) through (7c) =			**(7) $**

Do not include amount on the lines with a letter beside the number. Round to the nearest whole dollar. Do not enter a negative number. If any line item is a negative, enter "0" on that line.
Add lines (1) through (7) and enter the amount in Box A =

Box A
Available Individual Equity in Assets
$

NOTE: If you or your spouse are self-employed, Sections 4, 5, and 6 must be completed before continuing with Sections 7 and 8.

Section 4 **Self-Employed Information**

If you or your spouse are self-employed (e.g., files Schedule(s) C, E, F, etc.), complete this section.

Is your business a sole proprietorship?
☐ Yes ☐ No

Address of Business *(If other than personal residence)*

Name of Business

Business Telephone Number ( ) -	Employer Identification Number	Business Website		Trade Name or DBA
Description of Business	Total Number of Employees	Frequency of Tax Deposits	Average Gross Monthly Payroll $	

Do you or your spouse have any other business interests? Include any interest in an LLC, LLP, corporation, partnership, etc.
☐ Yes *(Percentage of ownership:* *)* Title:
☐ No

Business Address *(Street, City, State, ZIP code)*

Business Name	Business Telephone Number ( ) -	Employer Identification Number

Type of business *(Select one)*
☐ Partnership ☐ LLC ☐ Corporation ☐ Other ____________

Section 5 **Business Asset Information *(for Self-Employed)***

List business assets such as bank accounts, tools, books, machinery, equipment, business vehicles and real property that is owned/leased/rented. If additional space is needed, attach a list of items. Do not include personal assets listed in Section 3.

Round to the nearest whole dollar. Do not enter a negative number. If any line item is a negative number, enter "0".

☐ Cash ☐ Checking ☐ Savings ☐ Money Market/CD ☐ Online Account ☐ Stored Value Card		
Bank Name	Account Number	(8a) $
☐ Cash ☐ Checking ☐ Savings ☐ Money Market/CD ☐ Online Account ☐ Stored Value Card		
Bank Name	Account Number	(8b) $
	Total bank accounts from attachment	(8c) $
	Add lines (8a) through (8c) =	**(8) $**

Section 5 *(Continued)* **Business Asset Information *(for Self-Employed)***

Description of asset:

Current Market Value		Minus Loan Balance	*(if leased or used in the production of income, enter 0 as the total value)*	
$	X .8 = $	– $	=	(9a) $

Description of asset:

Current Market Value		Minus Loan Balance	*(if leased or used in the production of income, enter 0 as the total value)*	
$	X .8 = $	– $	=	(9b) $

Total value of assets listed from attachment [current market value X .8 minus any loan balance(s)]	(9c) $
Add lines (9a) through (9c) =	**(9) $**
IRS allowed deduction for professional books and tools of trade –	(10) $
Enter the value of line (9) minus line (10). If less than zero enter zero. =	**(11) $**

Notes Receivable

Do you have notes receivable? ☐ Yes ☐ No

If yes, attach current listing that includes name(s) and amount of note(s) receivable.

Accounts Receivable

Do you have accounts receivable, including e-payment, factoring companies, and any bartering or online auction accounts? ☐ Yes ☐ No

If yes, you may be asked to provide a list of your account(s) receivable.

Do not include amounts from the lines with a letter beside the number [for example: (9c)].
Round to the nearest whole dollar.
Do not enter a negative number. If any line item is a negative, enter "0" on that line.
Add lines (8) and (11) and enter the amount in Box B = **Box B** Available Business Equity in Assets $

Section 6 **Business Income and Expense Information *(for Self-Employed)***

If you provide a current profit and loss (P&L) statement for the information below, enter the total gross monthly income on line 17 and your monthly expenses on line 29 below. Do not complete lines (12) - (16) and (18) - (28). You may use the amounts claimed for income and expenses on your most recent Schedule C; however, if the amount has changed significantly within the past year, a current P&L should be submitted to substantiate the claim.

Round to the nearest whole dollar. Do not enter a negative number. If any line item is a negative number, enter "0".

Business Income *(You may average 6-12 months income/receipts to determine your Gross monthly income/receipts.)*	
Gross receipts	(12) $
Gross rental income	(13) $
Interest income	(14) $
Dividends	(15) $
Other income	(16) $
Add lines (12) through (16) =	**(17) $**

Business Expenses *(You may average 6-12 months expenses to determine your average expenses.)*	
Materials purchased *(e.g., items directly related to the production of a product or service)*	(18) $
Inventory purchased *(e.g., goods bought for resale)*	(19) $
Gross wages and salaries	(20) $
Rent	(21) $
Supplies *(items used to conduct business and used up within one year, e.g., books, office supplies, professional equipment, etc.)*	(22) $
Utilities/telephones	(23) $
Vehicle costs *(gas, oil, repairs, maintenance)*	(24) $
Business Insurance	(25) $
Current Business Taxes *(e.g., Real estate, excise, franchise, occupational, personal property, sales and employer's portion of employment taxes)*	(26) $
Secured debts *(not credit cards)*	(27) $
Other business expenses *(include a list)*	(28) $
Add lines (18) through (28) =	**(29) $**

Round to the nearest whole dollar.
Do not enter a negative number. If any line item is a negative, enter "0" on that line.
Subtract line (29) from line (17) and enter the amount in Box C = **Box C** Net Business Income $

Section 7 Monthly Household Income and Expense Information

Enter your household's gross monthly income. The information below is for yourself, your spouse, and anyone else who contributes to your household's income. The entire household includes spouse, non-liable spouse, significant other, children, and others who contribute to the household. This is necessary for the IRS to accurately evaluate your offer.

Monthly Household Income

Round to the nearest whole dollar.

Primary taxpayer Wages $ ______ + Social Security $ ______ + Pension(s) $ ______ + Other Income *(e.g. unemployment)* $ ______ Total primary taxpayer income =	(30) $
Spouse Wages $ ______ + Social Security $ ______ + Pension(s) $ ______ + Other Income *(e.g. unemployment)* $ ______ Total spouse income =	(31) $
Additional sources of income used to support the household, e.g., non-liable spouse, or anyone else who may contribute to the household income, etc.	(32) $
Interest and dividends	(33) $
Distributions *(e.g., income from partnerships, sub-S Corporations, etc.)*	(34) $
Net rental income	(35) $
Net business income from Box C	(36) $
Child support received	(37) $
Alimony received	(38) $
Round to the nearest whole dollar. Do not enter a negative number. If any line item is a negative, enter "0" on that line. **Add lines (30) through (38) and enter the amount in Box D =**	Box D Total Household Income $

Monthly Household Expenses

Enter your average monthly expenses.

Note: For expenses claimed in boxes (39) and (45) only, you should list the full amount of the allowable standard even if the actual amount you pay is less. You may find the allowable standards at http://www.irs.gov/Businesses/Small-Businesses-&-Self-Employed/Collection-Financial-Standards.

Round to the nearest whole dollar.

Food, clothing, and miscellaneous *(e.g., housekeeping supplies, personal care products , minimum payment on credit card). A reasonable estimate of these expenses may be used.*	(39) $
Housing and utilities *(e.g., rent or mortgage payment and average monthly cost of property taxes, home insurance, maintenance, dues, fees and utilities including electricity, gas, other fuels, trash collection, water, cable television and internet, telephone, and cell phone).*	(40) $
Vehicle loan and/or lease payment(s)	(41) $
Vehicle operating costs *(e.g., average monthly cost of maintenance, repairs, insurance, fuel, registrations, licenses, inspections, parking, tolls, etc.).* A reasonable estimate of these expenses may be used.	(42) $
Public transportation costs *(e.g., average monthly cost of fares for mass transit such as bus, train, ferry, taxi, etc.). A reasonable estimate of these expenses may be used.*	(43) $
Health insurance premiums	(44) $
Out-of-pocket health care costs *(e.g. average monthly cost of prescription drugs, medical services, and medical supplies like eyeglasses, hearing aids, etc.)*	(45) $
Court-ordered payments *(e.g., monthly cost of any alimony, child support, etc.)*	(46) $
Child/dependent care payments *(e.g., daycare, etc.)*	(47) $
Life insurance premiums	(48) $
Current monthly taxes *(e.g., monthly cost of federal, state, and local tax, personal property tax, etc.)*	(49) $

Section 7 Monthly Household Income and Expense Information *(Continued)*

Secured debts *(e.g., any loan where you pledged an asset as collateral not previously listed, government guaranteed Student Loan)*	(50) $
Enter the amount of your monthly delinquent State and/or Local Tax payment(s)	(51) $
Round to the nearest whole dollar. Do not enter a negative number. If any line item is a negative, enter "0" on that line. **Add lines (39) through (51) and enter the amount in Box E =**	Box E Total Household Expenses $
Round to the nearest whole dollar. Do not enter a negative number. If any line item is a negative, enter "0" on that line. **Subtract Box E from Box D and enter the amount in Box F =**	Box F Remaining Monthly Income $

Section 8 Calculate Your Minimum Offer Amount

The next steps calculate your minimum offer amount. The amount of time you take to pay your offer in full will affect your minimum offer amount. Paying over a shorter period of time will result in a smaller minimum offer amount.

Round to the nearest whole dollar.

If you will pay your offer in 5 or fewer payments within 5 months or less, multiply "Remaining Monthly Income" *(Box F)* by 12 to get "Future Remaining Income" *(Box G)*. Do not enter a number less than $0.

Enter the total from Box F $	**X 12 =**	**Box G Future Remaining Income** $

If you will pay your offer in 6 to 24 months, multiply "Remaining Monthly Income" (Box F) by 24 to get "Future Remaining Income" (Box H). Do not enter a number less than $0.

Enter the total from Box F $	**X 24 =**	**Box H Future Remaining Income** $

Determine your minimum offer amount by adding the total available assets from Box A and Box B (if applicable) to the amount in either Box G or Box H.

Enter the amount from Box A plus Box B (if applicable) $	+	**Enter the amount from either Box G or Box H** $	=	**Offer Amount** **Your offer must be more than zero ($0). Do not leave blank. Use whole dollars only.** $

If you cannot pay the Offer Amount shown above due to special circumstances, explain on the Form 656, Offer in Compromise, Section 1, Low Income Certification. You must offer an amount more than $0.

Section 9 Other Information

Additional information IRS needs to consider settlement of your tax debt. If you or your business are currently in a bankruptcy proceeding, you are not eligible to apply for an offer.

Are you the beneficiary of a trust, estate, or life insurance policy?
☐ Yes ☐ No

Are you currently in bankruptcy?
☐ Yes ☐ No

Have you filed bankruptcy in the past 10 years?
☐ Yes ☐ No

Discharge/Dismissal Date *(mm/dd/yyyy)*

Location Filed

Are you or have you been party to a lawsuit?
☐ Yes ☐ No
If yes, date the lawsuit was resolved: *(mm/dd/yyyy)*

In the past 10 years, have you transferred any assets for less than their full value?
☐ Yes ☐ No
If yes, date the asset was transferred: *(mm/dd/yyyy)*

In the past 3 years have you transferred any real property (land, house, etc.)?
☐ Yes ☐ No
If yes, list the type of property and date of the transfer.

Have you lived outside the U.S. for 6 months or longer in the past 10 years?
☐ Yes ☐ No

Do you have any funds being held in trust by a third party?
☐ Yes ☐ No If yes, how much $ Where:

Section 10 Signatures

Under penalties of perjury, I declare that I have examined this offer, including accompanying documents, and to the best of my knowledge it is true, correct, and complete.

Signature of Taxpayer	Date *(mm/dd/yyyy)*
Signature of Spouse	Date *(mm/dd/yyyy)*

Remember to include all applicable attachments listed below.

- ☐ Copies of the most recent pay stub, earnings statement, etc., from each employer
- ☐ Copies of the most recent statement for each investment and retirement account
- ☐ Copies of the most recent statement, etc., from all other sources of income such as pensions, Social Security, rental income, interest and dividends (including any received from a related partnership, corporation, LLC, LLP, etc.), court order for child support, alimony, and rent subsidies
- ☐ Copies of bank statements for the three most recent months
- ☐ Copies of the most recent statement from lender(s) on loans such as mortgages, second mortgages, vehicles, etc., showing monthly payments, loan payoffs, and balances
- ☐ List of Notes Receivable, if applicable
- ☐ Verification of delinquent State/Local Tax Liability, if applicable
- ☐ Documentation to support any special circumstances described in the "Explanation of Circumstances" on Form 656, if applicable
- ☐ Attach a Form 2848, *Power of Attorney*, if you would like your attorney, CPA, or enrolled agent to represent you and you do not have a current form on file with the IRS.
- ☐ Completed and signed Form 656

Form **433-B**

(Rev. December 2012)

Department of the Treasury
Internal Revenue Service

Collection Information Statement for Businesses

Note: *Complete all entry spaces with the current data available or "N/A" (not applicable). Failure to complete all entry spaces may result in rejection of your request or significant delay in account resolution.* **Include attachments if additional space is needed to respond completely to any question.**

Section 1: Business Information

1a Business Name

1b Business Street Address

Mailing Address

City State ZIP

1c County

1d Business Telephone ( )

1e Type of Business

1f Business Website (web address)

2a Employer Identification No. (EIN)

2b Type of entity *(Check appropriate box below)*

☐ Partnership ☐ Corporation ☐ Other

☐ Limited Liability Company (LLC) classified as a corporation

☐ Other LLC - Include number of members

2c Date Incorporated/Established

mmddyyyy

3a Number of Employees

3b Monthly Gross Payroll

3c Frequency of Tax Deposits

3d Is the business enrolled in Electronic Federal Tax Payment System (EFTPS) ☐ **Yes** ☐ **No**

4 Does the business engage in e-Commerce *(Internet sales)* If yes, complete 5a and 5b. ☐ **Yes** ☐ **No**

	PAYMENT PROCESSOR *(e.g., PayPal, Authorize.net, Google Checkout, etc.)* Name and Address *(Street, City, State, ZIP code)*	Payment Processor Account Number
5a		
5b		

CREDIT CARDS ACCEPTED BY THE BUSINESS

	Type of Credit Card *(e.g., Visa, Mastercard, etc.)*	Merchant Account Number	Issuing Bank Name and Address *(Street, City, State, ZIP code)*
6a			Phone
6b			Phone
6c			Phone

Section 2: Business Personnel and Contacts

PARTNERS, OFFICERS, LLC MEMBERS, MAJOR SHAREHOLDERS, ETC.

7a Full Name
Title
Home Address
City State ZIP
Responsible for Depositing Payroll Taxes ☐ **Yes** ☐ **No**

Social Security Number
Home Telephone ( )
Work/Cell Phone ( )
Ownership Percentage & Shares or Interest
Annual Salary/Draw

7b Full Name
Title
Home Address
City State ZIP
Responsible for Depositing Payroll Taxes ☐ **Yes** ☐ **No**

Social Security Number
Home Telephone ( )
Work/Cell Phone ( )
Ownership Percentage & Shares or Interest
Annual Salary/Draw

7c Full Name
Title
Home Address
City State ZIP
Responsible for Depositing Payroll Taxes ☐ **Yes** ☐ **No**

Social Security Number
Home Telephone ( )
Work/Cell Phone ( )
Ownership Percentage & Shares or Interest
Annual Salary/Draw

7d Full Name
Title
Home Address
City State ZIP
Responsible for Depositing Payroll Taxes ☐ **Yes** ☐ **No**

Social Security Number
Home Telephone ( )
Work/Cell Phone ( )
Ownership Percentage & Shares or Interest
Annual Salary/Draw

Section 3: Other Financial Information *(Attach copies of all applicable documents)*

8 **Does the business use a Payroll Service Provider or Reporting Agent** *(If yes, answer the following)* ☐ Yes ☐ No

Name and Address *(Street, City, State, ZIP code)*	Effective dates *(mmddyyyy)*

9 **Is the business a party to a lawsuit** *(If yes, answer the following)* ☐ Yes ☐ No

☐ Plaintiff ☐ Defendant	Location of Filing	Represented by	Docket/Case No.
Amount of Suit $	Possible Completion Date *(mmddyyyy)*	Subject of Suit	

10 **Has the business ever filed bankruptcy** *(If yes, answer the following)* ☐ Yes ☐ No

Date Filed *(mmddyyyy)*	Date Dismissed *(mmddyyyy)*	Date Discharged *(mmddyyyy)*	Petition No.	District of Filing

11 **Do any related parties** ***(e.g., officers, partners, employees)*** **have outstanding amounts owed to the business** *(If yes, answer the following)* ☐ Yes ☐ No

Name and Address *(Street, City, State, ZIP code)*	Date of Loan	Current Balance As of ______ *mmddyyyy*	Payment Date	Payment Amount
		$		$

12 **Have any assets been transferred, in the last 10 years, from this business for less than full value** *(If yes, answer the following)* ☐ Yes ☐ No

List Asset	Value at Time of Transfer	Date Transferred *(mmddyyyy)*	To Whom or Where Transferred
	$		

13 **Does this business have other business affiliations** ***(e.g., subsidiary or parent companies)*** *(If yes, answer the following)* ☐ Yes ☐ No

Related Business Name and Address *(Street, City, State, ZIP code)*	Related Business EIN:

14 **Any increase/decrease in income anticipated** *(If yes, answer the following)* ☐ Yes ☐ No

Explain *(Use attachment if needed)*	How much will it increase/decrease	When will it increase/decrease
	$	

15 **Is the business a Federal Government Contractor** *(Include Federal Government contracts in #18, Accounts/Notes Receivable)* ☐ Yes ☐ No

Section 4: Business Asset and Liability Information

16a **CASH ON HAND** *Include cash that is not in the bank* **Total Cash on Hand** $

16b **Is there a safe on the business premises** ☐ Yes ☐ No Contents

BUSINESS BANK ACOUNTS Include online and mobile accounts *(e.g., PayPal)*, money market accounts, savings accounts, checking accounts and stored value cards *(e.g., payroll cards, government benefit cards, etc.)*
List safe deposit boxes including location, box number and value of contents. Attach list of contents.

	Type of Account	Full Name and Address *(Street, City, State, ZIP code)* of Bank, Savings & Loan, Credit Union or Financial Institution	Account Number	Account Balance As of ______ *mmddyyyy*
17a				$
17b				$
17c				$
17d	**Total Cash in Banks** *(Add lines 17a through 17c and amounts from any attachments)*			$

ACCOUNTS/NOTES RECEIVABLE Include e-payment accounts receivable and factoring companies, and any bartering or online auction accounts. *(List all contracts separately including contracts awarded, but not started).* ***Include Federal, state and local government grants and contracts.***

	Name & Address *(Street, City, State, ZIP code)*	Status *(e.g., age, factored, other)*	Date Due *(mmddyyy)*	Invoice Number or Government Grant or Contract Number	**Amount Due**
18a	Contact Name Phone				$
18b	Contact Name Phone				$
18c	Contact Name Phone				$
18d	Contact Name Phone				$
18e	Contact Name Phone				$

18f Outstanding Balance *(Add lines 18a through 18e and amounts from any attachments)* $

INVESTMENTS List all investment assets below. Include stocks, bonds, mutual funds, stock options, certificates of deposit and commodities *(e.g., gold, silver, copper, etc.)*.

	Name of Company & Address *(Street, City, State, ZIP code)*	Used as collateral on loan	Current Value	Loan Balance	**Equity** Value Minus Loan
19a	Phone	☐ **Yes** ☐ **No**	$	$	$
19b	Phone	☐ **Yes** ☐ **No**	$	$	$

19c Total Investments *(Add lines 19a, 19b, and amounts from any attachments)* $

AVAILABLE CREDIT Include all lines of credit and credit cards.

	Full Name & Address *(Street, City, State, ZIP code)*	Credit Limit	Amount Owed As of ________ *mmddyyyy*	**Available Credit** As of ________ *mmddyyyy*
20a	Account No.	$	$	$
20b	Account No.	$	$	$

20c Total Credit Available *(Add lines 20a, 20b, and amounts from any attachments)* $

REAL PROPERTY Include all real property and land contracts the business owns/leases/rents.

	Purchase/ Lease Date *(mmddyyyy)*	Current Fair Market Value (FMV)	Current Loan Balance	Amount of Monthly Payment	Date of Final Payment *(mmddyyyy)*	**Equity** FMV Minus Loan
21a Property Description		$	$	$		$
Location *(Street, City, State, ZIP code)* and County	Lender/Lessor/Landlord Name, Address, *(Street, City, State, ZIP code)* and Phone Phone					
21b Property Description		$	$	$		$
Location *(Street, City, State, ZIP code)* and County	Lender/Lessor/Landlord Name, Address, *(Street, City, State, ZIP code)* and Phone Phone					
21c Property Description		$	$	$		$
Location *(Street, City, State, ZIP code)* and County	Lender/Lessor/Landlord Name, Address, *(Street, City, State, ZIP code)* and Phone Phone					
21d Property Description		$	$	$		$
Location *(Street, City, State, ZIP code)* and County	Lender/Lessor/Landlord Name, Address, *(Street, City, State, ZIP code)* and Phone Phone					
21e **Total Equity** *(Add lines 21a through 21d and amounts from any attachments)*						$

VEHICLES, LEASED AND PURCHASED Include boats, RVs, motorcycles, all-terrain and off-road vehicles, trailers, mobile homes, etc.

		Purchase/ Lease Date *(mmddyyyy)*	Current Fair Market Value (FMV)	Current Loan Balance	Amount of Monthly Payment	Date of Final Payment *(mmddyyyy)*	**Equity** FMV Minus Loan
22a Year	Make/Model		$	$	$		$
Mileage	License/Tag Number	Lender/Lessor Name, Address, *(Street, City, State, ZIP code)* and Phone Phone					
Vehicle Identification Number (VIN)							
22b Year	Make/Model		$	$	$		$
Mileage	License/Tag Number	Lender/Lessor Name, Address, *(Street, City, State, ZIP code)* and Phone Phone					
Vehicle Identification Number (VIN)							
22c Year	Make/Model		$	$	$		$
Mileage	License/Tag Number	Lender/Lessor Name, Address, *(Street, City, State, ZIP code)* and Phone Phone					
Vehicle Identification Number (VIN)							
22d Year	Make/Model		$	$	$		$
Mileage	License/Tag Number	Lender/Lessor Name, Address, *(Street, City, State, ZIP code)* and Phone Phone					
Vehicle Identification Number (VIN)							
22e **Total Equity** *(Add lines 22a through 22d and amounts from any attachments)*							$

BUSINESS EQUIPMENT AND INTANGIBLE ASSETS Include all machinery, equipment, merchandise inventory, and other assets in 23a through 23d. List intangible assets in 23e through 23g *(licenses, patents, logos, domain names, trademarks, copyrights, software, mining claims, goodwill and trade secrets.)*

	Purchase/ Lease Date *(mmddyyyy)*	Current Fair Market Value (FMV)	Current Loan Balance	Amount of Monthly Payment	Date of Final Payment *(mmddyyyy)*	**Equity** FMV Minus Loan
23a Asset Description		$	$	$		$
Location of asset *(Street, City, State, ZIP code)* and County	Lender/Lessor Name, Address, *(Street, City, State, ZIP code)* and Phone Phone					
23b Asset Description		$	$	$		$
Location of asset *(Street, City, State, ZIP code)* and County	Lender/Lessor Name, Address, *(Street, City, State, ZIP code)* and Phone Phone					
23c Asset Description		$	$	$		$
Location of asset *(Street, City, State, ZIP code)* and County	Lender/Lessor Name, Address, *(Street, City, State, ZIP code)* and Phone Phone					
23d Asset Description		$	$	$		$
Location of asset *(Street, City, State, ZIP code)* and County	Lender/Lessor Name, Address, *(Street, City, State, ZIP code)* and Phone Phone					
23e Intangible Asset Description						$
23f Intangible Asset Description						$
23g Intangible Asset Description						$
23h **Total Equity** *(Add lines 23a through 23g and amounts from any attachments)*						$

BUSINESS LIABILITIES Include notes and judgements not listed previously on this form.

Business Liabilities	Secured/ Unsecured	Date Pledged *(mmddyyyy)*	Balance Owed	Date of Final Payment *(mmddyyyy)*	Payment Amount
24a Description:	☐ Secured ☐ Unsecured		$		$
Name Street Address City/State/ZIP code Phone					
24b Description:	☐ Secured ☐ Unsecured		$		$
Name Street Address City/State/ZIP code Phone					
24c **Total Payments** *(Add lines 24a and 24b and amounts from any attachments)*					$

Form **433-B** (Rev. 12-2012)

Section 5: Monthly Income/Expenses Statement for Business

Accounting Method Used: ☐ Cash ☐ Accrual

Use the prior 3, 6, 9 or 12 month period to determine your typical business income and expenses.

Income and Expenses during the period *(mmddyyyy)* to *(mmddyyyy)*

Provide a breakdown below of your average monthly income and expenses, based on the period of time used above.

Total Monthly Business Income		**Total Monthly Business Expenses**	
Income Source	Gross Monthly	Expense items	Actual Monthly
25 Gross Receipts from Sales/Services	$	**36** Materials Purchased [1]	$
26 Gross Rental Income	$	**37** Inventory Purchased [2]	$
27 Interest Income	$	**38** Gross Wages & Salaries	$
28 Dividends	$	**39** Rent	$
29 Cash Receipts (Not included in lines 25-28)	$	**40** Supplies [3]	$
Other Income (Specify below)		**41** Utilities/Telephone [4]	$
30	$	**42** Vehicle Gasoline/Oil	$
31	$	**43** Repairs & Maintenance	$
32	$	**44** Insurance	$
33	$	**45** Current Taxes [5]	$
34	$	**46** Other Expenses (Specify)	$
35 **Total Income** (Add lines 25 through 34)	$	**47** IRS Use Only-Allowable Installment Payments	$
		48 **Total Expenses** (Add lines 36 through 47)	$
		49 **Net Income** (Line 35 minus Line 48)	$

1 **Materials Purchased:** Materials are items directly related to the production of a product or service.

2 **Inventory Purchased:** Goods bought for resale.

3 **Supplies:** Supplies are items used to conduct business and are consumed or used up within one year. This could be the cost of books, office supplies, professional equipment, etc.

4 **Utilities/Telephone:** Utilities include gas, electricity, water, oil, other fuels, trash collection, telephone, cell phone and business internet.

5 **Current Taxes:** Real estate, state, and local income tax, excise, franchise, occupational, personal property, sales and the employer's portion of employment taxes.

Certification: *Under penalties of perjury, I declare that to the best of my knowledge and belief this statement of assets, liabilities, and other information is true, correct, and complete.*

Signature	**Title**	**Date**

Print Name of Officer, Partner or LLC Member

After we review the completed Form 433-B, you may be asked to provide verification for the assets, encumbrances, income and expenses reported. Documentation may include previously filed income tax returns, profit and loss statements, bank and investment statements, loan statements, financing statements, bills or statements for recurring expenses, etc.

IRS USE ONLY *(Notes)*

Form **433-B (OIC)**
(Rev. February 2016)

Department of the Treasury — Internal Revenue Service

Collection Information Statement for Businesses

Complete this form if your business is a

- ▶ Corporation
- ▶ Partnership
- ▶ Limited Liability Company (LLC) classified as a corporation
- ▶ Other multi-owner/multi-member LLC

Note: If your business is a sole proprietorship or a disregarded single member LLC taxed as a sole proprietor (filing Schedule C, D, E, F, etc.), do not use this form. Instead, complete Form 433-A (OIC) Collection Information Statement for Wage Earners and Self-Employed Individuals.

Include attachments if additional space is needed to respond completely to any question.

Section 1 Business Information

Business Name		Employer Identification Number
Business Address *(street, city, state, zip code)*		County of Business Location
		Description of Business and DBA or "Trade Name"
Primary Phone ( ) -	Secondary Phone ( ) -	Mailing Address *(if different from above or Post Office Box number)*
Business website address		
Fax Number ( ) -		Does the business outsource its payroll processing and tax return preparation for a fee? ☐ Yes ☐ No If yes, list provider name and address in box below *(Street, City, State, ZIP Code)*
Federal Contractor ☐ Yes ☐ No	Total Number of Employees	
Frequency of Tax Deposits	Average Gross Monthly Payroll $	

Provide information about all partners, officers, LLC members, major shareholders (foreign and domestic), etc., associated with the business. Include attachments if additional space is needed.

Last Name	First Name	Title
Percent of Ownership and Annual Salary	Social Security Number - -	Home Address *(Street, City, State, ZIP Code)*
Primary Phone ( ) -	Secondary Phone ( ) -	
Last Name	First Name	Title
Percent of Ownership and Annual Salary	Social Security Number - -	Home Address *(Street, City, State, ZIP Code)*
Primary Phone ( ) -	Secondary Phone ( ) -	
Last Name	First Name	Title
Percent of Ownership and Annual Salary	Social Security Number - -	Home Address *(Street, City, State, ZIP Code)*
Primary Phone ( ) -	Secondary Phone ( ) -	

Section 2 Business Asset Information

Gather the most current statement from banks, lenders on loans, mortgages *(including second mortgages)*, monthly payments, loan balances, and accountant's depreciation schedules, if applicable. Also, include make/model/year/mileage of vehicles and current value of business assets. To estimate the current value, you may consult resources like Kelley Blue Book *(www.kbb.com)*, NADA *(www.nada.com)*, local real estate postings of properties similar to yours, and any other websites or publications that show what the business assets would be worth if you were to sell them. Asset value is subject to adjustment by IRS. Enter the total amount available for each of the following *(if additional space is needed, please include attachments)*.

Round to the nearest dollar. Do not enter a negative number. If any line item is a negative number, enter "0".

Cash and Investments *(domestic and foreign)*

☐ Cash ☐ Checking ☐ Savings ☐ Money Market/CD ☐ Online Account ☐ Stored Value Card		
Bank Name	Account Number	(1a) $
☐ Cash ☐ Checking ☐ Savings ☐ Money Market/CD ☐ Online Account ☐ Stored Value Card		
Bank Name	Account Number	(1b) $
☐ Cash ☐ Checking ☐ Savings ☐ Money Market/CD ☐ Online Account ☐ Stored Value Card		
Bank Name	Account Number	(1c) $
	Total bank accounts from attachment	(1d) $
	Add lines (1a) through (1d) =	**(1) $**
Investment Account: ☐ Stocks ☐ Bonds ☐ Other		
Name of Financial Institution	Account Number	
Current Market Value $ ______ X .8 = $ ______	Minus Loan Balance – $ ______ =	(2a) $
Investment Account: ☐ Stocks ☐ Bonds ☐ Other		
Name of Financial Institution	Account Number	
Current Market Value $ ______ X .8 = $ ______	Minus Loan Balance – $ ______ =	(2b) $
	Total investment accounts from attachment. [current market value X.8 minus loan balance(s)]	(2c) $
	Add lines (2a) through (2c) =	**(2) $**

Notes Receivable

Do you have notes receivable? ☐ Yes ☐ No

If yes, attach current listing which includes name, age, and amount of note(s) receivable.

Accounts Receivable

Do you have accounts receivable, including e-payment, factoring companies, and any bartering or online auction accounts? ☐ Yes ☐ No

If yes, you may be asked to provide a list of name, age, and amount of the account(s) receivable.

Section 2 *(Continued)* **Business Asset Information**

If the business owns more properties, vehicles, or equipment than shown in this form, please list on a separate attachment.

Real Estate *(Buildings, Lots, Commercial Property, etc.)*

Property Address *(Street Address, City, State, ZIP Code)*	Property Description	Date Purchased	
	Name of Creditor	Date of Final Payment	
	County and Country		
Current Market Value $ ______ X .8 = $ ______	Minus Loan Balance *(mortgages, etc.)* – $ ______	Total Value of Real Estate =	(3a) $
Property Address *(Street Address, City, State, ZIP Code)*	Property Description	Date Purchased	
	Name of Creditor	Date of Final Payment	
	County and Country		
Current Market Value $ ______ X .8 = $ ______	Minus Loan Balance *(mortgages, etc.)* – $ ______	Total Value of Real Estate =	(3b) $
Total value of property(s) listed from attachment [current market value X .8 minus any loan balance(s)]			(3c) $
		Add lines (3a) through (3c) =	**(3) $**

Business Vehicles *(cars, boats, motorcycles, trailers, etc.)*. If additional space is needed, list on an attachment.

Vehicle Make & Model	Year	Date Purchased	Mileage or Use Hours	
☐ Lease ☐ Loan	Monthly Lease/Loan Amount $	Name of Creditor	Date of Final Payment	
Current Market Value $ ______ X .8 = $ ______		Minus Loan Balance – $ ______	Total value of vehicle *(if the vehicle is leased, enter 0 as the total value)* =	(4a) $
Vehicle Make & Model	Year	Date Purchased	Mileage or Use Hours	
☐ Lease ☐ Loan	Monthly Lease/Loan Amount $	Name of Creditor	Date of Final Payment	
Current Market Value $ ______ X .8 = $ ______		Minus Loan Balance – $ ______	Total value of vehicle *(if the vehicle is leased, enter 0 as the total value)* =	(4b) $
Vehicle Make & Model	Year	Date Purchased	Mileage or Use Hours	
☐ Lease ☐ Loan	Monthly Lease/Loan Amount $	Name of Creditor	Date of Final Payment	
Current Market Value $ ______ X .8 = $ ______		Minus Loan Balance – $ ______	Total value of vehicle *(if the vehicle is leased, enter 0 as the total value)* =	(4c) $
Total value of vehicles listed from attachment [current market value X .8 minus any loan balance(s)]				(4d) $
			Add lines (4a) through (4d) =	**(4) $**

Section 2 *(Continued)*	**Business Asset Information**

Other Business Equipment
[If you have more than one piece of equipment, please list on a separate attachment and put the total of all equipment in box (5b)]

Type of equipment	
Current Market Value $ ________ X .8 = $ ________ Minus Loan Balance – $ ________ Total value of equipment *(if leased or used in the production of income enter 0 as the total value)* =	(5a) $
Total value of equipment listed from attachment [current market value X .8 minus any loan balance(s)]	(5b) $
Total value of all business equipment **Add lines (5a) and (5b) =**	**(5) $**
Do not include amount on the lines with a letter beside the number. Round to the nearest dollar. Do not enter a negative number. If any line item is a negative number, enter "0" on that line. **Add lines (1) through (5) and enter the amount in Box A =**	**Box A** Available Equity in Assets $

Section 3	**Business Income Information**

Enter the average gross monthly income of your business. To determine your gross monthly income use the most recent 6-12 months documentation of commissions, invoices, gross receipts from sales/services, etc.; most recent 6-12 months earnings statements, etc., from every other source of income (such as rental income, interest and dividends, or subsidies); or you may use the most recent 6-12 months Profit and Loss (P&L) to provide the information of income and expenses.

Note: If you provide a current profit and loss statement for the information below, enter the total gross monthly income in Box B below. Do not complete lines (6) - (10).

Gross receipts	(6) $
Gross rental income	(7) $
Interest income	(8) $
Dividends	(9) $
Other income *(Specify on attachment)*	(10) $
Round to the nearest dollar. Do not enter a negative number. If any line item is a negative number, enter "0" on that line. **Add lines (6) through (10) and enter the amount in Box B =**	**Box B** Total Business Income $

Section 4	**Business Expense Information**

Enter the average gross monthly expenses for your business using your most recent 6-12 months statements, bills, receipts, or other documents showing monthly recurring expenses.

Note: If you provide a current profit and loss statement for the information below, enter the total monthly expenses in Box C below. Do not complete lines (11) - (20).

Materials purchased *(e.g., items directly related to the production of a product or service)*	(11) $
Inventory purchased *(e.g., goods bought for resale)*	(12) $
Gross wages and salaries	(13) $
Rent	(14) $
Supplies *(items used to conduct business and used up within one year, e.g., books, office supplies, professional equipment, etc.)*	(15) $
Utilities/telephones	(16) $
Vehicle costs *(gas, oil, repairs, maintenance)*	(17) $
Insurance *(other than life)*	(18) $
Current taxes *(e.g., real estate, state, and local income tax, excise franchise, occupational, personal property, sales and employer's portion of employment taxes, etc.)*	(19) $
Other expenses *(e.g., secured debt payments. Specify on attachment. Do not include credit card payments)*	(20) $
Round to the nearest dollar. Do not enter a negative number. If any line item is a negative number, enter "0" on that line. **Add lines (11) through (20) and enter the amount in Box C =**	**Box C** Total Business Expenses $
Round to the nearest dollar. Do not enter a negative number. If any line item is a negative number, enter "0" on that line. **Subtract Box C from Box B and enter the amount in Box D =**	**Box D** Remaining Monthly Income $

Section 5 — Calculate Your Minimum Offer Amount

The next steps calculate your minimum offer amount. The amount of time you take to pay your offer in full will affect your minimum offer amount. Paying over a shorter period of time will result in a smaller minimum offer amount.

If you will pay your offer in 5 or fewer payments within 5 months or less, multiply "Remaining Monthly Income" (Box D) by 12 to get "Future Remaining Income." Do not enter a number less than zero.

Round to the nearest whole dollar.

Enter the total from Box D $	X 12 =	**Box E Future Remaining Income** $

If you will pay your offer in 6 to 24 months, multiply "Remaining Monthly Income" (Box D) by 24 to get "Future Remaining Income". Do not enter a number less than zero.

Enter the total from Box D $	X 24 =	**Box F Future Remaining Income** $

Determine your minimum offer amount by adding the total available assets from Box A to the amount in either Box E or Box F. Your offer amount must be more than zero.

Enter the amount from Box A * $	+	**Enter the amount from either Box E or Box F** $	=	**Offer Amount** **Your offer must be more than zero ($0). Do not leave blank. Use whole dollars only.** $

You must offer an amount more than $0.
***You may exclude any equity in income producing assets shown in Section 2 of this form.**

Section 6 — Other Information

Additional information IRS needs to consider settlement of your tax debt. If this business is currently in a bankruptcy proceeding, the business is not eligible to apply for an offer.

Is the business currently in bankruptcy?

☐ Yes ☐ No

Has the business ever filed bankruptcy?

☐ Yes ☐ No

If yes, provide:

Date Filed *(mm/dd/yyyy)* ________ Date Dismissed or Discharged *(mm/dd/yyyy)* ________

Petition No. ________ Location Filed ________

Does this business have other business affiliations *(e.g., subsidiary or parent companies)*?

☐ Yes ☐ No

If yes, list the Name and Employer Identification Number:

Do any related parties *(e.g., partners, officers, employees)* owe money to the business?

☐ Yes ☐ No

Is the business currently, or in the past, a party to a lawsuit?

☐ Yes ☐ No

If yes, date the lawsuit was resolved:

In the past 10 years, has the business transferred any assets for less than their full value?

☐ Yes ☐ No

If yes, provide date and type of asset transferred:

In the past 3 years have you transferred any real property (land, house, etc.)?

☐ Yes ☐ No

If yes, list the type of property and date of the transfer.

Has the business been located outside the U.S. for 6 months or longer in the past 10 years?

☐ Yes ☐ No

Does the business have any funds being held in trust by a third party?

☐ Yes ☐ No **If yes,** how much $ ________ Where: ________

Does the business have any lines of credit?

☐ Yes ☐ No **If yes,** credit limit $ ________ Amount owed $ ________

What property secures the line of credit? ________

Section 7	Signatures

Under penalties of perjury, I declare that I have examined this offer, including accompanying documents, and to the best of my knowledge it is true, correct, and complete.

Signature of Taxpayer	Title	Date *(mm/dd/yyyy)*

Remember to include all applicable attachments from list below.

- ☐ A current Profit and Loss statement covering at least the most recent 6–12 month period, if appropriate.
- ☐ Copies of the three most recent statements for each bank, investment, and retirement account
- ☐ If an asset is used as collateral on a loan, include copies of the most recent statement from lender(s) on loans, monthly payments, loan payoffs, and balances.
- ☐ Copies of the most recent statement of outstanding notes receivable.
- ☐ Copies of the most recent statements from lenders on loans, mortgages (including second mortgages), monthly payments, loan payoffs, and balances.
- ☐ Copies of relevant supporting documentation of the special circumstances described in the "Explanation of Circumstances" on Form 656, if applicable.
- ☐ Attach a Form 2848, Power of Attorney, if you would like your attorney, CPA, or enrolled agent to represent you and you do not have a current form on file with the IRS. Make sure the current tax year is included.
- ☐ Completed and signed Form 656

Collection Information Statement

Name(s) and Address	Your Social Security Number or Individual Taxpayer Identification Number	
	Your Spouse's Social Security Number or Individual Taxpayer Identification Number	
☐ If address provided above is different than last return filed, please check here	Your Telephone Numbers Home: ______ Work: ______ Cell: ______	Spouse's Telephone Numbers Home: ______ Work: ______ Cell: ______
County of Residence		

Enter the number of people in the household who can be claimed on this year's tax return including you and your spouse. Under 65 ____ 65 and Over ____

If you or your spouse are self employed or have self employment income, provide the following information:

Name of Business	Business EIN	Type of Business	Number of Employees *(not counting owner)*

A. ACCOUNTS / LINES OF CREDIT Include checking, online, mobile (e.g., PayPal) and savings accounts, Certificates of Deposit, Trusts, Individual Retirement Accounts (IRAs), Keogh Plans, Simplified Employee Pensions, 401(k) Plans, Profit Sharing Plans, Mutual Funds, Stocks, Bonds and other investments. If applicable, include business accounts. *(Use additional sheets if necessary.)*

Name and Address of Institution	Account Number	Type of Account	Current Balance/Value	Check if Business Account
				☐
				☐
				☐
				☐
				☐
				☐
				☐

B. REAL ESTATE Include home, vacation property, timeshares, vacant land and other real estate. *(Use additional sheets if necessary.)*

Description/Location/County	Monthly Payment(s)	Financing		Current Value	Balance Owed	Equity
		Year Purchased	Purchase Price			
☐ Primary Residence ☐ Other		Year Refinanced	Refinance Amount			
		Year Purchased	Purchase Price			
☐ Primary Residence ☐ Other		Year Refinanced	Refinance Amount			

C. OTHER ASSETS Include cars, boats, recreational vehicles, whole life policies, etc. Include make, model and year of vehicles and name of Life Insurance company in Description. If applicable, include business assets such as tools, equipment, inventory, etc. *(Use additional sheets if necessary.)*

Description	Monthly Payment	Year Purchased	Final Payment *(mo/yr)*	Current Value	Balance Owed	Equity
			/			
			/			
			/			
			/			
			/			
			/			
			/			

NOTES *(For IRS Use Only)*

TURN PAGE TO CONTINUE

D. CREDIT CARDS *(Visa, MasterCard, American Express, Department Stores, etc.)*

Type	Credit Limit	Balance Owed	Minimum Monthly Payment

E. BUSINESS INFORMATION Complete E1 for Accounts Receivable owed to you or your business. *(Use additional sheets if necessary.)* Complete E2 if you or your business accepts credit card payments.

E1. Accounts Receivable owed to you or your business

Name	Address	Amount Owed
	List total amount owed from additional sheets	
	Total amount of accounts receivable available to pay to IRS now	

E2. Name of individual or business on account

Credit Card *(Visa, Master Card, etc.)*	Issuing Bank Name and Address	Merchant Account Number

F. EMPLOYMENT INFORMATION If you have more than one employer, include the information on another sheet of paper. *(If attaching a copy of current pay stub, you do not need to complete this section.)*

Your current Employer *(name and address)*

How often are you paid? *(Check one)*
☐ Weekly ☐ Biweekly ☐ Semi-monthly ☐ Monthly
Gross per pay period ______
Taxes per pay period *(Fed)* ______ *(State)* ______ *(Local)* ______
How long at current employer ______

Spouse's current Employer *(name and address)*

How often are you paid? *(Check one)*
☐ Weekly ☐ Biweekly ☐ Semi-monthly ☐ Monthly
Gross per pay period ______
Taxes per pay period *(Fed)* ______ *(State)* ______ *(Local)* ______
How long at current employer ______

G. NON-WAGE HOUSEHOLD INCOME List monthly amounts. For Self-Employment and Rental Income, list the monthly amount received after expenses or taxes and attach a copy of your current year profit and loss statement.

Alimony Income		Net Rental Income		Interest/Dividends Income	
Child Support Income		Unemployment Income		Social Security Income	
Net Self Employment Income		Pension Income		Other:	

H. MONTHLY NECESSARY LIVING EXPENSES List monthly amounts. (For expenses paid other than monthly, see instructions.)

1. Food / Personal Care ***See instructions. If you do not spend more than the standard allowable amount for your family size, fill in the Total amount only.***

Food	
Housekeeping Supplies	
Clothing and Clothing Services	
Personal Care Products & Services	
Miscellaneous	
Total	

2. Transportation

Gas/Insurance/Licenses/Parking/ Maintenance etc.	
Public Transportation	

3. Housing & Utilities

Rent	
Electric, Oil/Gas, Water/Trash	
Telephone/Cell/Cable/Internet	
Real Estate Taxes and Insurance *(if not included in B above)*	
Maintenance and Repairs	
Total	

4. Medical

Health Insurance	
Out of Pocket Health Care Expenses	

5. Other

Child / Dependent Care	
Estimated Tax Payments	
Term Life Insurance	
Retirement *(Employer Required)*	
Retirement *(Voluntary)*	
Union Dues	
Delinquent State & Local Taxes *(minimum payment)*	
Student Loans *(minimum payment)*	
Court Ordered Child Support	
Court Ordered Alimony	
Other Court Ordered Payments	
Other *(specify)*	
Other *(specify)*	
Other *(specify)*	

Under penalty of perjury, I declare to the best of my knowledge and belief this statement of assets, liabilities and other information is true, correct and complete.

Your Signature	Spouse's Signature	Date

Instructions

Who should use Form 433-F?

Form 433-F is used to obtain current financial information necessary for determining how a wage earner or self-employed individual can satisfy an outstanding tax liability.

Note: *You may be able to establish an Online Payment Agreement on the IRS web site. To apply online, go to http://www.irs.gov, click on "I need to pay my taxes," and select "Installment Agreement" under the heading "What if I can't pay now?"*

If you are requesting an Installment Agreement, you should submit Form 9465, Installment Agreement Request, along with Form 433-F. (A large down payment may streamline the installment agreement process, pay your balance faster and reduce the amount of penalties and interest charged.)

After we review your completed form, we may contact you for additional information. For example, we may ask you to send supporting documentation of your current income or substantiation of your stated expenditures.

If any section on this form is too small for the information you need to supply, please use a separate sheet.

Section A – Accounts / Lines of Credit

List all accounts, even if they currently have no balance. However, do not enter bank loans in this section. Include business accounts, if applicable. If you are entering information for a stock or bond, etc. and a question does not apply, enter N/A.

Section B – Real Estate

List all real estate you own or are purchasing including your home. Include insurance and taxes if they are included in your monthly payment. The county/description is needed if different than the address and county you listed above. To determine equity, subtract the amount owed for each piece of real estate from its current market value.

Section C – Other Assets

List all cars, boats and recreational vehicles with their make, model and year. If a vehicle is leased, write "lease" in the "year purchased" column. List whole life insurance policies with the name of the insurance company. List other assets with a description such as "paintings", "coin collection", or "antiques". If applicable, include business assets, such as tools, equipment, inventory, and intangible assets such as domain names, patents, copyrights, etc. To determine equity, subtract the amount owed from its current market value. If you are entering information for an asset and a question does not apply, enter N/A.

Section D – Credit Cards

List all credit cards and lines of credit, even if there is no balance owed.

Section E – Business Information

Complete this section if you or your spouse are self-employed, or have self-employment income. This includes self-employment income from online sales.

E1: List all Accounts Receivable owed to you or your business. Include federal, state and local grants and contracts.

E2: Complete if you or your business accepts credit card payments (e.g., Visa, MasterCard, etc.).

Section F – Employment Information

If attaching a copy of current pay stub, you do not need to complete this section.

Section G – Non-Wage Household Income

List all non-wage income received monthly.

Net Self-Employment Income is the amount you or your spouse earns after you pay ordinary and necessary monthly business expenses. This figure should relate to the yearly net profit from Schedule C on your Form 1040 or your current year profit and loss statement. Please attach a copy of Schedule C or your current year profit and loss statement. If net income is a loss, enter "0".

Net Rental Income is the amount you earn after you pay ordinary and necessary monthly rental expenses. This figure should relate to the amount reported on Schedule E of your Form 1040 (do not include depreciation expenses). If net rental income is a loss, enter "0".

Other Income includes distributions from partnerships and subchapter S corporations reported on Schedule K-1, and from limited liability companies reported on Form 1040, Schedule C, D or E. It also includes agricultural subsidies, unemployment compensation, gambling income, oil credits, rent subsidies, Social Security and Interest/Dividends. Enter total distributions from IRAs if not included under Pension Income.

Instructions

Section H – Monthly Necessary Living Expenses

Enter monthly amounts for expenses. For any expenses not paid monthly, convert as follows:

If a bill is paid ...	Calculate the monthly amount by ...
Quarterly	Dividing by 3
Weekly	Multiplying by 4.3
Biweekly (every two weeks)	Multiplying by 2.17
Semimonthly (twice each month)	Multiplying by 2

For expenses claimed in boxes 1 and 4, you should provide the IRS allowable standards, or the actual amount you pay if the amount exceeds the IRS allowable standards. IRS allowable standards can be found by accessing http://www.irs.gov and entering "Collection Financial Standards" in the search field.

Substantiation may be required for any expenses over the standard once the financial analysis is completed.

The amount claimed for Miscellaneous cannot exceed the standard amount for the number of people in your family. The miscellaneous allowance is for expenses incurred that are not included in any other allowable living expense items. Examples are credit card payments, bank fees and charges, reading material and school supplies.

If you do not have access to the IRS web site, itemize your actual expenses and we will ask you for additional proof, if required. Documentation may include pay statements, bank and investment statements, loan statements and bills for recurring expenses, etc.

Housing and Utilities – Includes expenses for your primary residence. You should only list amounts for utilities, taxes and insurance that are not included in your mortgage or rent payments.

Rent – Do not enter mortgage payment here. Mortgage payment is listed in Section B.

Transportation – Include the total of maintenance, repairs, insurance, fuel, registrations, licenses, inspections, parking, and tolls for one month.

Public Transportation – Include the total you spend for public transportation if you do not own a vehicle or if you have public transportation costs in addition to vehicle expenses.

Medical – You are allowed expenses for health insurance and out-of-pocket health care costs.

Health insurance – Enter the monthly amount you pay for yourself or your family.

Out-of-Pocket health care expenses – are costs not covered by health insurance, and include:

- Medical services
- Prescription drugs
- Dental expenses
- Medical supplies, including eyeglasses and contact lenses. Medical procedures of a purely cosmetic nature, such as plastic surgery or elective dental work are generally not allowed.

Child / Dependent Care – Enter the monthly amount you pay for the care of dependents that can be claimed on your Form 1040.

Estimated Tax Payments – Calculate the monthly amount you pay for estimated taxes by dividing the quarterly amount due on your Form 1040ES by 3.

Life Insurance – Enter the amount you pay for term life insurance only. Whole life insurance has cash value and should be listed in Section C.

Delinquent State & Local Taxes – Enter the minimum amount you are required to pay monthly. Be prepared to provide a copy of the statement showing the amount you owe and if applicable, any agreement you have for monthly payments.

Student Loans – Minimum payments on student loans for the taxpayer's post-secondary education may be allowed if they are guaranteed by the federal government. Be prepared to provide proof of loan balance and payments.

Court Ordered Payments – For any court ordered payments, be prepared to submit a copy of the court order portion showing the amount you are ordered to pay, the signatures, and proof you are making the payments. Acceptable forms of proof are copies of cancelled checks or copies of bank or pay statements.

Other Expenses not listed above – We may allow other expenses in certain circumstances. For example, if the expenses are necessary for the health and welfare of the taxpayer or family, or for the production of income. Specify the expense and list the minimum monthly payment you are billed.

Form **9465**

(Rev. December 2013)
Department of the Treasury
Internal Revenue Service

Installment Agreement Request

▶ Information about Form 9465 and its separate instructions is at *www.irs.gov/form9465.*
▶ If you are filing this form with your tax return, attach it to the front of the return.
▶ See separate instructions.

OMB No. 1545-0074

Tip: If you owe $50,000 or less, you may be able to establish an installment agreement online, even if you have not yet received a bill for your taxes. Go to IRS.gov to apply to pay online. **Caution:** *Do not file this form if you are currently making payments on an installment agreement or can pay your balance in full within 120 days. Instead, call 1-800-829-1040. Do not file if your business is still operating and owes employment or unemployment taxes. Instead, call the telephone number on your most recent notice. If you are in bankruptcy or we have accepted your offer-in-compromise, see* **Bankruptcy or offer-in-compromise,** *in the instructions.*

Part I

This request is for Form(s) (for example, Form 1040 or Form 941) ▶ and for tax year(s) (for example, 2012 and 2013) ▶

1a Your first name and initial | Last name | **Your social security number**

If a joint return, spouse's first name and initial | Last name | **Spouse's social security number**

Current address (number and street). If you have a P.O. box and no home delivery, enter your box number. | Apt. number

City, town or post office, state, and ZIP code. If a foreign address, also complete the spaces below (see instructions)

Foreign country name | Foreign province/state/county | Foreign postal code

1b If this address is new since you filed your last tax return, check here . . . . ▶ ☐

2 Name of your business (must be no longer operating) | Employer identification number (EIN)

3 Your home phone number | Best time for us to call

4 Your work phone number | Ext. | Best time for us to call

5 Name of your bank or other financial institution:

Address

City, state, and ZIP code

6 Your employer's name:

Address

City, state, and ZIP code

7 Enter the total amount you owe as shown on your tax return(s) (or notice(s)) **7**

8 Enter the amount of any payment you are making with your tax return(s) (or notice(s)). See instructions **8**

9 Subtract line 8 from line 7 and enter the result **9**

10 Enter the amount you can pay each month. Make your payments as large as possible to limit interest and penalty charges. **The charges will continue until you pay in full. If no payment amount is listed on line 10, a payment will be determined for you by dividing the balance due by 72 months** . . **10**

11 Divide the amount on line 9 by 72 and enter the result **11**

- If the amount on line 10 is less than the amount on line 11 and you are unable to increase your payment to the amount on line 11, complete and attach Form 433-F, Collection Information Statement.
- If the amount on line 10 is equal to or greater than the amount on line 11 but the amount you owe is greater than $25,000 but not more than $50,000, you must complete either line 13 or 14, if you do not wish to complete Form 433-F.
- If the amount on line 9 is greater than $50,000, complete and attach Form 433-F, Collection Information Statement.

12 Enter the date you want to make your payment each month. **Do not** enter a date later than the 28th ▶

13 If you want to make your payments by direct debit from your checking account, see the instructions and fill in lines 13a and 13b. This is the most convenient way to make your payments and it will ensure that they are made on time.

▶ **a** Routing number ☐☐☐☐☐☐☐☐☐

▶ **b** Account number ☐☐☐☐☐☐☐☐☐☐☐☐☐☐☐☐☐

I authorize the U.S. Treasury and its designated Financial Agent to initiate a monthly ACH debit (electronic withdrawal) entry to the financial institution account indicated for payments of my Federal taxes owed, and the financial institution to debit the entry to this account. This authorization is to remain in full force and effect until I notify the U.S. Treasury Financial Agent to terminate the authorization. To revoke payment, I must contact the U.S. Treasury Financial Agent at **1-800-829-1040** no later than 14 business days prior to the payment (settlement) date. I also authorize the financial institutions involved in the processing of the electronic payments of taxes to receive confidential information necessary to answer inquiries and resolve issues related to the payments.

14 If you want to make your payments by payroll deduction, check this box and attach a completed Form 2159, Payroll Deduction Agreement . . . . ☐

Your signature | Date | Spouse's signature. If a joint return, **both** must sign. | Date

For Privacy Act and Paperwork Reduction Act Notice, see instructions. Cat. No. 14842Y Form **9465** (Rev. 12-2013)

Part II **Additional information.** Complete this part only if you have defaulted on an installment agreement within the past 12 months and the amount you owe is greater than $25,000 but not more $50,000 and the amount on line 10 is equal to or greater than the amount on line 11. If you owe more than $50,000, complete and attach Form 433-F, Collection Information Statement.

15 In which county is your primary residence? [ ]

16a Marital status:
- ☐ Single. Skip question 16b and go to question 17.
- ☐ Married. Go to question 16b.

b Do you share household expenses with your spouse?
- ☐ Yes.
- ☐ No.

17 How many dependents will you be able to claim on this year's tax return? **17**

18 How many people in your household are 65 or older? **18**

19 How often are you paid?
- ☐ Once a week.
- ☐ Once every two weeks.
- ☐ Once a month.
- ☐ Twice a month.

20 What is your net income per pay period (take home pay)? . . . . **20** $

21 How often is your spouse paid?
- ☐ Once a week.
- ☐ Once every two weeks.
- ☐ Once a month.
- ☐ Twice a month.

22 What is your spouse's net income per pay period (take home pay)? . . . . **22** $

23 How many vehicles do you own? **23**

24 How many car payments do you have each month? **24**

25a Do you have health insurance?
- ☐ Yes. Go to question 25b.
- ☐ No. Skip question 25b and go to question 26a.

b Are your premiums deducted from your paycheck?
- ☐ Yes. Skip question 25c and go to question 26a.
- ☐ No. Go to question 25c.

c How much are your monthly premiums? . . . . **25c** $

26a Do you make court-ordered payments?
- ☐ Yes. Go to question 26b.
- ☐ No. Go to question 27.

b Are your court-ordered payments deducted from your paycheck?
- ☐ Yes. Go to question 27.
- ☐ No. Go to question 26c.

c How much are your court-ordered payments each month? . . . . **26c** $

27 Not including any court-ordered payments for child and dependent support, how much do you pay for child or dependent care each month? . . . . **27** $

RMS Tax Consulting LLC

We are not just writing this book and telling you what to do and then sending you off on your own. RMS Tax Consulting LLC is offering a special deal that will help you to help yourself in your IRS case. We offer this special one-hour consultation for $150 or two hours for $250. We will review your case and your IRS correspondence letters and then do a brief review of your financial and personal circumstances. We will advise you what you can expect and what you need to do to respond to the IRS. If we believe that the issue is too large for you to handle yourself, we have a qualified network of affiliates of retired and former IRS employees, certified public accountants, and bankruptcy and tax lawyers who we regularly work with and trust. We can represent you before the Internal Revenue Service.

Richard M. Schickel was a Senior Revenue Officer (Tax Collector) in IRS Collection for 33 years and retired in 2013. He has over 65 awards from the Department of Treasury and the Internal Revenue Service, including a medal and commendation from President Reagan and the Secretary of the Treasury for saving an 8-year-old girl from a house fire. Since his retirement, he formed RMS Tax Consulting LLC. He and his team are enrolled agents licensed to practice before the IRS in all 50 states. He has also written a book detailing his experiences of his life in the IRS, called *IRS Whistleblower,* which is available in bookstores and on Amazon. Richard worked Offer in Compromise cases, and individual and business tax balance due cases. He made 22 successful criminal fraud investigations referrals. He also wrote a book on financial analysis for the IRS called *The Asset Recovery Guide.* This later became the basis for the Internal Revenue Manual Financial Analysis Handbook (IRM 5.15.1)

William Dieken was a Senior Revenue Agent in IRS who conducted field audits on individuals and businesses for 34 years. He was also an IRS instructor and coach who trained dozens of employees.

Lauri Goff was a Revenue Agent and President of the Oklahoma chapter of the National Treasury Employees Union. She retired from the IRS in 2015 after 34 years. She also instructed many IRS classes and served as a negotiator with the union on numerous occasions.

Guadalupe Aguirre was a Senior Tax Compliance Officer (TCO) (Office Auditor) in the office audit section of IRS. She retired in 2013 with 26 years of experience.

Kay Deters was a Senior Tax Compliance Officer in the office audit section who retired from IRS after 27 years.

Reina Fregoso was a Senior Revenue Officer in IRS Collection for 32 years. She was also an instructor and coach that trained and mentored new employees. She worked as an Offer in Compromise Specialist and Recruiter for the Southwestern states.

Our website can be found at www.RMS-Consulting.net.

Index

Made in the USA
Middletown, DE
14 December 2022

18496547R00241